WOMEN AND THE GIFT

Women and the Gift

BEYOND THE GIVEN AND ALL-GIVING

Edited by Morny Joy

INDIANA UNIVERSITY PRESS
Bloomington and Indianapolis

This book is a publication of

Indiana University Press
Office of Scholarly Publishing
Herman B Wells Library 350
1320 East 10th Street
Bloomington, Indiana 47405 USA

iupress.indiana.edu

Telephone orders   800-842-6796
Fax orders   812-855-7931

LIBRARY OF CONGRESS CATALOGING-IN-PUBLICATION DATA

Women and the gift : beyond the given and all-giving / edited by Morny Joy.
    pages   cm
  Includes bibliographical references and index.
    ISBN 978-0-253-00663-9 (cloth : alk. paper) — ISBN 978-0-253-00664-6 (pbk. : alk. paper) — ISBN 978-0-253-01033-9 (e-book) 1. Women—Psychology. 2. Generosity. 3. Magnanimity. I. Joy, Morny, editor of compilation.
  HQ1206.W8742 2013
  155.3'33—dc23   2013006921

  1 2 3 4 5 18 17 16 15 14 13

CONTENTS

ACKNOWLEDGMENTS

I would first like to thank all of the contributors to this volume for their patience and commitment during the years that it took to bring this project to fruition. Then I would like to thank profusely my husband, John King, for his assistance in all things electronic and technical, as well as for his constant supportive presence. Finally, I am indebted to the anonymous final reader of the volume whose searching questions prodded me to clarify my own position and refine my arguments in the introduction to the volume.

WOMEN AND THE GIFT

Introduction

Morny Joy

"Gift" is a word with many different resonances—of celebration, of appreciation and thanks, of farewell, of sharing, of reward, even of compensation. Yet it can also have less positive connotations of indebtedness as an obligation to reciprocate in kind, or in excess. There are also warnings about the duplicitous motives of certain people bearing gifts—the Greeks with the Trojan horse come to mind. Finally there is Pandora, so aptly named, perhaps the prototype for women's ambivalent relation to the gift—at once bountiful yet potentially malevolent. In the latter half of the twentieth century, however, the association of women with the gift has been the focus of a number of studies by male thinkers, such as Jacques Derrida ([1978] 1979, [1991] 1992b) and Georges Bataille ([1957] 1987, 1985). In their writings women were portrayed as emblematic of a mode of excess. Their idealized evocations of women and the "feminine" also promoted a notion of giving without any expectation of return.[1] Such depictions, however, had nothing to do with women themselves, as women were not consulted about being represented in this manner. It is intriguing to surmise the motives for this development. It could be interpreted as a protest against the exploitation of women, or perhaps as a rebuttal of bourgeois complacency, or maybe even as a rejection of obsessive late capitalism. Such extravagant gestures, however, were also in the French tradition of elaborate commentary on the classic book of Marcel Mauss, *The Gift* ([1924] 1990).

Mauss's work, however, did not concern itself with women, except for a few minor references. It was written from ethnological, sociological, and historical perspectives, exploring variations on the theme of the gift so as to appreciate its "aesthetic, moral, religious, and economic motivations" (Mauss [1924] 1990, 107). His reflections ranged from commentary on studies of the indigenous peoples of North America, Oceania, and Australia written by earlier ethnographers to historical examination of Roman and Germanic legal systems. It was Claude Lévi-Strauss, a former student of Mauss, who proposed in *The Elementary Structures of Kinship* ([1949] 1969) that women, as gifts given in marriage, constituted the gift par excellence, thus establishing the foundation for premonetary exchange systems. His suggestion was certainly controversial—today as much for its colonialist views as for its provocative assumptions about women. This legacy underlies and inevitably influences much contemporary discussion about women and the gift. Undoubtedly Mauss's and Lévi-Strauss's proclamations about the gift do provide a provocation to revisit their data, as well as to try and extricate any further deliberations on this topic from their own Eurocentric preoccupations.

Recent studies, such as *The Potlatch Papers,* by Christopher Bracken (1997), have been extremely helpful in indicating some of Mauss's and Lévi-Strauss's more dubious colonialist claims. Bracken also points to a contradiction inherent in locating their project at the limits of "western" thought as it encounters "the other."[2] He demonstrates that these limits are actually protective boundaries that indeed impede the possibilities for learning anything from other peoples. Bracken describes how "the gift" is symptomatic of the implicit prejudices of western thought and language in attempts to define other peoples in relation to its presumed self-image. His discussions of the "potlatch" ceremony and western efforts to contain and define the perceived profligate waste involved—both literally and legally—are telling. Bracken's analyses of the writings of Gilbert Sproat, a nineteenth-century government agent; of the anthropologist Franz Boas; and even of Derrida's more recent commentary on Mauss actually expose these writers' inability to discern and express the potlatch's meaning, as it will forever exceed their grasp (Bracken 1997, 48–49, 153–62). Yet such appropriations of indigenous peoples' traditions still continue to service western desires and designs, be they neocolonial, ethnological, or deconstructive.

So why write a book on women and the gift today? Where does it belong, if not in the history of such deceptive and compromised enterprises? It is only too apparent that there can no longer be any appeal today to women to provide a figure of infinite generosity, although there are still contemporary writers, such as Genevieve Vaughan (1997, 2007), who believe they can. Nor can one presume in this age of über-commodification, of continued exploitation by neocolonial interests in a globalized world,[3] to introduce a theory exempt from any complicity—of either an intellectual or a material nature.

The first response to such challenges would be to note that although such thinkers as Hélène Cixous in "Sorties" (Cixous 1986), Luce Irigaray ([1977] 1985, [1987] 1993), Marilyn Strathern (1988), and Annette Weiner (1976) have passionately written on aspects of the gift and its relation to women, there has not been a comprehensive collection that appraises women's own interventions both on the gift itself and on the pronouncements made by the men. Of itself, however, such a rationale alone is not persuasive. So, while the stated intention of the volume is to provide a forum for present-day women scholars to reflect on the nature of the gift, its aspirations are more ambitious. The hope is that the book will appeal to readers of many backgrounds who want to understand how women are defining their roles and making considered responses to the challenges of contemporary existence. These challenges include relationships of care, fidelity, generosity, and trust, such as the gift often evokes. The list of topics discussed is not exhaustive, but it does represent the most prominent ideas and ideals that have been advanced recently. The crucial question is whether in this alleged postmodern, postcolonial, postfeminist, and postsecular age, these issues can engage the hearts and intellects of like-minded women.

In earlier commentaries, especially those on the work of Marcel Mauss and Claude Lévi-Strauss, the gift was employed to ascribe certain roles for women, as well as to designate attributes considered appropriate for a docile and amenable female character. Then the writings of Derrida and Bataille introduced a new model of femininity—where women's extravagant generosity subverted former constraints. These pronouncements were declared by male scholars in the absence of women themselves and without regard for their own input. It is time to undertake a thorough evaluation of all such artificial constructs. To reflect on women and the gift today is to conduct a careful, if not rigorous, examination in light of all that has been learned by women from many years of feminist interrogation. What recommendations can be distilled from the proverbial blood, sweat, and tears that have been expended in the past forty years as women have struggled to achieve integrity and recognition? These have not been easy years, and it is necessary to remain constantly on alert against ongoing forays such as the backlash in the name of "postfeminism." Nevertheless, a goodly measure of wisdom and insight has been acquired. The essays in this book attest to this wisdom as women honestly and attentively strive to discern ways of flourishing in relationships—with one another, with men, with other sentient beings in the cosmos—in ways that celebrate life. The gift thus serves as an indicator that can help to conceive of relations that are affirmative and non-exploitative, where there is trust, respect, and reciprocity. Above all, the writings in this book attest to a need for tolerance and openness. Such recommendations help to foster an orientation that would recognize differences and allow them to exist in a non-coercive space that does not stipulate any exclusionary sex-specific or gender-appropriate requisites for admittance.

Some essays in this volume speak to new inclusions, while others draw attention to continued exclusions. The gift has indeed had a checkered history. It is crucial to be aware that, as formerly, it can be specious in its intentions and detrimental in its effects. Ever mindful of such deviations, it is also important to acknowledge that the gift, in the form of testimonials to past violations and omissions, can foster reconciliation.

A PERSONAL ITINERARY

My own attraction to this topic was prompted by a conference on the gift in which I participated, organized by Professor Constantin Boundas at Trent University in 1996.[4] At that conference, where most attendees were philosophers, only a few papers mentioned women and the gift, although efforts had been made to include this topic. Similarly, in the resulting publication of seventeen articles in an issue of the journal *Angelaki* (2001), there was little analysis.[5] Alan Schrift, a conference participant, also subsequently edited a volume, *The Logic of the Gift* (1997), in which he acknowledged the importance of the question of gender and the gift by including excerpts from the published work of Hélène Cixous and Luce Irigaray.[6] Their ideas stimulated me to investigate this phenomenon further.

Over the intervening years I invited a number of women colleagues to offer their reflections on this relationship of women to the gift. The response was overwhelming. This present volume is the first of two. It is mainly theoretical in nature: it principally addresses philosophical ideas about women and the gift. The second volume, which will be published in the near future, is more concrete in its approach. It comprises a survey of different varieties of gifts—both material and figurative, many of them unacknowledged or deliberately overlooked—that have been contributed by women to various religions of the world.

The first volume, however, is not overtly religious, but ranges over a number of disciplines, eliciting responses from women as they evaluate certain presumptions concerning the ways women stand in relation to the gift. Often such presumptions are not particularly affirmative. Even when they do seem initially positive, on further reflection they tend to define women in ways that regard their qualities as subsidiary, or as lacking in the more robust attributes that characterize masculinity. Such implications of inferiority did not start with Mauss's book—in fact he rarely mentions women—or with the work of his commentators. Insofar as both philosophy and religion are concerned, women's role as "the lesser vehicle," with reference to both her mind and her body, has been amply described in western literature from the time of the Greeks.[7] The first chapter in this volume, by Deborah Lyons, succinctly articulates the position that women, and the gifts they have provided since the time of Pandora, have been held in highest suspicion.

A BRIEF HISTORICAL OVERVIEW

This attitude of suspicion, however, is not the only negative value ascribed to women. In the western tradition, there is ample evidence that, from the era of the early church fathers, women were deemed subordinate. Their bodies were suspect, and their minds, specifically their reasoning abilities, were regarded as deficient. Church fathers such as Augustine and Jerome (fifth century CE) associated sexuality with sin and women as temptation incarnate.[8] Aquinas later adapted Aristotle's rather bizarre biological designations of male and female characteristics as proof of women's lack.[9] Certain types of penitential practices were recommended to curb these wayward tendencies, but basically there was a belief in the early church that women could attain sainthood only by forsaking their deviant feminine form and taking on aspects of a virile masculinity. This view was extant in later centuries, though it was not universal.

In an article on Carolingian hagiography of women, Julia M. H. Smith provides a description of the conventions that informed this tradition:

> Patristic writers adapted to their own purposes a classical vocabulary which identified right moral action with masculinity and deemed moral weakness a characteristic of women. . . . Manly action manifested the strength and virtue necessary to pursue the ascetic life. . . . Jerome and others elaborated the theme of *femina virilis* or *virago,* the manly woman, whose ascetic prowess transcended her gender. (Smith 1995, 18)

Yet these recommendations of a needed asceticism and control of women took another anomalous direction. Women, who were expected to be subservient to men in all things, could find an earthly form of redemption in their role as a mother. Both early and late medieval hagiographies exhorted women—those who did not enter nunneries—to follow the example of Mary, the mother of Jesus, who was depicted as living an exemplary life of humility, purity, and sacrifice. Mary's boundless love for her son and excessive suffering at his death was proposed as a model of the sacrificial love that women should imitate to fulfill their maternal mandate. At the same time, Mary's virginal status was incongruously extolled as constituting the model of chastity to which women should aspire.[10] These idealized projections of maternity were not especially practical for the average woman, either then or now, as it deprived her of access to any form of independent activity. Such restrictions virtually dictated that the better part of women's endowments, or gifts, were to be exercised in the service of men and their families. As such, it amounted to a mode of giving as self-sacrifice.

Although there have been exceptions, this version of women as "all-giving," encouraging self-abnegation, has sustained many of the world's religions over the centuries. From the sixteenth to eighteenth centuries, however, women did begin to experiment in ways that challenged these formulas, as Erica Longfellow has illustrated in her writing on early modern England (2004).[11] Remnants of the social attitudes and the cultural structures that have enforced these restrictive measures, however, can still be found today in fundamentalist forms of both eastern and western religions. This is only too evident in their concerted opposition to women's access to both birth control and abortion counseling.[12]

Another predominant feature of women's role in relation to the gift is that of being given away, i.e., "the given." This feature is graphically described by Lévi-Strauss in *The Elementary Structures of Kinship* ([1949] 1969).[13] Lévi-Strauss's designation of women as the pawns in whatever matrimonial arrangements are determined by the men of the tribe, in the name of incest prohibition, does not allow women any basis of agency. Yet the work of Annette Weiner, in her study of Trobriand Island women, demonstrates that in this society, women certainly could, and did, wield power in ways that refute Lévi-Strauss's facile generalization.[14] It does need to be noted, unfortunately, that, in certain contemporary religions, such arrangements continue. Many women have little or no say in their being traded or given away in marriage, functioning simply as tokens in agreements that confirm patriarchal and/or tribal allegiances.

Both of the above stereotypes—of women as "all-giving" or "given"—may seem somewhat arcane to many young women in the present-day secularized west, where Eve Ensler's *The Vagina Monologues* (1998) has been performed worldwide to appreciative audiences.[15] This has occurred at the same time that second-wave feminists are both worried and critical of the behavior of young women in western countries, citing both "raunch culture" and the cult of the perfect or ideal body. The first of these concerns, that of "raunch culture," indicates a number of young women's practices—from going to male strip clubs, to attending bare-it-all gatherings occurring under the salubrious title of "Girls Gone Wild,"[16] to imitating role models such as Britney Spears and Miley Cyrus—all of which are justified by the rhetoric of "individual choice" and self-empowerment. Natasha Walter has addressed these issues in her book *Living Dolls: The Return of Sexism* (2010). As she observes ruefully: "The rise of hypersexual culture is not proof that we have reached full equality; rather it has reflected and exaggerated the deeper imbalances of power in our society" (8). She later elaborates on the detrimental effects that this shift has on women: "By co-opting the language of choice and empowerment, this culture creates smoke and mirrors that prevent many people from seeing just how limiting such so-called choices can be" (39). In many cases of self-expression, as described by Walter (2010, 28–35), the existence of free choice would appear to be conspicuously absent.

The second and related form of worrisome behavior is connected to extreme dieting and constant critical self-appraisal, resulting in low self-esteem for young women and even girls. Many young women have a negative relation to their bodies, finding them wanting according to highly artificial constructs of "the body beautiful." Such images are relentlessly promoted by all forms of media. These two examples may seem somewhat removed from the topic of the gift, but my reasons for introducing them at this juncture have to do with the form of co-optation of women and girls that is involved in the two cases. For what is patently apparent behind both the contemporary slogans, as well as the simplifications coded by "the given" and the "all-giving," is a stark fact. This is that women's emotions and energies are being both contained and directed by a system that is basically controlled by men. Contemporary young women and their bodies are being packaged, or commodified, to fit the needs of a consumer market that caters to the desires of men. It is indeed troubling that women, whether as gifts or as goods, have not yet escaped from insidious bonds that can dictate their destiny.

From this perspective, it is then quite fascinating to review the present-day literature on women and the gift, particularly that written by men. The major problem with such work—be it concerned with either theoretical or practical matters, or even when it's idealistic in its exhortations—is that, by excluding the voices of women, it presumes to speak for them. It raises a significant question: In what way are such recommendations any different from the decrees of religious or authority figures that continue to dictate the terms of a woman's life? Keeping these reflections and questions in mind, I will give a brief survey of certain recent works, by men as well as women, before introducing the essays in this volume. The intent is not to dismiss such thinkers peremptorily, but to try and understand how such ideas and ideals arose and still continue to be circulated and considered as appropriate. In undertaking this exercise, my own approach, informed by a hermeneutics of suspicion, in the manner of Paul Ricoeur, seeks to uncover not just conscious, but unconscious motivations.[17] It will also seek to discern whatever lingering romantic conventions or misogynistic attitudes endure behind the rationalizations and idealizations that align women with an expansive orientation of gift-giving.

Many contemporary thinkers who have engaged with Marcel Mauss's seminal work *The Gift* ([1924] 1990) have taken issue with his findings and/ or with the interpretations of commentators of more recent vintage. Among the many fascinating titles presently in circulation are *The Enigma of the Gift,* by Maurice Godelier ([1996] 1999); *The World of the Gift,* by Jacques T. Godbout ([1992] 1998); *The Gift: Imagination and the Erotic Life of Property,* by Lewis Hyde (1983); *The Gift: An Interdisciplinary Perspective,* edited by Aafke E. Komter (1996); *The Question of the Gift: Essays across the Disciplines,* edited by Mark Osteen (2002); *The Logic of the Gift,* by Alan Schrift (1997); and *The Work of the Gift,* by Scott Cutler Shershow (2005). All attempt to revisit Mauss's deliberations on the gift and rework his ideas so as to render them accessible to a contemporary audience. Perhaps, however, the most illuminating exploration of the gift in recent years has been Marcel Hénaff's *The Price of Truth* ([2002] 2010). Hénaff's subtle and penetrating reading of Mauss, and also of later respondents to Mauss, makes many routine remarks, such as "There is no such thing as a free gift"[18] or "any gift that has an expectation of a return, is not a gift,"[19] appear somewhat simplistic, if not trite. For what Hénaff has endeavored to portray is the complex and multifaceted dimensions that inform Mauss's analysis, at the same time as he refines and expands certain of Mauss's somewhat limited observations.

Probably the most dramatic clarification that Hénaff makes is that gift-giving, as described by Mauss, is not a preliminary form of contemporary market exchange. It is sufficient unto itself as a ceremonial mode of sumptuary gift-giving, undertaken first to establish alliances and then to initiate further exchanges that cement this relationship. What is at stake is reciprocal recognition, rather than commercial trade, which would involve exchange of goods with economic value. As Hénaff further explains: "The good offered is not considered something to be consumed but is presented as a mark of respect, as an expression of the desire to honour the existence and status of the other, and finally as testimony to an alliance" (Hénaff [2002] 2010, 153). In this sense the gift is at once incommensurable and priceless. As Hénaff then observes: "There is no gift economy" (153). This is a brilliant insight that rebuts the earlier elaborations of many thinkers. It also clarifies Mauss's own equivocations (Mauss [1924] 1990, 100–108), as well as certain statements of his commentators who have idealized the gift as involving an archaic and less avaricious mode of economy, in contrast to present-day business dealings.

Hénaff also realizes that something of major importance is occurring with marriage: "Matrimonial alliance is the highest and most decisive form of the relationship of recognition between groups that reciprocal ceremonial gift exchange constitutes" (Hénaff [2002] 2010, 143). To appreciate the full import of this gesture, it is necessary to explore certain of Hénaff's other careful qualifications of Mauss's depiction of gift-giving as a "total social fact" (Mauss 1990, 16). Hénaff qualifies Mauss's claim by insisting that this form of gift-giving is not "totalizing" in any absolute sense. Instead, for Hénaff, "[i]t is a total social fact because it involves the entire society and society as a whole (even if it does not constitute everything in this society): it is not a marginal or private phenomenon but an institutional one" (Hénaff 2010, 153). Yet, as Hénaff further clarifies, such exchanges "do not amount to a total social phenomenon because they do no more than create or preserve bonds between local groups or persons" (154).

Another, more exalted element is nevertheless involved. This element, however, needs amplification in order to grasp what Mauss's enigmatic references to other relations might signify. In this connection Hénaff further refines Mauss's explanation of "total" as encompassing more than a merely mortal realm. He states: "Ceremonial gift exchange would not be total if it were not cosmic" (2010, 129). This cosmic affiliation evokes an even grander scale within which gift-giving also takes place: "Besides the system of reciprocal exchanges between humans, a different system is constituted that involves humans in their relationship to deities" (150). This relationship to deities, to which Mauss also alludes, but which he does not develop in great detail (Mauss 1990, 20–22), has certain symbolic ties that distinguish it from the more mundane reciprocal human interactions connected to the gift. As Hénaff explains:

> Whereas the former system, symmetrical and horizontal, ensures social life in the present and only concerns relationships between humans, the latter, asymmetrical relationships and vertical, seems designed to confront the permanence of the community through time . . . [E]ven beyond this permanence, what is at stake is establishing a bond with the deities to which the group owes its existence and identity and on which its fate depends. (2010, 150)

There is not the space to pursue this crucial connection with deities at length, but central to the process, as Mauss also perceived, are specific precious items associated with the gods. These items, which Mauss named *sacra,* guarantee the identity and continuity of a particular society or group. But, as Hénaff himself acknowledges, it was the anthropologist Annette Weiner who first labeled such goods "inalienable" (Weiner 1976, 149). They constitute the symbolic bedrock of a group, and they do not circulate. Such sacred objects represent not just allegiance to the gods, but a recognition that humanity's very existence derives from these beings, as does their integrity and survival as a people. Hénaff recognizes that this divine relationship encompasses the whole of the cosmic realm: "Furthermore, the alliance to which the precious goods kept within the group are a testament expresses this requirement: reciprocity must bond together not only humans and gods or humans with each other but all living beings, every element, and the totality of the world: this is the first gift" (2010, 152).

Such a panorama of the interweaving strands of gods and humans with all living things delineates a cosmic design that is complex in its demands and inexhaustible in its possible combinations. As Hénaff discerns, there is a mode of reciprocity that is integral to this special relationship. Often it takes the form of rituals of gift exchange, even sacrifice.[20] Hénaff's account, then, does not reduce the world to a finely calibrated structural system of checks and balances, as does Lévi-Strauss's, but he appreciates that from the beginning, people have honored the gift of life, which is incalculable. Hénaff captures the wonder and extraordinary reach of this originary gift. "The anthropology of gift exchange offers a different interpretation: spirits and deities are conceived of and named as the addressors of this inaugural, constant, and infinite gift of which humans know that they are the addressees" (2010, 151).

It is within this cosmic framework that the full significance of marriage is realized. To support this, Hénaff states: "Because the wives are essential to the group's existence, the group's very being is at stake in the recognition ensured by matrimonial alliance" (2010, 143). But although Hénaff recognizes the importance of Weiner's work on "inalienable goods" (1992), he misses a golden opportunity when he does not engage further with Weiner's profound insights about women. And this is, unfortunately, the major omission in Hénaff's work. He could have used Weiner's findings to help him incorporate the roles of women as active partners and even power brokers in the exchange of gifts at both the material and the symbolic levels. Annette Weiner has demonstrated that women are just as capable as men of being full participants in procedures of gift-giving. They are agents in a process which confirms their own symbolic worth in both the horizontal and the vertical dimensions of gift exchange. Weiner describes the way in which marriage provides the context in which a woman can display, manipulate, and channel the power of Trobriand *womanness*. As Weiner observes:

The power of Trobriand women, from a cultural view, is not merely a fact of biology. Rather, the value of *womanness* is identified through the cultural symbols of her wealth—skirts and bundles which serve to objectify this transformation. *The value of womanness, not women,* is what men gain at marriage, and this value is now exploited in a positive sense by women themselves on every level. (1976, 230)

It needs to be acknowledged, however, that the Trobriand society that informed Weiner's portrayal of women both as actors and as having access to negotiations of power was a matrilineal society. As such, it accorded women a high status (Weiner 1976, 225, 228). Women partake in activities that establish their symbolic worth, where they both negotiate respect and have their integrity affirmed. This takes place on two planes. Weiner's depiction of the intricate maneuvers involved in these activities does acknowledge women as serious players in horizontal gift exchange, while a higher symbolic level also pervades these material transactions.[21] Weiner elaborates on the significance for both men and women:

One must understand the power structure in which Trobriand women operate in order to understand how Trobriand men perceive themselves. Nature exists in order to be shaped and transformed to serve one's purposes. All manner of human resources and energy is turned to this effort. The basic premise on which this effort is sustained is the regeneration of human beings. The symbolic qualities of exchange objects mirror the preoccupation with the developmental cycle of life and death. Stone axe blades (male wealth), skirts and bundles (female wealth), and yams (the composite of male and female wealth) constitute the basic artifacts of Trobriand exchange, and each object symbolically represents some measure of regeneration. (1976, 231)

She then concludes that in these multifaceted arrangements "Trobriand women participate on both social and cosmic planes" (231). Her further remarks to the effect that, in Trobriand society, "the female domain, the regenesis of human life, is accorded primary value" (234) attest to the fact that women are specifically revered for their intimate connection with birth and life within a regenerative cosmic framework. Thus: "Perpetuation of life or human survival is given far more transcendental significance than is the kind of immortality found in objects or in 'cultural' survival. Therefore women, innately tied to the continuity of life, remain the locus for the means by which human survival transcends itself" (234).[22]

Women are specifically honored for this revered power of cosmic connection. Yet it would seem that while Weiner did discern and communicate, for the first time, the symbolic status of such "womanness," she did not detect the actual process of recognition that Hénaff understands to be taking place. This is possibly because at the time Weiner wrote, the current scholarship on recognition was not available.[23] But there could be other reasons. It is apparent that Hénaff does not seem to accord women the same powerful and respected status that Weiner does. This raises pertinent questions about the implications of Hénaff's work for women in the course of recognition that he so ably defines. For Henaff's conclusions would seem to point in the direction that, when women are married in ceremonial exchanges, they need not be regarded simply as commodities. But though Hénaff acknowledges that "[m]atrimonial alliance is the highest and most decisive form of the relationship of recognition between groups that reciprocal ceremonial gift exchange constitutes" (2010, 143), he does not analyze women's role in the ceremony. He also does not state, as does Weiner, that women themselves are active participants in marriage, bringing their own worth and integrity to the agreement. In Hénaff's portrayal, women could thus still function as pawns, as they do in Lévi-Strauss. This is because Hénaff does not mention the symbolic status and special cosmic connection that Weiner so powerfully ascribes to women. It could well be that Hénaff is not willing to concede that women are sufficiently qualified to be a part of a process of recognition, and that such proceedings are reserved for men. Hénaff's silence on these issues is puzzling, as he is not unaware of Weiner's work. It raises the issue of not only Hénaff's, but also male scholars' lack of acknowledgment of women's work, let alone gifts—in all their different dimensions of existence and regeneration—about which Weiner wrote so passionately.

Weiner's most relevant critical observations concern the omission of data about women from most male-authored anthropological studies, from the discipline's beginnings to the time of her writing in the 1970s. Weiner poses certain questions which address issues that are at the heart of this volume. The first concerns both the omission of women from anthropological studies until quite recently, and the biases and distortions that do appear. She states:

> In all major areas within our discipline, we have re-evaluated and reformulated nineteenth-century theories of society and culture. But we have accepted almost without question the nineteenth-century western legacy that had effectively segregated women from positions of power. We have subjected early missionary and travelers' documents to a careful evaluation

of their bias toward the "native." But have we equally considered the effects of their bias toward women? (1976, 228)

Weiner's work alerts scholars not only to the fact that women have often been absent from scholarly work but also that, even when they do appear, the conventions of the scholar's own period tend to color the descriptions of their role. She was also one of the first to raise the problem of the rather startling interpretive presumptions that inform many early accounts of other cultures. This involves the human propensity—which is not limited to anthropologists—to shape received data in accordance with the myopic constructs and assumptions of one's own culture. Weiner's indictment on this score is at once acute and damning:

> The Trobriand who say they exchange for "love" or "generosity" are following a myth that serves in their society to hide a reality of self-interest. The anthropologist who then insists on labeling this act as a "gift" seems to be perpetuating the Trobriand natives' myth. But this is probably only incidental to what she or he is doing. In weaving the "gift" myth, is not the anthropologist hiding a reality that concerns *his* or *her* role in *his* or *her* society? (1976, 221)

The predicament that Weiner discusses here is also central to the problematic nature of the gift in relation to women. Her work addresses the unexamined presuppositions with which a scholar approaches a topic, and not simply those of gender. In affirming the latent prejudices inherent in any work of scholarship, she does not let women themselves off the hook. Her reflections on what is at stake in interpretations of the gift cut to the core of the way that unreflective views tend to curtail much-needed in-depth investigations into unwarranted assumptions and superficial generalizations. Weiner's contributions remain particularly relevant for contemporary studies on the gift.

BUSINESS AS USUAL?

Similar shortcomings are much in evidence in a number of recent treatments of women and the gift by male scholars. It is in this context that I will discuss the work of Jacques Derrida as well as that of Georges Bataille. I choose these two male thinkers because, for different reasons, I regard them as two of the most troublesome writers in their treatment of women and the gift.

Derrida does deserve to be given the benefit of the doubt in that I believe he does have women's interests at heart. Nevertheless he is extremely gratuitous, in a negative fashion, in his invocations of women in connection with both the gift and deconstruction itself. In *Spurs* ([1978] 1979), Derrida takes his direction from Nietzsche, adapting the latter's equivocations on woman and truth to his own deconstructive ends.

> There is no such thing as the essence of woman because woman averts, she is averted of herself, out of the depths, endless and unfathomable, she engulfs and distorts all vestige of essentiality, of identity, of property. . . . There is no such thing as the truth of woman, but it is because of that abyssal divergence of the truth, because that untruth is "truth." Woman is but one name for that untruth of truth. (Derrida [1978] 1979, 51)

In many ways, by thus associating women with deconstruction, Derrida believed that he was paying women a compliment. Building on this somewhat contentious basis of woman's relation to truth, in *Given Time* ([1991] 1992b), Derrida extrapolates from a letter of Madame de Maintenon, the wife of Louis XIV, who appears to be trapped in a paradoxical situation. She writes that she cannot give her time to a cause she wants to support, a school for impoverished genteel girls, because the king takes up all of it ([1991] Derrida 1992b, 3–4). This is the type of statement Derrida revels in, making the most of various contrary statements in a literalist sense, with their obviously irreconcilable conclusions. But inevitably there is more at stake. Derrida's further inference is that a woman does not have time, because the king—patriarchy personified—does not grant it to her. Consequently, there can be no (free) gift from a woman who does not have either the freedom or the time to bestow it. Yet, Derrida has perhaps tripped himself up in this attempt at ingenuity in portraying women in relation to the gift. Indeed, as Annette Weiner has shown, women need not be so circumscribed when it comes to gift-giving. In addition, the work of Marcel Hénaff has also provided a valuable insight into the basic problem of Derrida's dealings with the gift. Hénaff has shown in Derrida's experiments on the gift that "[t]he aporia he presented as a radical objection to ritual gift exchange as described by Mauss was based on a serious misunderstanding; this was associated with a constant suspension regarding the very idea of reciprocity, always reduced to a self-interested movement of returns to the self, whereas reciprocity in ceremonial gift exchange actually belongs to a logic of glorious and generous reply" (Hénaff 2010, 231–32).

Derrida's work is based on a simplistic dichotomy between gift and exchange. For his purpose, a purely disinterested gift is impossible because all gifts have expectations of recompense. This marks them inevitably as forms of exchange. Any notion of genuine reciprocity is thus excluded. Yet women writers, especially Weiner (1976) and Eleanor Burke Leacock (1981), have illustrated that neither women nor gifts need necessarily be imprisoned by a system that, despite its deconstructive veneer, still constructs the world according to mutually exclusive or self-preoccupied categories.

Bataille is another matter altogether. He was fascinated by Mauss's description of potlatch ceremonies of the Northwest Coast indigenous people of Canada. He interpreted potlatch's wanton expenditure as a supreme gesture, celebrating excess and superfluity, even going to the extreme of total destruction. He postulated that all societies could function according to this surplus energy and its associated lavish devastation. Such activities were extolled by Bataille, specifically in contrast to the current repressive regimes he posited as characterizing both religion and capitalism. The figure of women was also central to this vision, representing a similar gesture in the mode of extreme profligacy. The prostitute, in particular, features as the victim nonpareil, the ultimate gift in an economy of transgression. At times it would seem that Bataille's depiction of such a worldview was deliberately exaggerated—stock tactics of an agent provocateur. There is, however, a major problem with Bataille's excessive indulgences. This is that they involved exploitation, whether conscious or otherwise. It was not only women who were degraded by his efforts. His extreme interpretation of potlatch as a prodigality that verged on parody was an unwarranted appropriation of the cultural practices of the Northwest Coast aboriginal peoples of Canada. They were wrenched from their specific context to suit his own extravagant, if not perverse, ends.

In contrast to these male theorists, contemporary women thinkers who reflect on the gift prefer to explore certain more affirmative aspects. As my principal examples, I will now introduce the work of Luce Irigaray and Hélène Cixous, though I do address their work in more detail in the final chapter in this volume. In many ways their work can be understood as a response to the French tradition of reflection on the gift, and its post-Mauss commentators, from Lévi-Strauss to Bataille and Derrida in particular. Nevertheless, in their dependence on their predecessors' views and definitions, they run the serious risk of committing similar appropriative errors.

Luce Irigaray, in "Women on the Market" ([1977] 1985), takes issue with both Lévi-Strauss and Marx, castigating the former for reducing women to exchange value and the latter for framing women as fetishistic commodities. In both instances, women are viewed as commercial products or objects of desire that circulate according to market values. This market, in Irigaray's view, operates according to standards set by a male-ordered economy. This is a realm, according to Irigaray, that is controlled by the "Law of the Father" or the (Lacanian) Phallus. Irigaray's solution to this domination, which I have commented on elsewhere (Joy 2008), is for women themselves "to go to market." They will not act, however, in accordance with the current exchange model, but will introduce another set of values. These would reflect a set of ideals where indeed recognition between partners as egalitarian participants has become possible. Irigaray describes this changed mode of interaction which surpasses any notion of one-sided interest. Irigaray's work, nevertheless, remains reliant on the same dichotomy between gift and exchange as does Derrida's:

> It would entail, beyond the enslavement to property, beyond the subject's submission to the object . . . becoming capable of giving and receiving, of being active and passive, of having an intention that stays attuned to inter-actions, that is, of seeking a new economy of existence or being which is neither that of mastery nor slavery but rather of exchange with no precon-stituted object—vital exchange, cultural exchange, of words, gestures etc., an exchange thus able to *communicate* at times, to commune . . . beyond any exchange of objects. ([1992] 1996, 45)

Obviously Irigaray's vision assumes that a type of revolution has taken place, where women have come into their own, and have assumed their rightful place as co-creators not just of life itself, but of the way that society is ordered. Such a woman, according to Irigaray, has also accomplished "the perfection of her gender." In using this phrase, Irigaray intends to say that women need to free themselves from patriarchal precedents. Her whole oeuvre is dedicated to helping women achieve this end. She uses her own personal journey as an illustration of the tasks that need to be undertaken. Through a process of careful self-analysis that also included yoga and medi-tation, Irigaray deconstructed what she termed "the fabricated character of my own feminine identity" (2000, 147). At the same time, she undertook a reassessment of the absolutist values promulgated by the Law of the Father, with their inevitable dualist dichotomies. Her own solution was based on a redefinition of Hegel's concept of recognition—especially the Marxist mate-rialist interpretation that had found favor in France as a result of Alexandre Kojève's Parisian lectures (1969) during the 1930s. Instead, Irigaray encour-ages a relationship between a man and a woman where each affirms the integrity of the other. In her view this can only happen once women have been able to establish their own sense of identity or autonomy.

This is an attractive proclamation—that women can decide and shape their own subjectivity. Yet there are a number of specific behaviors and atti-tudes Irigaray recommends for women to accomplish such perfection. This is where Irigaray's work becomes somewhat controversial. This is because her support of a woman's "perfection of her gender" entails the adoption of a radical notion of gender difference between the male and female sexes. As she asserts: "The whole of humankind is composed of men and women and nothing else" (1996, 47). Such a declaration borders on biological essentialism. There is also a set of specific "feminine" qualities and behaviors that Irigaray promotes, or even prescribes, as most appropriate for women. The reason for such partiality is that she does not approve of women's claims to equality, assuming that this will lead to women becoming the same as men. But this is a mistaken idea, as she misinterprets formal equality on issues under the law, such as pay equity, as being identical with biological features. As a result, Irigaray can often be understood as simply reasserting traditional "feminine" attributes that connect women with "a culture of the earth, the body, life, peace" ([1987] 1993, 190). Such prescriptions would deny women the opportunity to explore values other than those conventionally ascribed to them. Nonetheless, Irigaray's incisive criticism of the gender blindness of male scholars on the topic of the gift remains a valuable contribution.

Hélène Cixous also contests what she considers a "masculine" economy— one founded on "the fear of expropriation, of separation, of losing the attribute" (1986, 80). Economies of exchange, then, on Cixous's account, cannot but exclude the motivations of generosity that inspire the gift. By way of comparison, according to Cixous, a feminine economy is one that does not calculate, does not expect a return. As a result, the gifts that women give do not have exchange value, but reflect a non-possessive amplitude that affirms life. As proposed by Cixous, in its finest form gift-giving would appear to be quintessentially "feminine" in its trademark concern for the other. This expansiveness draws upon virtually inexhaustible if not incalculable resources.[24] Cixous elaborates:

> How does she give? What are her dealings with saving and squandering reserve, life, death? She too gives *for.* She too, with open hands, gives herself—pleasure, happiness, increased value, enhanced self image. But she doesn't try to "recover her expenses." She is able not to return to herself, never settling down, pouring out, going everywhere to the other. She does not flee extremes; she is not the being-of-the-end (the goal), but she is how-far-being-reaches. (1984, 87)

While the reflections of Irigaray and Cixous were startling in their originality and extravagance at their first appearance, over the years their division into "masculine" and "feminine" worldviews has come to appear somewhat indulgent, if not dangerous. In their simplicity, their respective frameworks can encourage a form of dualism that entrenches sexual stereotypes, even if "masculine" and "feminine" attributes need not necessarily be viewed as always applicable to the male and female of the species—there is an overlapping, even identification at times. This sets up a binary of male/exchange (bad) and woman/gift (good). There is also a dichotomy posited, as with Derrida, between the gratuitous gift and economies that calculate a return. The extremes to which these distinctions can be misapplied are evident in Genevieve Vaughan's various studies of gift-giving.

BACK TO BASICS

In her work, Vaughan (1997; 2007) seeks to reinstall gift-giving as a mode of selfless, unilateral generosity that is a unique quality belonging to women. In contrasting her definition of the gift with commercial exchange, Vaughan waxes lyrical in her appreciation of the all-giving mother, utterly devoted to satisfying the needs of her child, as a revered exemplar of gift-giving. Such selfless service is praised as being far superior to the competitive, self-centered, profit-driven capitalist exchange model that is identified as patriarchal. This stark contrast is somewhat alarming, not just in its diagnostic opposition, but also in its recommended solution. Vaughan's basic strategy is to reclaim the values of mothering as the epitome of gift-giving. One reason for such an undertaking is that Vaughan asserts that both mothering and gift-giving have been discredited and co-opted by capitalism for its own profiteering ends. As Vaughan asserts: "Gift-giving has been given many names that bring it into the Patriarchal Capitalist fold, like 'profit,' 'housework,' 'morality,' 'charity,' 'remittances,' 'solidarity,' 'political commitment,' even 'love'" (Vaughan 2007, 24). Vaughan believes that by calling attention to this process, i.e., the assimilation of terms connected with the maternal by capitalism, such subversion can be recognized and right order re-established. "I believe that in discussing the gift economy we are naming something that we are already doing but which is hidden under a variety of names, and is disrespected as well as misconstrued" (2007, 1).

In some ways this assertion is not quite as fanciful as it first appears. Such vacillation is not exactly absent from the work of Mauss himself. In his book, *The Work of the Gift* (2005), Scott Cutler Shershow has detected a similar tendency in Mauss. (Yet in Mauss's own reflections, things are not quite as clear-cut as they are for Vaughan.) Shershow rightly identifies a "totalizing" impulse that informs Mauss's interpretation of the gift as an exercise in the service of a disciplinary grand narrative, i.e., that of anthropology itself.[25]

At the same time, however, Shershow discerns a strange ambivalence that disturbs this absolutist pretension. Indeed, this incongruity may well have escaped Mauss's own awareness. On the one hand, Shershow reads in Mauss's interpretation a nostalgic celebration of an era when gift-giving seemed less mercenary than in his own time, and he asserts that much could be learned by his contemporaries about the spirit in which such transactions took place. On the other hand, there is also evident in Mauss a more pragmatic notion. This is that one can rediscover today a continuity of certain practices that existed in such past times. On this account, there is no need to keep searching elsewhere to find more appropriate practices for present needs. They have always been part of "our" culture. In other words, different modes of exchange did once exist and have continued to exist, possibly in camouflage, until today. But Mauss is not entirely forthright on these matters, especially in his conclusion, where he seems to want to have the best of both worlds.

Similarly in Vaughan's version, as in many readings of Mauss, there seems to be a constant slippage between the uses of gift and exchange, and their respective values. Initially Vaughan posits that gift-giving has always existed and that capitalist patriarchy is a later deviation that needs to be reformed. In this telling, it seems that gift is free from pecuniary concerns, while exchange is compromised by monetary matters. At other times, however, gift and exchange are posited as part of a continuum whereby the pristine gift can either be viewed as a preliminary form of contemporary capitalism, or as being in need of liberation from accumulated venal practices (Vaughan 2007, 24–25).

Christopher Bracken makes an observation that is helpful in understanding why such ambiguous readings of Mauss may occur. He notes: "Mauss makes it clear from the outset that his aim is to learn why in certain premodern, and non-western societies total services are exchanged not *as* gifts, but *as if* they were gifts" (1997, 155). It is perhaps a failure to distinguish this subtlety in Mauss's work that could well be responsible for the many subsequent indiscriminate interpretations of gift and exchange, especially by those who posit them as mutually exclusive.

Yet while at times Vaughan's views may owe something to such purported equivocations in Mauss's text—conscious or otherwise—her own final recommendations regarding the gift and exchange are quite straightforward. I am sympathetic to Vaughan's intention to rehabilitate other values than those of graft and greed that have become synonymous with contemporary global capitalism. It is difficult, however, to comprehend how her proposal of restoring a society that is dedicated solely to gift-giving could succeed. The inversion she recommends would seem to be based on a wishful fantasy of a "pure gift" that has probably never existed. Vaughan endeavors to reform today's crass commercialism by rejecting all exchange as a virtual tool of patriarchy. But it would seem that a more nuanced, or realistic, assessment of what is actually at stake is needed. Marcel Hénaff has definitely helped to amplify certain dimensions of Mauss's interpretation of the gift, especially the dynamics of recognition as enacted in the forms of ceremonial gift-giving. He also describes how such gift-giving has always co-existed with trade and forms of market exchange. Indeed, there may well be instances of intersecting mutual interests. As a result, not all exchange conforms to the extremes of crass contemporary capitalism as Vaughan implies.

There is another problematic aspect in Vaughan's program. It is also hampered by her identification of the ideals that she attributes to mothering as also belonging to indigenous peoples. Such an association is reminiscent of Mauss's own nostalgia for a bygone age of innocence. Vaughan declares: "Indigenous and matriarchal cultures, based more on *gift-giving*, had and have very different worldviews that honor and sustain life, create lasting community and foster abundance for all" (2007, 2–3). Such a universal statement belies the fact that many societies of indigenous peoples throughout the world continue to witness to varied expressions of both honoring life and exchanging goods. While it needs to be observed that certain contemporary deviations could be attributable to the effects of colonialism,[26] all indigenous peoples cannot be regarded as conforming since time immemorial to an archaic and exotic ideal of generous gift-giving. There have been many anthropological studies of precolonial patriarchal cultures, including those of the Nuer peoples of Africa, that support this (Meeker 1989). Even the work of Peggy Reeves Sanday (1981, 2011), whose studies on existing matriarchies contest the ubiquity of patriarchy, attests to its existence in many early communities.

A further difficulty evident in Vaughan's work is her complaint that many contemporary discussants of the gift do not perceive the logic of exchange as a major problem and, as a result, have not made the obviously needed link between mothering and gift-giving as the solution to society's woes (1997, 22). There is no compelling reason, however, why such a connection should be made by scholars. Some scholars, such as Hyde (1983) and Godbout (1998), worried by the contemporary commercialized aspects of the gift, instead look to aesthetic and other life-affirming naturalistic modes as possible correctives. Others describe extremely problematic contemporary issues of women in relation to commodification and trafficking, but do not prescribe gift-giving as a solution.[27] Their recommendations favor changes to the demands associated with male privilege; they do not recommend gift-giving as a solution. In all of these cases it is difficult to appreciate how an idealized view of mothering as unilateral giving could come to the rescue of current societal practices. The evidence for a prehistoric matriarchy and its gift-giving propensity is scanty at best and selective in its references. Inevitably, without a very detailed and comprehensive analysis of the variable economic, political, and societal arrangements of early peoples in their diverse geographical locations, any assertions of an essentialist nature regarding their gifts and exchange practices are extremely dubious.

THE CARING HYPOTHESIS

Nonetheless, the question of what prevents scholars from appreciating an association of gift-giving with mothering introduces a fiercely contested topic in feminist circles. This is because it assumes that there are specific characteristics associated with mothering that deserve not only recognition but general cultivation. Such a conviction recalls the controversy that began with the work of Sara Ruddick (1989) and Virginia Held (1993), and which, in fact, continues to this day. In a recent special issue of *Hypatia* (Gruen and Wylie 2010), celebrating its twenty-fifth year of publication, a number of women scholars revisited Ruddick's work. This task was undertaken in the context of ongoing study and the developing of new insights on this issue. Yet it seems that the initial problematic remains controversial, not simply with the construct of "motherhood" itself, but also with the various tenets, such as caring, that are attributed to mothering. In Ruddick's work, the main assumption on her part was that certain practices that she associated with "mothering" were regarded as compatible with peace-making, rather than with gift-giving. Ruddick further identified this peace-making with Mahatma Gandhi's practices of nonviolence (*ahimsa*). She encouraged the universal adoption of such practices. In the recent *Hypatia* issue, one contributor returns to Alison Bailey's comments on the false universalism that pervades Ruddick's project. Bailey states: "By conflating these two voices [one that emerges from personal experience, and the other the voice of the near-universal moral theorist], Ruddick lets her own experience stand in for the experiences of mothers in general" (Bailey quoted in Keller 2010, 836). While it cannot be said that Genevieve Vaughan similarly advances her own experience of mothering as a universal prescription, it appears that she similarly selects one specific characteristic of motherhood, gratuitous gift-giving, as definitive for all women, and deems it suitable for global adoption.

Susan Mendus, in her book, *Feminism and Emotion: Readings in Moral and Political Philosophy* (2000), makes some trenchant remarks that are applicable to shortcomings in the work of both Ruddick and Vaughan. Firstly, Mendus is concerned that a woman's identity appears to be primarily dictated by her role as the bearer of and carer for children, thereby either ignoring or dismissing the putative identity of a childless woman, whether this condition is the result of choice or barrenness (2000, 102–103). Mendus further considers this conflation as not just "simplistic and unitary" (100), but as intrinsically romantic (104). For Mendus, such a position glorifies domesticity at the expense of other roles and activities, such as political involvement, that could well prove necessary for a woman's survival (104). Finally, it idealizes mothering and fails to take into account the conflict and frustrations often involved in it (104).

In another article in the same volume of *Hypatia,* María Lugones, who does not specifically cite Ruddick, draws attention to the hierarchical dichotomies that are implicit in such forms of the universalizing of caregiving. As a consequence, "women at the intersection of race, class, and gender, nonwhite, black, mestiza, indigenous and Asian women," become virtually invisible or impossible to acknowledge, because they do not fall into the established ideal categories (2010, 755). Lugones's main criticism is that such a mode of colonial or selective thinking still intrudes today. It prevents many women from witnessing to disparate ways of being and thinking that existing empirical research fails to acknowledge. Another significant aspect that Lugones's work raises in relation to Vaughan's and Ruddick's definitions of motherhood are their Eurocentric presumptions. This can be detected most especially in their respective univocal value systems, but also, in Vaughan's case, in her unqualified identification of gift-giving with indigenous peoples. Such colonialist tendencies still surface in much literature on the gift.

MATERNITY AND ITS DISCONTENTS

Perhaps the most noticeable defect in Vaughan's position, however, is that she seems totally unaware that today, mothering has lost something of its former rosy glow. It is no longer collectively acclaimed as a selfless yet self-fulfilling task. This can be attributed to a number of realistic books by young women reporting from the trenches of contemporary motherhood, among them Maushart (1999) and Crittenden (2001). These books are not necessarily hostile to motherhood, but they are unsentimental assessments by young contemporary mothers of the thankless way in which they believe they are treated by their society. What these women have realized is that the needs of motherhood are a very low priority in most social systems, with funding for child care being a particular problem. The working world also largely refuses to adapt its policies to allow flexibility for mothers who want to continue their careers. Yet this is not all. What these young women have come

to understand is that while women have taken upon themselves a disproportionate amount of responsibility in the maintenance of familial duties—
where care and compassion still feature prominently in the guidance literature—recompense for such an undertaking is negligible. As Crittenden has
observed: "The gift of care can be both selfless and exploited" (2001, 4). This
is all too obvious in the lack of public support systems that provide aid—be
it of psychological or practical nature—in times of stress. This demonstrates
that women's basic needs are disregarded and they are left to fend for themselves. In other words, women's gifts in this vital area can indeed be praised
as unilateral, but only because such gifts are taken for granted. Many women
today are protesting this benign neglect or deliberate indifference that takes
advantage of their services. Susan Maushart is quite explicit in her diagnosis
of one of the very basic needs that continue to be ignored.

> The question "What do women want?" which vexed Freud, and countless
> millions of males since Freud, can be answered very simply in the case of
> postpartum females. What they want is sleep, and if not sleep then at least
> undisturbed rest. And in a nuclear family structure in which a woman is
> solely responsible for infant care both day and night, she is not likely to get
> either of these for a long, long time. (1999, 302)

Maushart is just as explicit in her depiction of the realities of power that are
involved, or rather not involved, for women who choose to mother and are
thereby automatically relegated to the private sphere.

> Some observers have argued that the social contract called patriarchy rests
> on a trade-off in which the control by men of the "means of production" (of
> social and economic power) compensates for female control of the "means
> of reproduction." While impossible to verify or refute empirically, for me the
> theory makes intuitive sense. It is this trade-off that ensures that the hand
> that rocks the cradle does *not* rule the world, or at least not absolutely or for
> long. From this point of view, the familiar formulations of gender-specific
> spheres of endeavor—the domestic versus the economic; the heart versus
> the head; nature versus culture—reflect more than a division of labor. They
> reflect a primary division of power. (1999, 49)

POWER DYNAMICS

A careful analysis shows quite bluntly that the culturally specific niceties
Vaughan promotes in relation to unilateral maternal gift-giving utterly fail

to take into consideration the imbalance of power that is involved. There are dynamics of power involved in all such gift-giving, not solely in the naked power politics of economic dealings—even if their modalities of operations are somewhat different. Michel Foucault has acutely analyzed the inevitable maneuvers of power as they influence even the most trivial levels of activity. The use and abuse of power in relation to the contemporary dynamics of human relations, especially those that address issues of equality and integrity in relationships, needs to be accorded the same scrutiny that Weiner applied to Trobriand women.[28]

Annette Weiner has described precisely the negotiations of power that Trobriand women engaged in, with their husbands as well as with other women. The identities (or subjectivities) of these women are shown as deeply implicated in both private and public realms, thus affirming their integrity within an overarching cosmology. The Trobriand women she described, however, did have the advantage of living in a society that honored women and respected their contributions. Yet it is not simply the act of giving that confers affirmation on women; giving as an activity must be respected as positive and incorporated into a society's value system. The realpolitik demanded in daily life in contemporary western society with its multilayered and intertwined worlds of economics, politics, and the law—to name but a few of its spheres of influence—does not facilitate a similar study today. Yet a few have undertaken such research, using the gift as a guiding indicator.

Aafke Komter, in her edited volume *The Gift: An Interdisciplinary Perspective* (1996), has attempted, from a sociological perspective, to delineate four different ways that women may negotiate power within the framework of today's heterogeneous society. Her work makes some excellent observations on the possibilities available for women and their advantages as well as disadvantages. Yet there is a familiar dichotomy that informs her work. Her principal recommendation is that women, though they remain principally affiliated with giving, should attempt to participate in the activities of those domains that are connected to the market. Yet she warns: "In giving much to others, women incur the risk of losing their own identities, given their unequal societal and economic power compared with men" (130–31). While Komter's sociological approach is descriptive rather than diagnostic, it nonetheless appears to acquiesce to the dominant values of contemporary society. Women remain basically identified with private caring, men with the public market economy. Although Komter is sympathetic to women's dilemma and advocates change, she does not investigate why these values still persist, apparently almost impervious to change. Ultimately, then, her conclusions are not particularly inspiring.

At the heart of the matter, however, there remains a vital question as to why most western institutions, despite more than forty years of feminist activism, still do not accord women due respect and compensation for their services, whether they are in the workforce or on the home front. Why does sexual bifurcation still continue, despite the explorations in gender-bending instigated by Judith Butler in her book *Gender Trouble* (1990)? There is always recognition of some progress, though the intransigence on certain issues of women's integrity remains firm. The lack of constructive response to feminist recommendations, particularly in trying to realign aspects of the public/private separation, is perplexing. It is symptomatic of something far more complex than the clichés of sexism that basic analyses identify as the problem. There remains a deeply embedded strain of misogyny in most western cultural institutions where the real sources of power are located. One thing is clear, however, and this is that the situation will not be remedied by continued selfless giving as it is presently conceived. The worry is that these views are still being circulated, even in quite recent empirical studies.

SCIENCE TO THE RESCUE

As part of a search for deeper insight into this continuing quandary, the recent work of two women scholars, Cordelia Fine (2010) and Rebecca Jordan-Young (2010), has been immensely helpful. They are both extremely critical of the recent biological essentialism that assumes gender attributes are largely predetermined before birth. This has been promoted in the work of scholars such as Simon Baron-Cohen (2005) and Louann Brizendine (2007). Fine and Jordan-Young are also both scathing in their evaluations of the lack of proper protocols in much of the empirical research involved, as well as of the exaggerated claims that result from these findings. Their investigative research work builds on the earlier research assessments of Anne Fausto-Sterling, especially her book, *Sexing the Body: Gender Politics and the Construction of Sexuality* (2000). In an earlier work, Fausto-Sterling had herself remarked on other faulty findings, most of which focused on proving distinct "brain-sex" determinants of males and females. She then asked:

> What is the untrained onlooker to make of all this? Are these examples of "science corrupted," as one historian has called the misrepresentation of women in scientific studies, or do such cases provide evidence for a rather different view of science—one in which the scientists themselves emerge as cultural products, their activities structured, often unconsciously, by the great social issues of the day? (1992, 8–9)

Such observations are of critical importance, for while nobody is denying that there are definite differences between males and females that result from the effects of hormones and neurons, sociobiologists and cognitive scientists seem determined to eliminate any reference to their own biases. Ironically it is Baron-Cohen's and Brizendine's own unrecognized social conditioning that may indeed be interfering with certain of their findings. Presuppositions as to what constitutes appropriate "masculine" and "feminine" behavior are all too evident. Fine will refer to this bias as "neurosexism," while Jordan-Young employs the term "sex-typed interest."

It is very disheartening to read their evaluations of the results from the PET scans, fMRIs, and various types of tests on infants undertaken by Baron-Cohen and Brizendine. Many of these tests are on newborn babies, given the assumption that no socialization can have yet taken place. These tests, however, simply confirm most of the present stereotypes about male and female differences. This is that males have a higher Systemizing Quotient (SQ) while females have an Empathizing Quotient (EQ). (Fine's account of the actual testing on one-and-a-half-day-old infants is particularly entertaining, if not also sobering in its implications [2010, 110–15].) Much of the research seems bent on confirming that an in utero testosterone surge "masculinizes" the fetal brain. In this strictly determined binary division of the sexes there is little, if any, attention paid to the lives of lesbians and gays, to intersexuals and transsexuals, as if their experiences do not count.

In connection with this inquiry on women, care, and the gift, and its actual relation to women's temperaments, it is the emphasis on the so-called Empathizing Quotient that is perhaps the most distressing. The principal claim is that these tests prove women are hardwired for caring for others. It is not that caring and empathy are intrinsically bad things, but when it appears that social scientific resources are heavily concentrated on continuing a misguided tradition, there is cause for deep suspicion. Why the seemingly desperate need to make assertions, be they "scientific" or God-given, to affirm women's more caring disposition? In these experiments, specific contexts are also discounted on the supposed grounds of objectivity. Because of this, many influences attributable to cultural conditioning are overlooked. Ultimately, all this amounts to the fact that women, because of a purported emotional inheritance, are still expected to carry a disproportionate load of the moral burden of care and concern for humanity. Such injustice unfortunately continues to be defended on scientific grounds that, as Fausto-Sterling, Fine, and Jordan-Young demonstrate, do not withstand rigorous investigation.

The only ray of light, if that is the appropriate phrase, is the recent vogue in empathy studies. One recent volume comes from the primatologist Frans de Waal (2009), another from the all-purpose trendsetter and analyzer of these developments, Jeremy Rifkin (2009). De Waal's basic premise in *The Age of Empathy* is that many primates have exhibited cooperative tendencies and empathy, so not all nature is brutish and only promotes survival of the fittest. At least it is something of a corrective to *The Naked Ape* (1999), but in both books an underlying variant of the naturalist fallacy seems to assume that as it goes with apes, so it is with humans. Rifkin, in a futurist mode in *The Empathic Civilization* (2009), prescribes empathy as a necessary ingredient for human survival as well as the planet's. In his entrepreneurial style, Rifkin automatically assumes it will be business-philanthropist types, such as Bill Gates or Warren Buffett, who will lead the way, while new empathic management styles in business will change the face of capitalism. Perhaps benevolent gift-giving without profit-seeking will automatically follow. Again it seems that a utopian fantasy prevails and, as in Vaughan's scenario, chances of its arrival are slim. The irony in this case, however, is that when the knights of capitalism ride to the rescue, all the feminine gender-specific aspects of empathy and caring, so pervasive in neuroscience, seem to be entirely forgotten.

INTIMATIONS OF OTHERNESS

In many of the recent discussions on care, gender, and the gift, philosophical concerns seem to have faded into the background. This is particularly disheartening as both care and the gift are intimately related to issues of intersubjectivity and ethics from a philosophical perspective. Rosalyn Diprose (2002) and Lisa Guenther (2006) are two exceptions to this trend. They both incorporate an ethical direction toward others, grounded in revised notions of the thought of Emmanuel Levinas, principally as presented in *Totality and Infinity* ([1969] 1991). In this, they are similar to Marcel Hénaff, who also appeals to Levinas in concluding his observations in *The Price of Truth* (2010), claiming that such an ethics is at the heart of his own project. Yet the Levinasian project is troublesome for women, with its privileging of male views on maternity and his ideal of "love without concupiscence."[29] Thus, although I am very much an admirer of Levinas, I have nevertheless taken him to task for certain views on women and the "feminine" as exemplars of extreme responsibility (Joy 2006a, 72–88). My problem with Levinas is that, as a woman, I balk at both his idealizations and his ethical injunction to be both passive and fully responsible for the other, to the extent that I am virtually at the other's disposal. Such an orientation sounds all too familiar, in line with the expected self-sacrificial orientation of women over the centuries.

Nevertheless, as I have also commented, Levinas's ethical challenge could be regarded as a fitting exhortation to men to reform their own ethical dispositions, especially in their relations to women. Diprose and Guenther, however, have proposed other emendations to Levinas's ethical endorsements that summon justice as a supplement and relevant support for women today.

Diprose's and Guenther's important books seek to "rescue" the gift from a number of the misappropriations that identify it with women and/or the "feminine." They both strive to reinterpret the gift as a gesture of radical generosity. At the same time, however, they are extremely wary about adopting any position that would presume to depend on women as a source of unstinting yet unrewarded generosity. Diprose and Guenther modify and reframe, respectively, Levinas's ideas, especially on the topic of justice. These revisions allow for a more equitable understanding of human relationships represented in terms of the gift. Both their works also defer to the work of Derrida on the aporia of the gift, which leads to inevitable problems. This is because they still envision the gift only as something that can be given without calculation, as an act of selfless magnanimity.

Diprose's work, *Corporeal Generosity: On Giving with Nietzsche, Merleau-Ponty, and Levinas* (2002), is principally concerned with portraying a new ontology of the gift, which she aligns with generosity. She believes that generosity can inform personal, social, and even political activity. At the heart of her work is an endeavor to reframe generosity so that it is appreciated as embracing bodily and affective elements that foster new ways of being and understanding through relationships with others. Diprose emphasizes the "ineradicable difference" (2002, 184) of the other as informing her model of intersubjective relations, as well as "a passionate politics of transformation" (187). Her final position in revising the gift as generosity is a fascinating blend of Derrida, Merleau-Ponty, and Levinas—with qualified help from Nietzsche's notion of self-overcoming and his praise of a generous attitude (12–13; 23–25).

Diprose initially justifies her adaptation of Levinas's notion of responsibility as resonating with her own understanding of generosity. "Levinas describes subjectivity . . . in terms of generosity as I understand it. His work lends itself to a philosophy of the gift, insofar as he bases a sociality that does not absorb difference on giving to the other without expectation of return" (2002, 13). In stressing the "ineradicable difference" of the other, Diprose melds two different meanings associated with Levinas's originary ethics. The first posits the other as that which disturbs one's egotistic preoccupations and conceptual certainties. The second prescribes an attitude of radical generosity, as maternity, that informs one's openness to and hospitable reception of others.[30] But Diprose worries that Levinas's ethical injunction and its emphasis on passivity does not pay sufficient attention to the corporeal and affective elements of interpersonal relationships. (Diprose quotes Levinas: "I am given to the other unconditionally through passive sensibility" [179].) To "flesh out" the actual dynamics of such relations, Diprose turns to Merleau-Ponty as a way to move beyond Levinas's own depiction. Diprose invokes Merleau-Ponty's notion of intersubjectivity—or, more precisely, intercorpo-reality—to provide insight into the active dimensions of personal encounter whereby: "bodily identity is never individual; it is intersubjective: based on the non-volitional generosity of intercorporeality fashioned with reference to the social and familial situation" (68–69). Generosity, in Diprose's analysis, is always embodied or corporeal—something Levinas does not observe.

Diprose also includes a further dimension, likewise undeveloped in any detail by Levinas. This is that of transformation: "The other side of the story is that my body identity is transformed in this performance through the world of the other" (70). Such interactions and transformative aspects of interpersonal/social relationships have major implications for Diprose's work. This is because Diprose realizes that there can be psychological and social interference both in relationships and in their potential transformation. Again Diprose turns to Merleau-Ponty because he recognizes that social norms and prohibitions can influence sensibility, hence perception, and consequently intersubjective relations. In some cases sensibility may not necessarily open to the other, because in Merleau-Ponty's view, "social sedimentation," in the form of inflexible norms and prohibitions, can prove to be obstructive. Diprose proposes that intervention is required to disturb such sedimentations if one is "to remain open to new modalities of being" (72), and hence to transformation. It is here that Diprose's ontology and politics make their appearance, as she is aware that Levinas's position of passivity is insufficient to sustain such activism, however vigilant it may be.

It is in this context that Diprose also raises the problem of the "asymmetry of the gift," that is, the way that, according to convention, social gifts have been designated to reward the privileged and exclude minorities. She investigates such occurrences in relation not only to women, but also to the indigenous peoples of Australia (148–59). Such imbalances need to be addressed. This marks Diprose's move beyond Levinas's ethics—including his maternal extravagances—to an ontology and politics with a special concern for justice. She criticizes both Levinas's understanding of justice and his separation of ethics and ontology (180–81). As she observes: "As Levinas is concerned with the order of responsibility rather than with its content, with ethics understood as radical generosity rather than ontology and politics, it is necessary to move beyond his thinking" (141–42).

Diprose introduces a more dynamic model that treats the personal as the political, and also supports an activist stance to combat inequitable distribution. From Levinas's perspective, Diprose has made a step that entails an "ontological closure." (This is the closure that comes from a totalizing system such as Levinas criticizes, where decisions are made in accordance with legal dictates and a general rule.)[31] Although Levinas concedes that justice is necessary, often framing his discussion in terms of a "third" (or plurality) who intervenes in one's singular ethical relation to the other, he is adamant about the primacy of ethics. He has stated, however, that "[j]ustice is impossible without the one that renders it finding himself in proximity [to the other]. His function is not limited to 'the function of judgment,' the subsuming of particular cases under a general rule" ([1974] 1998, 159). Diprose is adroit in calling on Derrida and his sense of a "justice that is to come" to sustain her own appeal to ethics and justice. In so doing, she does not necessarily dismiss the relationship of proximity and "non-indifference to difference," insofar as it implies a radical openness to the other. But she also insists on transformation. In summoning Derrida's messianic ideal of justice that can never be realized, but always impels social action toward a futural justice, Diprose also avoids closure.[32] Finally, such activity is in keeping with Diprose's appreciation of generosity as a gift that is both embodied and material. She justifies her approach, in using this politically sensitive notion of generosity: "The analysis maintains a focus on the theme of social justice by framing the development of the concept of corporeal generosity in terms of particular social issues and political problems concerning sexual difference, sexuality and cultural difference" (150).

In Diprose's development, the gift takes on new resonances, beyond Levinas's recommendations of responsibility and hospitality. It allows that transformation can be a felicitous result of personal interaction. This transformation can happen not simply by dedication to the subjective sensibilities of other human beings, but also by reform of unjust societal preferences that restrict their range of experience, and of being. Generosity is then a gift of openness and attention to the other that can foster transformation in the name of justice. Perhaps one of the more intriguing conclusions of her work is that this mode of generosity is not necessarily a virtue specific to women. As a result, Diprose can situate feminist approaches as constituting one of the discourses that need to be embraced as a previously marginalized voice of the other—a caution overlooked in Levinas. Her work is thus a major contribution to deliberations on women and the gift.

Lisa Guenther's work, *The Gift of the Other: Levinas and the Politics of Reproduction* (2006), is another close reading of Levinas's books, and another feminist response to his ideas. It focuses specifically on the contested topic of motherhood, understood as "the gift of the Other" (2006, 2). Her intention is to examine Levinas's observations on both paternity and maternity so as to "problematize any stable, unambiguous interpretation of femininity in his work" (7). Principally, however, Guenther provides new perspectives that enrich feminist work concerned with an ethics of birth and a politics of reproduction. In reforming certain of Levinas's more suspect claims about women and the "feminine,"[33] Guenther also helps to clarify the way that an ethical understanding of maternity, in relation to the gift, might actually be expressed. Here, Guenther enlists justice for her cause, as does Diprose.

By way of introduction it seems appropriate to begin with Guenther's startling proviso in her introduction. Here she indicates immediately that she will not endorse Levinas's romantic evocation of maternity as the epitome of total responsibility for the other—the gift nonpareil. Guenther states: "Without a situation of reproductive justice—in which women have access to a meaningful range of reproductive choices that take into account differences in race, income, mobility, and sexuality—the ethics of birth [I outline] could have profoundly unethical and unjust consequences for women" (8).

It is with this stipulation in mind that Guenther first explores Levinas's preferential treatment of paternity in *Totality and Infinity* ([1969] 1991). Ironically, in Guenther's reading, the intense attention Levinas pays to father and son makes fecundity and giving birth appear to be a virtual male preserve. "In *Totality and Infinity,* parenthood is understood almost exclusively as the transcendent relation of a father to his son. Despite the implicit figuration of given birth as a welcome from the feminine Other, *giving* birth would seem to be a wholly masculine affair" (75). As a result, women's role is marginalized and admonitions even issued regarding her potential interference, if *eros* is profaned.[34]

Nevertheless, as mentioned above, there is a place for woman in Levinas's scheme, as representative of the munificent welcome of hospitality, of unconditional acceptance of the stranger. Yet Guenther then circumspectly notes that in this context a woman is neither the proprietor of the dwelling nor the head of the family. As such, woman exemplifies the unacknowledged expenditure of time and energy that provides food, shelter, and other amenities to guests. This is similar to her indispensable but seemingly subsidiary role in the birth of a son. "The encounter of the feminine beloved may be necessary for paternity, just as the welcome of the feminine in the home was necessary for ethics; however here, as before, the serious business of ethics is left to the men" (89). Guenther understands both of these illustrations as evidence of a basic flaw in Levinas's work that institutes a mode of social asymmetry. This easily mutates into a political bias where the status of women's essential con-tributions to domestic maintenance is reduced to a token of self-sacrificial duty/responsibility.

Yet in her own search for justice, Guenther makes a surprising move when she responds to Levinas's expression "like a maternal body," which he uses in his second major book, *Otherwise than Being* ([1974] 1998, 67). As she suc-cinctly states: "*Like* opens up a gap between maternity as a biological fact and as ethical responsibility" (7). This implies that maternity need not be taken literally, and that it can be applied to both men and women. Consequently, in Guenther's reading, the command to welcome the stranger, in the man-ner of maternal hospitality, can be understood as a mandate "to be femi-nized by the Other" (6). As a non-patriarchal step toward equity, this move broaches extremely sensitive territory for both men and women. Guenther is well aware of this. One immediate question is, How can a non-gender-specific and gift-oriented ethics address women's long-neglected service in mothering humanity? Another, of equal importance, arises: How will such "feminine" values be appropriated by men who fear their virility is threat-ened? Guenther treads carefully through this minefield. Her comments cen-ter on clarifying her own appreciation of motherhood on ethical, political, and judicial grounds.

Guenther first raises the issue of the way that the command of maternal hospitality registers differently for women themselves, given their ability to give birth both literally and figuratively. This raises further provocative issues about the relevance of physical maternity. Guenther responds: "Where power is shared unequally across gender, race and class lines, it seems naïve and even dangerous to claim that birth is a gift for which no adequate reciproca-tion is possible" (8). Yet if maternity and the generosity of the gift, especially in accord with responsibility and hospitality are to be recommended as a possible orientation for men, something else is obviously needed. For Guen-ther, this requisite addition is justice. As a result, any universal injunction of maternal welcome could only occur in an equitable world. This would inevitably imply that Levinas's previous stress on paternity and sons would also have to be extended to mothers and daughters. Yet Guenther is not forthcoming about the way that men can be persuaded to accept such a radi-cal move, attractive as it may sound theoretically. This matter of the actual acceptance of maternal hospitality and its implementation by both men and women is perhaps the weakest point of her position.

Ultimately, Guenther's argument for a feminist vision of maternal ethics and a politics of reproduction entails that ethics, even when as inexorable as Levinas's, cannot be implemented without a concomitant appeal to justice.

The gift, as an inexhaustible maternity, as total responsibility, as hospitality without reserve, cannot be idealistically invoked unless a thorough contextual and historical evaluation is first undertaken. Guenther's vigorous arguments on behalf of those whose gifts have been unrecognized, which she supports by a demand for justice, have definite similarities to Diprose's call for justice and the inclusion of all marginalized others:

> Precisely because it calls for such inordinate goodness, Levinas's ethics of radical responsibility . . . requires a politics of justice to address and critique the unshared social burden that is often heaped on certain groups of people: women, workers, black and brown people, anyone whose contribution to collective life goes regularly unnoticed or unreciprocated. (Guenther 2006, 140)

Both Diprose and Guenther, from different perspectives, summon justice to amend Levinas's asymmetrical ethical dispensation. In one sense they each attempt to resolve the core problem presented by Diane Perpich as it relates to women and care in Levinas's work. Perpich states: "That Levinas employs the figure of *the feminine* to bridge the gap between ontology and ethics—a gap he elsewhere implies is unbridgeable—is not incidental" (2008, 104). Perpich further discusses how Levinas employs *the feminine* in a way that allows his theory to succeed—though some would argue it doesn't—while women themselves are actually excluded from undertaking this move from ethics to ontology (108). The invocation of justice by Diprose and Guenther, and the move beyond ethics, is a welcome development that addresses Levinas's blind spots in relation to women.

FINAL QUALIFICATIONS

There still remains one final predicament at the heart of both Diprose's and Guenther's work. This is that they both accept Derrida's aporia between the gift (that must be without calculation) and exchange (that expects remuneration). As Hénaff argued earlier, Mauss did not necessarily have this distinction in mind, and the affiliations involved are far more complex. As Hénaff also described earlier, it was recognition that animated many of the interactions Mauss described. Thus Derrida's stark distinction needs to be called into question. (It could still serve as a heuristic tool, to indicate certain contemporary aberrations in capitalism, but even as a broadly based insight it is simplistic at best.) Derrida's designation of the gift as selfless and without need of remuneration is particularly problematic for women, who could still be urged, whether or not men join them in this task, to give without restriction. This seems an inordinate demand, especially if it is expected in an equitable society. In contrast, it would seem that, for both Diprose and Guenther, what women are seeking in such an equitable society is recognition of their integrity. In this setting, any further admonitions to selflessness would seem somewhat anachronistic. Respect and concern for the other as irreducible and recognition of their integrity in an equitable society would alleviate Derrida's requirement of selflessness and infinite largesse.

It is perhaps time, then, to explore what a reclamation of recognition in relation to the gift, within a transformed and just society, could effect. For certain revisions in the definition of the gift and its requirements—especially the demand of selflessness—do need to be initiated. Its relation to recognition also warrants further investigation. Fortunately, there are recent works that do focus on recognition (Honneth 1996, Nussbaum 1999, Ricoeur 2005). Yet many discussions on recognition today have centered mainly on rights talk in the political sphere. At a basic level, rights would imply that all human beings are entitled to the same basic freedoms as oneself. While extremely laudatory, such a statement can seem empty in the face of states that refuse to enact them or even violate them without compunction. From a postcolonialist perspective, rights also have been criticized for their universal claims that basically reflect a western viewpoint. In addition, from a more communitarian perspective, rights entitlements have been criticized for their co-optation by an individualistic agenda. Rights may thus be necessary, but not sufficient, if recognition and the gift are to be revised to accommodate an intersubjective element. A revised appreciation of recognition, then, could to help fill in the gaps, the areas that basic assumptions of rights do not necessarily cover. The Hegelian version of recognition, however, has also been criticized for its patronizing aspects. Kelly Oliver, in *Witnessing: Beyond Recognition,* captures this nuance particularly well. "The very notion of recognition as it is deployed in various contemporary theoretical contexts is, then, a symptom of the pathology of oppression itself" (2001, 9). For Oliver, the act of recognition can simply endorse the dominant culture's superiority. She continues: "If recognition is conceived as being conferred on others by the dominant group, then it merely repeats the dynamic hierarchies, privilege and domination" (9).

It may be that Paul Ricoeur's model of recognition as a gift can, in some measure, begin to aid in a reformulation of recognition that avoids such traps (Ricoeur 2005, 257–63).[35] His arguments in *The Course of Recognition* (2005) are inevitably complex, and unfortunately there is not sufficient space to examine them in detail. Ultimately, however, he proposes that recognition needs to be grounded in a reciprocal relationship, inspired by a passion for justice. It features a caring and non-narcissistic subject in communication with an irreducible other(s). Such an understanding of recognition would then no longer reinforce elitist ways of granting admission only when prescribed standards of conformity are met. It would also provide the basis for an ethics not only of compassion and generosity, but one that honors the integrity of another person in a way that also respects his or her differences. This understanding of an ethical foundation would be in keeping with Hénaff's observation about recognition as it functions in Mauss: that by bestowing a gift on the other, one is "honoring the existence and status of the other" (Hénaff 2010, 153).

Would this revision of a formalist version of recognition be sufficient to bring about more nuanced appreciations of the gift in relation to women, especially in their roles as givers? On this subject both Hénaff' and Ricoeur are silent. But this is where the work of Diprose can prove especially helpful, even if she does not supply the solution herself. First, Diprose can be of assistance because she insists on transformation—experienced not just in personal encounters, but also as a result of social reforms in the cause of justice. Other resources of a more subjective nature in her work could help to construe a non-self-sacrificial option for women. One term Diprose uses, borrowed from Levinas, is the "ineradicable difference" of the other person (2002, 184). She also speaks of an orientation of "radical openness to the other" (180). These two expressions need not necessarily imply that a giver of a gift, in acting in accordance with both of these dispositions, is someone who is utterly self-sacrificial. Such a woman could certainly maintain a generous and non-egotistical disposition, but not to the point of total self-abnegation in service to the other. Insofar as these dispositions enhance one's interpersonal relationships with irreducible others in their "ineradicable difference," there is no reason why transformation, of oneself and of another, could not occur. A gift, then, need not always be selfless. Diprose herself does not claim this, but it is a plausible reading. Such an interpretation would signal a vast step forward, and many of the contributors to this volume would not disagree with this less exacting orientation.

One final qualification needs to be added to these intensely abstract qualifications. This is because the personal dimension, which does not need to justify itself theoretically, but instead relates details of a discerning and even intimate nature, is lacking. Such details, however, are patently evident in many of the suggestions offered by the contributors to this volume. Their awareness testifies to the fact that though justice, recognition, and rights may be recommended at the societal level, insights of a more personal nature can prove extremely beneficial. These disclosures help to illuminate other aspects of the gift and reveal its possibilities for transformation. Continued discussions at a theoretical level, though indispensable, can often prove frustrating. So, instead of continuing to seek more comprehensive or better elucidations of rights and recognition in relation to the gift, it is especially appropriate to turn now to the words of wisdom disclosed by the women contributors.

CONTRIBUTIONS

Deborah Lyons's introductory essay on the gift journeys back to the beginnings of the western heritage: to Greece. She describes how women—as daughters, wives, and sisters—are often represented in ancient Greek literature as gifts to be exchanged among men: as objects rather than subjects. Occasionally, however, women do become agents. They participate in exchanges that have serious consequences both for themselves and for their male relations. Lyons examines the role gender plays in these dynamics of exchange, primarily in Homeric epic, but also in several later works. Analyzing this material in light of cross-cultural evidence about gender, kinship, and exchange, she illustrates how anxiety about women's role in exchange is closely linked to ancient Greek ideas about marriage, as well as the sexual division of labor. Overall, the attitude is ambivalent, with a marked tendency towards anxiety.

Lyons first examines the *Iliad,* which establishes women's status as gifts, prizes, or booty. Women move as objects from one man to another through exchange or theft. From the abduction of Helen, which begins the Trojan War, to the quarrel over Briseis that threatens Greek victory, the circulation of women is a central theme of the poem. Objects of exchange only, women are not allowed any autonomy. Lyons then turns to the *Odyssey,* which, with its more domestic focus on Penelope waiting and weaving, offers an alternative perspective. Here, reciprocity becomes a major concern, and women are depicted as economic actors for the first time in Greek literature. This is because Odysseus, in journeying back to his wife and homeland, enters into a network of exchange relations with different women. Lyons observes that, not coincidentally for a poem that so often depicts its female characters from all classes working at the loom, the gifts women give men are predominantly textiles (soft wealth). In contrast, the gifts given by men are usually metal objects (durable wealth). Cloth seems to have been the only wealth over which women had any control. Men, in contrast, even when they are not the producers of precious metal objects, can freely dispose of them.

The poem nevertheless betrays hesitation about women's role in gift exchange, as summed up in the enigmatic phrase "on account of womanly gifts." It is used to allude to specific episodes of treachery in which gifts to a woman induce her to betray a close male relative; for instance, Astyoche betrays her son (*Odyssey* 11.521) and Eriphyle her husband *Odyssey* 15.247). Lyons ponders the origin of this suspicion about women and exchange. She remarks that Jean-Pierre Vernant, a French classical scholar, has reflected on the contradictory nature of the woman as both symbol of family continuity and circulating commodity. Because a daughter must leave her natal family to enter into that of her husband, the woman remains an outsider, a potential double agent. Lyons remarks on the fact that the integrity of the lineage she has entered depends on her fidelity to her husband, and this fidelity is seen as closely linked to her role as guardian of the household possessions, both material and symbolic (*Odyssey* 1.178–79, 19.525–27). In fact, a women's infidelity is nearly always linked to the giving or getting of inappropriate gifts. For instance, Eriphyle accepts a golden necklace and betrays her husband; Helen's abduction by Paris is accompanied by the theft of valuables from Menelaos's house. In these instances of betrayal, the gifts in question are inappropriate because they are not textile, and also because they circulate between the woman and a man who is not her husband. In a fascinating twist, however, it appears that by entering into an adulterous relationship, women are temporarily able to overturn the usual relations between men and women and create a new economy of gender, one in which they can give themselves away.

In concluding, Deborah Lyons observes that it is the initial circulation of women that makes marriage possible, but this association of women with circulation marks both their vulnerability and their untrustworthiness. It is the threat of this continued circulation which makes women not only objects of exchange, but also subjects; not only gifts but also givers, sometimes with deadly results. Hence the underlying distrust and anxiety that is so evident in early Greek portrayals of women and the gift. Even their limited autonomy, however, does not appear to have resulted in any abiding changes in the gender economy, but only in a reallocation of resources. Lyons demonstrates quite convincingly that the relationship of woman and the gift has been a contentious one from the very beginning.

Lorraine Markotic begins by acknowledging that a good number of Nietzsche's writings are not only sexist, but misogynist. At the same time, she points out that there are numerous writings by Nietzsche on women that are simply ambiguous. Nietzsche's aphoristic style contributes to this, and he himself worried that his writings would be misinterpreted. He insists that individual aphorisms should not be isolated from broader thematic concerns. As a result, certain philosophers have considered not only what Nietzsche wrote about women, but the concept of "woman" or the "feminine," and its associations. From this perspective, a number of Nietzsche's concepts could traditionally be associated with a notion of the "feminine" (though Nietzsche himself would hardly have formulated it this way). In addition, Nietzsche's critique of objectivity and reason, his emphasis on the Dionysian, his interest in metaphor and language, his consideration of questions of style, and his attention to the body could also appear as more compatible with a "feminine" rather than a "masculine" philosophy.

It is along these lines that Markotic elaborates on ways in which Nietzsche's ideas on the gift and gratitude can be regarded as "feminine." Furthermore, she states that they contain elements that could even be considered feminist. In line with Alan Schrift's demonstration that Nietzsche's concept of generosity can be said to involve a "feminine economy" of giving, Markotic attempts to show how Nietzsche's formulation of what is involved in a gift—giving and receiving, generosity and gratitude—entail a "feminine" notion of the gift.

It is specifically in Nietzsche's treatment of gratitude that his ideas could be coded as "feminine" (regardless of the sex of the people involved). For Nietzsche contends that a gift should not lead to one's rejecting the gift or taking it for granted out of fear that one will consequently relinquish independence, self-sufficiency, and completeness. Nor should there be so strong an attachment to the idea of self-reliance that one is unable to acknowledge and feel grateful for what has been received. Nietzsche's portrayal of gratitude also suggests that taking something for granted, not noticing that it was what one needed or what one wanted, is a weakness. Indeed, giving thanks can be considered a kind of strength. It is also a kind of generosity. By instigating reflection on the sensitivity required to be both a gracious giver and a gracious receiver, Nietzsche further provokes thinking about the intricacies involved, plus the resistances to being both a gracious and grateful receiver of gifts. Perhaps what is of most interest in Nietzsche's writings is that this appreciation opens the possibility that generosity and the gift need not be always marked as a prerogative of women.

While the concept of the gift, and the notion of giving, have been increasingly explored by philosophers (Derrida, Marion, Levinas, Bataille), Nietzsche examines not only giving but also receiving and the notion of gratitude. Nietzsche insists that we should not take for granted what we receive. Markotic then suggests that rather than seeing gratitude as opposed to giving, one can consider it a form of giving, insofar as it involves giving acknowledgment or giving thanks. For Nietzsche giving and generosity are crucial concepts, but so too is gratitude, and Markotic argues that they are connected. Her chapter is an attempt to break away from the sexual stereotyping that unfortunately dominates many reflections on the gift. At the same time it opens up further discussion of the way that "feminine" and "masculine" can be attributed when they are not simply identified with biological markers.

Nancy J. Holland frames her chapter as a belated token of thanks to Sarah Kofman for two gifts she received from her. One of these was to affirm Holland's intuition that whenever Derrida wrote on the gift, he was also writing about Woman/women. Their status, as with all other figures of Derridean possibility/impossibility, was to undermine the "phallogocentric" system that Derrida dates from the time of Plato. Yet Holland asks whether Woman/ women can feature in the guise of both gift and poison, among many other deconstructive terms, in a system from which they have been excluded from its beginnings. She wonders if Derrida, with his constant play of ellipses, has not become entangled in his own elliptical ruse. Must women only feature as a cipher? Must he always speak on their behalf? This is especially evident in Derrida's response when receiving the Adorno Prize in 2001. How could Derrida have been so blind to their names, to the gifts of actual women—he who so carefully indicated others' blind spots? But this is not a cause for Holland to reject Derrida out of hand, as she invokes another mode of Derridean possibility/impossibility, that of forgiveness. Holland's contribution, then, is a fitting tribute to Derrida and his own incisive yet elusive insights.

In introducing her contribution, Kathleen O'Grady cites a line in Marcel Mauss's *The Gift* that always interrupts her concentration. She rereads this quote: "Now in our view one of the most important acts noted . . . and one which throws a strong light on sexual relationships, is the *mapula,* the sequence of payments by a husband to his wife as a kind of salary for sexual services" (Mauss [1924] 1990, 39). This is one of very few references made by Mauss to an economy of the gift that *includes* women, yet he does not develop it, except in a sweeping reference to the power of this information to "throw a strong light on sexual relationships" generally. O'Grady reflects on the lack of commentary about this example where women are depicted as objects of male desire and recompense, yet seem to be viewed as without desire themselves.

By way of contrast, O'Grady explores Julia Kristeva's deliberations on the female subject, and, in a delightful inversion of Mauss, predicates the logic of "the gift" itself on woman's *desire*. She demonstrates that Kristeva's conception of the gift contests Mauss's. O'Grady argues that Kristeva's conception of the gift is a "for-giving" which operates on the logic of love, established and expressed through the metaphoric function of language. Her particular focus is Kristeva's *Soleil Noir,* where Kristeva first presents her notion of melancholia as an inability to accept the "gift of love." Kristeva then proposes an aesthetic-theology of "forgiveness" as a possible solution. O'Grady's essay, which explores Kristeva's preoccupations with the wounds of love, highlights the fact that the gift can be reconceived in ways that evoke generosity and forgiveness. It also allows that women's desire need not be equated with unrestrained passion or concupiscence. Instead it can be appreciated as a love that is related to forgiveness and gratitude that mediate as gifts. Kristeva appreciates such generous ways of being that enhance rather than eradicate the yearning for plenitude that suffuses human existence.

Mariana Ortega addresses the work of Heidegger which provides a different perspective on the gift. She first observes that beginning with Mauss, and then in Lévi-Strauss, Derrida, and Irigaray, the gift is presented, or presents itself. Yet it is eluded, or it eludes us. It is thus not a nicely wrapped box that, when opened, automatically presents a clear, obvious, or beautiful content. Questions of meaning, intention, obligation, elision, come to mind. In this way, the gift, a symbol of sociality, altruism, love, may not simply represent a purer, more authentic, economy than capitalist avarice. For Ortega, it could also indicate a history of past bloodshed and colonialism; so that nostalgia for a bygone ideal of the gift may well prove to be an illusion.

At the same time, however, Ortega appreciates that the gift can be a gift of disclosure, of an understanding of life itself, as a gift of being. She reflects on Heidegger's postulates of *Es gibt* and *Ereignis,* and on what he was trying to convey by these expressions. In one sense it was an attempt to open up a world, of being/Being, as a way of experiencing the wonder of existing. For Heidegger this was the gift of existence, of being able to realize one's "ownmost possibilities." Such an offering is, for Heidegger, the most meaningful, as it allows us to have an understanding of ourselves in relation to others and our world.

Yet other questions arise for Ortega about the way in which we can relate to this gift. She introduces a number of puzzles: To whom does this gift present itself? To the *Dasein* that Heidegger describes? Yet who is perhaps not included? Ortega is concerned about the *Dasein* that Heidegger fails to describe. These are beings whose primary way of dealing with the world is not "ready-to-handness," but a constant clashing with the environment, given their multicultural, even "multiplicitous," status.

Ortega thus problematizes the Heideggerian analysis by examining the manner in which multicultural, multiplicitous beings inhabit the world—as different modes of being-in-the-world. She believes that there is a vital need to reinterpret the Heideggerian analysis of both *Dasein* and the gift of being in the light of these multivalent ways of being. In concluding her essay, Ortega presents a multiplicitous woman's understanding of the gift: this is the Hispanic Gloria Anzaldúa's *mestiza* way. This is not so much a gift of being, but rather a gift of creative celebration. In this manner, Ortega again brings into focus the issue of ethnocentrism of many interpretations of the gift—interpretations that have been questioned by women anthropologists such as Annette Weiner and Marilyn Strathern. Ortega's chapter is a careful criticism of Heidegger's limited interpretation of Being. Yet, at the same time, it is a poetic evocation of multiplicitous ways that human beings can celebrate the wondrous gift of life.

Maria Cimitile commences her chapter on Irigaray and Heidegger by noting that some thematizations of Mauss's notion of the gift focus on the workings of power that underlie the gift and gift-giving. In contrast, however, she presents Ralph Waldo Emerson's view that a true gift is unnecessary and excessive. He also states that if it is a true gift, then it is a gift of the self, that is, selfless. Emerson thus establishes the distinction, elaborated by Derrida, that a gift differs radically from an exchange. Cimitile's chapter adopts these two views of the gift to help frame the thought of Luce Irigaray and Martin Heidegger. Both thinkers, in Cimitile's reading, judge Mauss's view of the economy of the gift as a confining metaphysical system. For both thinkers the gift is an event, at once a propaedeutic measure and a future-oriented occasion. Yet they diverge on the manner of the gift's disclosure. Irigaray amends Heidegger's depiction. She views his understanding of the gift as situated squarely within a masculinist discourse, though masquerading as a neutral, apolitical, transcendental condition. Irigaray also voices her disagreement with Heidegger's further development of language and the event of Being as a private disclosure. Irigaray then delineates her own appreciation of a loving interrelationship between two people.

By focusing on Irigaray's engagement with Heidegger, Cimitile helps the reader to understand how Irigaray's assertion of two distinct yet interdependent worlds—of sexual difference—establishes a new foundation for a philosophy of being. This difference is the precondition for the emergence of love between two autonomous individuals. Such a relationship is only possible when the distinct difference of a person of the other sex is respected. Thus, while Heidegger believes humanity receives the gift of Being, Irigaray demonstrates that his depiction of the gift is specific only to man, not woman. Maria Cimitile indicates that for Irigaray, the full realization of the gift of Be-ing, of being human, will only occur when this gift is received by two fully realized subjectivities, representing two worlds—male and female.

Sal Renshaw's contribution explores Hélène Cixous's writings on the gift and love. If the gift per se is impossible, how then, Cixous asks, does one give? And by extension, how does one receive? Can otherness itself be a gift? And what of love? How should we understand a love that arrives, a love that preserves rather than annihilates the other who is loved? At the heart of these questions is a desire to source love and gifting in generosity, excess, and abundance. In many ways, much of Hélène Cixous's work can be understood as an ongoing exploration of the conditions of subjectivity that might make such loving/gifting possible. In this chapter Renshaw reflects on these questions via an engagement with Cixous and her animal loves. Cixous's writings on the dog of her childhood, Fips, and the cat who insisted on other love, the cat who became Thea, form the basis of a new chapter in Cixous's reflections on the conditions of subjectivity that might permit the radical gift of an other/love.

Rachel Muers introduces the work of John Milbank, a British social theorist and theologian. Muers concentrates on Milbank's approach, which he terms his "theopneumatics." It focuses on the idea of the gift and gift-exchange. In his work *Being Reconciled: Ontology and Pardon,* (2003) Milbank characterizes the gift/Spirit as "(relatively) feminine," and justifies doing so on both theological and ethical/political grounds. Muers also describes how, in his discussions of anthropology, Milbank makes frequent direct and indirect allusions to women as gifts in archaic/local gift economies. Central to his argument, as well as to his resistance to accusations that he uncritically reads the gift from a patriarchal perspective, is the assertion that women-as-gifts are not thereby made into "passive objects." (Perhaps because of his theological underpinnings, Milbank does not regard the gift as conveying the status of object.) Muers analyzes the "the gender of the gift" (a phrase from Marilyn Strathern) as it features in Milbank's thought. She questions to what extent his way of construing sexual difference in relation to gift-exchange represents (as he claims) an advance on modern manifestations of patriarchy. Muers proposes that as a purported intervention in feminist debates, Milbank's work could perhaps be viewed as an attempt to imagine a pristine relationship of "original peace" between two sexes. She views Milbank's position as having much in common with Irigaray's later writings on sexual difference. This position, Muers also suggests, shares some of the advantages of Irigaray's work, but also its disadvantages. In concluding, Rachel Muers suggests that by focusing on sexual difference and the relationship between the sexes, Milbank, like Irigaray, raises important questions about the complicity of certain feminist discourses in modern erasures of real difference. Nevertheless, similarly to Irigaray, Milbank lays himself open to charges of heterosexism, and of reinscribing a traditional logic of complementarity that has been shown to have detrimental effects on women. Milbank's version of the gift, then, may not entirely escape the charge of confining women with gifts of a dubious provenance.

Victoria Barker states that Simone de Beauvoir must be counted as perhaps the founding figure of contemporary feminism. She does not examine notions of the gift in Beauvoir—basically because they are nowhere evident. Beauvoir refused to concede that women are born with innate qualities, instead declaring that they acquire them through socialization. She would have understood the gift, especially as it has been attached to women, simply as symptomatic of the characteristics she associated with the "eternal feminine." These feature as part of the mythology that ensnared women into a life of dependency. Beauvoir's life and work was a repudiation of such a self-sacrificial existence. Perhaps Beauvoir can be situated as an influential figure in opposition to the gift insofar as it is aligned with care and gratuitousness. Barker chooses instead to highlight a perspective which is crucial to understanding Simone de Beauvoir's work: the perspective of philosophical anthropology. Such an approach was crucial to the debunking of any "feminine" mythology. *The Second Sex,* in particular, responds to the advances in philosophical anthropology that dominated French thought in the first half of the last century.

Barker demonstrates that this anthropological perspective gave Beauvoir an extraordinary latitude in her analysis of "woman." It permitted her to highlight the commonality of literary and philosophical imagery of woman. It also allowed her to explore the analogies between the myth of woman and other myths that are central to philosophy: that of man's emergence from nature, that of the master's overcoming of the slave, and that of man's relationship to his God. This encouraged her to emphasize the central role of religion in the figuration of sexual difference. Barker claims that since Beauvoir's aim was not to understand religious commitment, but rather to diagnose and demystify it—in the manner of Feuerbach—the anthropological perspective was particularly appropriate (by contrast with the strictly phenomenological). Such an approach is obvious when Beauvoir demonstrates the way that the myth of God as transcendent (male) other reinforces that of woman as the absolute other of man, She views them as twin effects of the same idolatrous structure of thought. The connection between these two modes of otherness helps to explain Beauvoir's antagonism toward each form—and her wish to abolish them by means of demystification.

Yet Barker wonders how the demystification of "woman" can contribute to the overcoming of women's exclusion and inferiority. According to Barker, while this anthropological perspective provides an excellent tool for diagnosing the role of woman in the construction of social customs, it does not provide answers of a therapeutic nature. Barker then pursues several possible ways beyond this seeming impasse and considers the resources that philosophical anthropology can supply to Beauvoir's affirmation of woman as subject. In Barker's view, Beauvoir's interpretation is deeply indebted to her insistence on the future dimension of the meaning of "woman," that deferred time that will allow women to confront the question of what woman "will have become." Indeed, the chapters in this volume could be considered as a careful evaluation of women's progress in this direction.

In the final chapter, I address the worrisome notions of the gift as they derive from the findings of the early anthropologists that informed Mauss's reflections. From a postcolonial position, their reliability is questionable. Contemporary commentators such as Annette Weiner (1976) and Christopher Bracken (1997) both raise the issue of the colonial lens through which most of these early studies were filtered. They also raise the crucial question of the wisdom of using such ideas as the basis for present-day speculations. Weiner has shown most convincingly that, in regard to women's relations to the gift, in certain instances the anthropologists were negligent if not erroneous. Their views appear to be projections resulting from presuppositions of their western heritage. It is from this perspective that I examine the contributions of both Hélène Cixous and Luce Irigaray to the contemporary debate—examining their innovations, as well as some questionable attributions and deductions. Their work definitely marks a positive step in that women themselves are now undertaking creative analyses on their behalf. Nevertheless, by taking certain of their male predecessors at their word, they risk adopting colonialist views or resorting to stereotypes of a binary nature in their discussions of the nature of the gift. Extreme vigilance will always be necessary.

CONCLUSION

The contributions of Hélène Cixous and Luce Irigaray, as well as those of Julia Kristeva, have initiated dialogue, and often disagreements, among women. It is to be expected that these discussions will not always be harmonious, but it is now women themselves who are resisting and debating their situation, independent of previous male prescriptions. It is only in this way that the dubious legacy of past prejudices and elisions can be rejected and revised. As I described earlier, the recent work of Cordelia Fine (2010) and Rebecca Jordan-Young (2010) helps to dispel such inaccuracies. Their keen evaluations also help to lay the foundations for more finely tuned research practices, and less biased approaches in regard to the basic biological data. This book was inspired by the hope that the essays in this volume can contribute to further rich research and innovative reflection.

This volume has given pride of place to women's voices that are at times theoretical, philosophical, and, in one case, theological. All of them are not simply grappling with intellectual issues, but seeking to find a way to express their knowledge of ways of relating, of interacting, that resonate with life and love, that honor women's experience. They are rueful, poignant, angry, hopeful, and daring, and resourceful as they give voice to contemporary women's aspirations and misgivings. All are deeply concerned with perhaps the most precious of all gifts, transformation, not just of oneself, but also of others and society. The transformation they seek, then, is not necessarily only for themselves, but for others of all dispensations, as well as for future generations. Their impetus is the desire that men and women may inhabit a just world and may enjoy its plentiful resources in an equitable manner.

In concluding this introduction, I would like to return to the work of Mariana Ortega in this volume. This is because Ortega asks the most searching of questions. In her chapter she worries about the endless theorizing about the gift, and she considers the purpose that this serves. What is at stake in this fascination with the gift, even though in the greater scheme of things its audience is indeed small and exclusive? Why such a great concern about a correct/precise/pure definition? What can be gained by further discussions, even if by women? She also worries about the later Heidegger and his isolated poetic quest, removed from everyday language and his fellow human beings. Basically these concerns revolve around the diminution that excessive theorizing and solitude can produce. It can deaden the gift of life and the life-force that should animate all our activities.

At the same time, Ortega is troubled by exclusion of multicultural ways of being. In rejecting such narrowness, such austerity, Ortega summons the Hispanic poet-writer Gloria Anzaldúa as an exemplar of someone who celebrates existence in words that reverberate with love of the world. For Ortega, Anzaldúa gives of herself, with a delight in sharing that is not sacrificial but exultant, and so opens a world for us that exceeds narrow intellectual and political formulas. In the light of Mariana Ortega's contribution, the gift can be appreciated as a cipher, as an indicator of women's situation—and of their vibrant ways of being in the world on their own terms, rather than those of others. My hope is that this volume on the gift and its multiplicitous meanings can bring a vitality to future discussions and human interactions concerning this at once evocative and provocative subject.

NOTES

1. The term "feminine" is particularly troubling, as evidenced by the various debates concerning sex and gender. Formerly, it was used to name gender attributes that pertained to women. Yet the much-disputed sex/gender distinction did help to

allay its normative force. From a feminist perspective, today neither "sex" nor "gender" is regarded as free from cultural biases. The "feminine," used either figuratively or substantively, must always be regarded with suspicion; even its regulative ideals are no longer enforced.

2. The term "western" in this context carries with it the presumption of superiority that has been called to account by critics using approaches informed by critiques of Orientalism and postcolonialism. See Joy (2003).

3. The word "neocolonialism" is employed today to refer to the operations of international capitalism and globalization, which are viewed as operating in a manner similar to the earlier exploitations of colonialism.

4. The conference on the gift was held at Trent University, Peterborough, Ontario, in May 1996. According to Constantin Boundas, the principal convenor, it was prompted by an impulse to explore, in this age of globalization, the fact that "it seems that alternatives to dominant utilitarian ethics, to political economy solidly grounded on commodity exchange and to the view of human beings as rational maximizers of their own advantage, continue to beckon us post moderns" (Boundas 2001, 1).

5. Selected conference papers, with some additional essays, were published in the journal *Angelaki* 6 (2) (2001) with an introduction by Constantin Boundas, under the title *Gift, Theft, Apology*.

6. In the actual conference proceedings, an article by Schrift that examined certain ideas in Cixous's work on the gift and expenditure was included. See Schrift (2001).

7. I still regard Julia O'Faolain and Lauro Martines's volume, *Not in God's Image* (1973), as one of the best surveys of this topic.

8. Rosemary Ruether (1974) provides a succinct overview of these developments.

9. For a fine perspective of the medieval ideals and changes, see McLaughlin (1974). Aristotle's *Generation of Animals* makes some extraordinary statements such as this one: "Though once birth has taken place everything reaches its perfection sooner in females than in males—e.g. puberty, maturity, old age—because females are weaker and colder in their nature; and we should look upon the female state as being as it were a deformity, though one which occurs in the ordinary course of nature." See Aristotle (1953, 460–61).

10. This original ideal was just one of several recommended facets of Mary's life. Works that help to understand the variety of such ideals are Penny S. Gold (1985, 43–75) and Christiania Whitehead (2000).

11. In her book *Women and Religious Writing in Early Modern England,* Erica Longfellow declares: "This book thus marks the bold claim that women participated in defining what it meant to be a woman and how a woman ought to behave. They were not victims but agents in a continued process of changing gender relations . . . Their poetry thus demonstrates that both women's writing and the categories of gender were not incidental, but were crucial to the formation of Christian piety and Christian virtue in the early modern period" (2004, 212).

12. For excellent surveys of fundamentalism and its views on women see Brasher (1997) and DeBerg (2000).

13. Lévi-Strauss presents his evaluation of this procedure: "The prohibition of incest is less a rule prohibiting marriage with the mother, sister or daughter, than a rule obliging the mother, sister or daughter to be given to others. It is the supreme

rule of the gift, and it is clearly in this aspect, too often unrecognized, which allows its nature to be understood" (1969, 481).

14. Annette Weiner in *Women of Value, Men of Renown* states: "Through annual harvests of yams and women's activities in mortuary distributions, women are given public recognition for the active, pivotal role they play, a role demonstrating the worth of men in their lives and, equally, their own sociocultural value. Throughout a marriage women and men have equal negotiating power" (1976, 230).

15. In 1998, Ensler created V-Day, an organization focused on combating violence against women. On St. Valentine's Day (V-Day) in 2002, over a thousand performances of *The Vagina Monologues* (2007) took place throughout the world.

16. For an excellent overview of these movements see Ariel Levy (2005).

17. Paul Ricoeur introduced this term in his work on Freud, *Freud and Philosophy: An Interpretation* (1970), where he referred to the masters of suspicion, Nietzsche, Marx, and Freud himself.

18. While Mary Douglas's exploration of this theme in her foreword (1990) to the latest edition of Mauss's *The Gift* (1990) is not without merits, its applications are limited.

19. Hénaff totally disagrees with this premise, on which Derrida bases his analysis of the gift. Hénaff observes: "In short, whereas throughout *The Gift* Mauss was at pains to demonstrate that these offerings were inseparable from public expressions of generosity, prestige, honor, the granting of trust, promises of fidelity, and the creating and reinforcing of bonds, Derrida interpreted the entire language of the gift as a language of trade and profit" (2009, 221).

20. Hénaff acknowledges, as does Mauss, that sacrifice is one of the ways that the debt to the gods is returned (Mauss 1990, 19–23). Hénaff again refines the way that this relationship can be appreciated, especially from a religious studies perspective. "Before the movement of goods between humans through gifts and countergifts, a first gift came from the ancestor or the gods; the latter symbolized by the *sacra,* and humans reply to it through offerings, words of gratitude, prayers, and in certain cases sacrifices. What are these gifts? Narratives, prayers and rituals help provide an answer: these gifts are life, the natural world, and other human beings but also the civilized arts—everything as it is, including the ambiguous gifts of death and disease, adversity and destruction" (Hénaff 2010, 151–52).

21. Marilyn Strathern expands on Weiner's model, specifically in relation to the complex details of sister/brother/husband relations in connection with the gift and the production of children. I will not expound on these qualifications as my emphasis is solely on demonstrating the role of women specifically as givers, and Strathern's anthropological points refine rather than reject this situation (1988, 231–40). I thank Thorgeir S. Kolhus for drawing my attention to this.

22. Central to women's power is their link to the notion *dala.* Weiner describes this dynamic element: "*Dala* refers both to identity conceived through women and to property (i.e. land, decorations and names) controlled by men. But in the male domain, this property is lent to others of different *dala* blood. Without women to recover property and reproduce, *dala* is lost. . . . Therefore land does not provide a transcendental identity in the way that women's regenerative ability maintains the continuity of *dala* identity" (1976, 232).

23. Both Honneth (1996) and Ricoeur (2005) have written extensively on this topic.

24. Neither Cixous nor Irigaray is particularly exact in her dealings with gender, and there is a constant slippage in their work between actual women and the term "feminine," which may or may not be confined to females. I have written about this problem and concerns about the use of gender. See Joy (2006b).

25. Shershow comments: "The special thesis in its broadest form—that an economy of gift exchange united a whole range of otherwise disparate archaic cultures—is itself finally subordinate to a disciplinary imperative that is a commitment to the production of anthropological knowledge in general" (2005, 109).

26. A number of books have been written by indigenous women in Canada today that testify to this colonial problem. Emma LaRocque, a Métis scholar, relates the predicament of many aboriginal women in Canada today: "Racism and sexism found in the colonial process have served to dramatically undermine the place and value of women in Aboriginal cultures, leaving us vulnerable both within and outside our communities. Not only have native women been subjected to violence in both white and Native societies, but we have also been subjected to patriarchal policies that have dispossessed us of our inherited rights, lands, identities, families" (1996, 11).

27. Gayle Rubin's 1975 essay on the symbolic exchange of women in patriarchal societies was a landmark. In a recent collection of essays (2011), Rubin both comments on this earlier work and traces the changes that have since taken place in the sex trade, i.e., the actual buying and selling of women.

28. There have been a number of works that analyze the dynamics of power and their implications for women, employing Foucault's critical apparatus. Amy Allen's *The Politics of Our Selves* (2007) is both an excellent overview and an innovative contribution.

29. In the chapter on Irigaray and Levinas in my *Divine Love,* I compare their respective attitudes on love and eros (Joy 2006a, 65–75).

30. Diprose justifies this position: "Levinas describes subjectivity . . . in terms of generosity as I understand it. His work lends itself to a philosophy of the gift, insofar as he bases a sociality that does not absorb difference on giving to the other without expectation of return" (2002, 13).

31. See Levinas (1978, 159).

32. For Derrida's work on justice see 1992a. There are those, however, who question Derrida's understanding of messianism. See Smith (1998).

33. The slippage between the use of the terms "woman" and "feminine" is quite marked in Levinas. At times it is difficult to know if he is speaking figuratively or literally.

34. See Joy (2006a, 68–72).

35. Ricoeur understands his version of recognition and intersubjectivity as an attempt to mediate two forms of asymmetry between self and other: that of Husserl, who locates the ego or self as the principal site of reference, and that of Levinas, who gives the other person priority (2005, 260).

REFERENCES

Allen, Amy. 2007. *The Politics of Our Selves: Power, Autonomy, and Gender in Contemporary Critical Theory.* New York: Columbia University Press.
Aristotle. 1953. *Generation of Animals.* Trans. A. L. Peck. Cambridge, MA: Harvard University Press.

Baron-Cohen, Simon. 2004. *The Essential Difference: Male and Female Brains and the Truth about Autism.* New York: Basic Books.

Bataille, Georges. [1957] 1987. *Eroticism.* Trans. M. Dalwood. London: Mario Boyas.

———. 1985. *Visions of Excess: Selected Writings.* Trans. A. Stoekl. Manchester, UK: Manchester University Press.

Boundas, Constantin. 2001. "Gift, Theft, Apology." *Angelaki* 6/2: 1–5.

Bracken, Christopher. 1997. *The Potlatch Papers: A Colonial Case History.* Chicago: University of Chicago Press.

Brasher, Brenda E. 1997. *Godly Women.* Camden, NJ: Rutgers University Press.

Brizendine, Louann. 2007. *The Female Brain.* New York: Three Rivers Press.

———. 2012. *The Male Brain.* New York: Three Rivers Press.

Butler, Judith. 1990. *Gender Trouble.* New Haven, CT: Yale University Press.

Cheal, David. 1988. *The Gift Economy.* London: Routledge.

Cixous, Hélène. 1986. "Sorties." In *The Newly Born Woman,* by Hélène Cixous and Catherine Clément. Trans. Betsy Wing. Minneapolis: University of Minnesota Press. 63–132.

———. 1998. "From My Menagerie to Philosophy." In *Stigmata: Escaping Texts.* London: Routledge. 173–94.

Crittenden, Ann. 2001. *The Price of Motherhood: Why the Most Important Job in the World Is Still the Least Valued.* New York: Metropolitan Books.

DeBerg, Betty A. [1990] 2000. *Ungodly Women: Gender and the First Wave of American Fundamentalism.* Macon, GA: Mercer University Press.

Derrida, Jacques. [1978] 1979. *Spurs: Nietzsche's Styles.* Trans. B. Harlow. Chicago: University of Chicago Press.

———. [1991] 1992b. *Given Time 1: Counterfeit Money.* Trans. Peggy Kamuf. Chicago: University of Chicago Press.

———. 1992a. "Force of Law: The 'Mystical Foundation of Authority.'" In *Deconstruction and the Possibility of Justice,* ed. Cornell Drucilla et al. New York: Routledge. 3–67.

———. [1992] 1995. *The Gift of Death.* Trans. David Wills. Chicago: University of Chicago Press.

de Waal, Frans. 2009. *The Age of Empathy.* New York: Harmony Books.

Diprose, Rosalyn. 2002. *Corporeal Generosity: On Giving with Nietzsche, Merleau-Ponty, and Levinas.* Albany: State University of New York Press.

Douglas, Mary. 1966. *Purity and Danger: An Analysis of Concepts of Pollution and Taboo.* London: Routledge & Kegan Paul.

———. 1990. "Foreword." In *The Gift: The Form and Reason for Exchange in Archaic Societies,* by Marcel Mauss. London: Routledge. ix–xiii.

Ensler, Eve. 2007. *The Vagina Monologues.* New York: Random House.

Fausto-Sterling, Anne. 1992. *Myths of Gender.* New York: Basic Books.

———. 2000. *Sexing the Body: Gender Politics and the Construction of Sexuality.* New York: Basic Books.

Fine, Cordelia. 2010. *Delusions of Gender: The Real Science behind Sex Differences.* London: W. W. Norton.

Godbout, Jacques T. [1992] 1998. *The World of the Gift.* Trans. Donald Winkler. Montreal: McGill–Queen's University Press.

Godelier, Maurice. [1996] 1999. *The Enigma of the Gift.* Trans. Nora Scott. Chicago: University of Chicago Press.

Gold, Penny Schine. 1985. *The Lady and the Virgin: Image, Attitude and Experience in Twelfth Century France.* Chicago: University of Chicago Press.

Gregory, C. A. 1982. *Gift and Commodities.* London: Academic Press.

Gruen, Lori, and Wylie, Alison, eds. 2010. "Feminist Legacies / Feminist Futures." 25th Anniversary Issue, *Hypatia* 4 (25).

Guenther, Lisa. 2006. *The Gift of the Other: Levinas and the Politics of Reproduction.* Albany: State University of New York Press.

Held, Virginia. 1993. *Feminist Morality: Transforming Culture, Society, and Politics.* Chicago: University of Chicago Press.

———. 2005. *Ethics of Care.* Oxford: Oxford University Press.

Hénaff, Marcel. [2002] 2010. *The Price of Truth: Gift, Money and Philosophy.* Trans. J.-L. Morhange with A.-M. Feenberg-Dion. Stanford, CA: Stanford University Press.

———. 2009. "The Aporia of Pure Giving and the Aim of Reciprocity." In *Derrida and the Time of the Political,* ed. Peng Cheah and Suzanne Guerlac. Durham, NC: Duke University Press. 215–34.

Honneth, Axel. 1996. *The Struggle for Recognition: The Moral Grammar of Social Conflicts.* Trans. Joel Anderson. Cambridge, MA: MIT Press.

Hyde, Lewis. 1983. *The Gift: Imagination and the Erotic Life of Property.* New York: Vintage Books.

Irigaray, Luce. [1977] 1985. "Women on the Market." *This Sex Which Is Not One.* Trans. C. Porter with C. Burke. Ithaca, NY: Cornell University Press. 170–91.

———. [1987] 1993. *Sexes and Genealogies.* Trans. G. C. Gill. New York: Columbia University Press.

———. [1992] 1996. *I Love to You.* Trans. Alison Martin. New York: Routledge.

———. 2000. *Why Different? A Culture of Two Subjects.* New York: Semiotext(e).

Jordan-Young, Rebecca. 2010. *Brain Storm: The Flaws in the Science of Sex Difference.* Cambridge, MA: Harvard University Press.

Joy, Morny. 2003. "Postcolonialism and Gender Reflections." In *Challenges to Method in Religion,* ed. U. King and T. Beattie. London: Continuum. 28–39.

———. 2006a. *Divine Love: Luce Irigaray, Women, Gender and Religion.* Manchester, UK: Manchester University Press.

———. 2006b. "Gender and Religion: A Volatile Mixture," *Temenos* 42 (1): 7–30.

———. 2008. "Women, Sacrifice and Transcendence." In *Women and the Divine,* ed. Gillian Howie and J'annine Jobling. London: Palgrave Macmillan. 13–25.

Keller, Catherine. 2010. *Apophatic Bodies: Negative Theology, Incarnation, and Relationality.* New York: Fordham University Press.

Kojève, Alexander. 1969. *Introduction to the Reading of Hegel: Lectures on the Phenomenology of Spirit.* Trans. James A. Nichol. Ithaca, NY: Cornell University Press.

Komter, Aafke E., ed. 1996. *The Gift: An Interdisciplinary Perspective.* Amsterdam: Amsterdam University Press.

LaRocque, Emma. 1996. "The Colonization of a Native Woman Scholar." In *Women of First Nations: Power, Wisdom and Strength,* ed. Christine Miller and Patricia Chuchryk. Winnipeg: University of Manitoba Press. 11–17.

Leacock, Eleanor Burke. 1981. *Myths of Male Dominance: Collected Articles on Women Cross-Culturally.* New York: Monthly Review Press.

Lévi-Strauss, Claude. [1949] 1969. *The Elementary Structures of Kinship*. Trans. J. H. Bell, J. R. von Sturmer, and R. Needham. Boston: Beacon Press.

Levinas, Emmanuel. [1969] 1991. *Totality and Infinity: An Essay on Exteriority*. Trans. Alphonso Lingis. Pittsburgh: Duquesne University Press.

———. [1974] 1998. *Otherwise than Being or Beyond Essence*. Trans. Alphonso Lingis. Dordrecht: Kluwer Academic.

Levy, Ariel. 2005. *Female Chauvinist Pigs: Is Raunch Culture the New Women's Liberation?* New York: Simon & Schuster.

Longfellow, Erica. 2004. *Women and Religious Writing in Early Modern England*. Cambridge: Cambridge University Press.

Lugones, María. 2010. "Toward a Decolonial Feminism." *Hypatia* 25 (4): 742–67.

Maushart, Susan. 1999. *The Mask of Motherhood*. New York: Vintage.

Mauss, Marcel. [1924] 1990. *The Gift: The Form and Reason for Exchange in Archaic Societies*. Trans. W. D. Halls. Foreword by Mary Douglas. London: Routledge.

McLaughlin, Eleanor Como. 1974. "Equality of Souls, Inequalities of Sexes: Women in Medieval Theology." In *Religion and Sexism: Images of Women in the Jewish and Christian Traditions,* ed. R. R. Ruether. New York: Simon and Schuster. 213–66.

Meeker, Michael E. 1989. *The Pastoral Son and the Spirit of Patriarchy*. Madison: University of Wisconsin Press.

Mendus, Susan. 2010. *Politics and Morality*. Malden, MA. Polity Press.

Morris, Desmond. 1999. *The Naked Ape: A Zoologist's Study of the Human Animal*. New York: Delta.

Nussbaum, Martha. 1999. *Sex and Social Justice*. Oxford: Oxford University Press.

O'Faolain, Julia, and Lauro Martines, eds. 1973. *Not in God's Image: Women in History from the Greeks to the Victorians*. New York: Harper & Row.

Oliver, Kelly. 2001. *Witnessing: Beyond Recognition*. Minneapolis: University of Minnesota Press.

Osteen, Mark, ed. 2002. *The Question of the Gift: Essays across the Disciplines*. London: Routledge.

Perpich, Diane. 2008. *The Ethics of Emmanuel Levinas*. Stanford, CA: Stanford University Press.

Ricoeur, Paul. [1965] 1970. *Freud and Philosophy: An Interpretation*. Trans. D. Savage. New Haven, CT: Yale University Press.

———. 1992. *Oneself as Another*. Trans. Kathleen Blamey. Chicago: University of Chicago Press.

———. [2004] 2005. *The Course of Recognition*. Trans. David Pellauer. Cambridge, MA: Harvard University Press.

Rifkin, Jeremy. 2009. *The Empathic Civilization: The Race to Global Consciousness in a World in Crisis*. New York: Penguin.

Rubin, Gayle S. 1975. "The Traffic in Women: Notes on the 'Political Economy' of Sex." In *Toward an Anthropology of Women,* ed. Rayna Reiter. New York: Monthly Review Press. 157–210.

———. 2011. *Deviations: A Gayle Rubin Reader*. Durham, NC: Duke University Press.

Ruddick, Sara. 1989. *Maternal Thinking: Toward a Politics of Peace*. Boston: Beacon Press.

Ruether, Rosemary Radford. 1974. "Misogynism and Virginal Feminism in the Fathers of the Church." *Religion and Sexism: Images of Woman in the Jewish and Christian Traditions,* ed. Rosemary Radford Ruether. New York: Simon and Schuster. 150–83.

Sanday, Peggy Reeves. 1981. *Female Power and Male Dominance.* Cambridge: Cambridge University Press.

———. 2011. "Matriarchy." *Feminism and Religion.* July 29. http://feminismandreligion.com/2011/07/29/matriarchy-by-peggy-reeves-sanday/.

Schrift, Alan. 1997. *The Logic of the Gift: Toward an Ethic of Generosity.* New York: Routledge.

———. 2001. "Logics of the Gift in Cixous and Nietzsche: Can We Still Be Generous?" *Angelaki* 6 (2): 113–23.

Shershow, Scott Cutler. 2005. *The Work of the Gift.* Chicago: University of Chicago Press.

Smith, James K. A. 1998. "Determined Violence: Derrida's Structural Religion." *Journal of Religion* 78: 197–212.

Smith, Julia M. H. 1995. "The Problem of the Female Sanctity in Carolingian Europe c. 780–920." *Past and Present* 146 (1): 3–37.

Strathern, Marilyn. 1988. *The Gender of the Gift: Problems with Women and Problems with Society in Melanesia.* Berkeley: University of California Press.

Vaughan, Genevieve. 1997. *For-Giving: A Feminist Criticism of Exchange.* Austin, TX: Plainview/Anomaly Press.

———. 2002. "Mothering, Co-muni-cation and Gifts of Language." In *The Enigma of Gift and Sacrifice,* ed. Edith Wyschogrod, J.-J. Goux, and E. Boynton. New York: Fordham University Press. 91–113.

———. 2007. "Introduction." In *Women and the Gift Economy: A Radically Different Worldview Is Possible,* ed. Genevieve Vaughan. Toronto: Inanna Publications. 1–41.

Walter, Natasha. 2010. *Living Dolls: The Return of Sexism.* London: Virago Press.

Weiner, Annette. 1976. *Women of Value, Men of Renown: New Perspectives of Trobriand Exchange.* Austin: University of Texas Press.

———. 1992. *Inalienable Possessions: The Paradox of Keeping-While-Giving.* Berkeley: University of California Press.

Whitehead, Christiania. 2000. "A Fortress and a Shield." In *Writing Religious Women: Female Spiritual and Textual Practices in Late Medieval England,* ed. Denis Renevey and Christiania Whitehead. Toronto: University of Toronto Press. 109–32.

ONE

Pandora and the Ambiguous Works of Women: All-Taking or All-Giving?

Deborah Lyons

Δὼς ἀγαθή, ἅρπαξ δὲ κακή, θανάτοιο δότειρα
[Give is a good girl, but Take is bad. She is a giver of death.]
—HESIOD, WORKS AND DAYS

Women in ancient Greek myth and literature are often represented as gifts to be exchanged among men, as objects rather than subjects. When they do become active agents of exchange, these exchanges often have serious negative consequences for themselves and their male relations. Together, these attitudes are part of a larger pattern of undervaluing the contributions of women. Analyzing this material in light of cross-cultural evidence about gender, kinship, and exchange, I will show that anxiety about women's role as exchange object and as exchanger is closely linked to ancient Greek ideas about marriage and the gendered division of labor. What is more, it is already encoded in the first appearance of woman as recounted in two seventh-century BCE texts—the *Theogony* and the *Works and Days*—attributed to the Boeotian poet Hesiod. In the first of these, woman remains nameless; only in the second is she given the name Pandora.

These texts, which are the primary focus of this chapter, place the creation of woman and the evils she brings to men within the history of relations between men and gods. The creation of woman—by the command of Zeus—is presented as part of a theodicy that indicates the extent to which what modern readers think of as "myth" deals with concepts of a religious nature. While "myth" meant something very different to an ancient Greek ear, and there was no word for "religion," these two categories are very closely related in archaic Greece. It should be remembered that the concepts under discussion—specifically the divine dispensation establishing the difficult lot of mortals—are part of what a modern audience would recognize as a religious discourse.[1]

The misogynist tradition embodied by Hesiod does not go completely unchallenged in archaic Greek culture. Not only does Homeric epic present a more nuanced picture—as I will show toward the end of this chapter—but even within Hesiod's text it is possible to find traces of a tension between negative and positive views of women's contributions to human economy and human existence. In order to understand why the association with women and resources is so fraught with anxiety, it is necessary to consider the contradictions embedded in the institution of marriage.

Claude Lévi-Strauss (1969) saw "woman" as the exchange object par excellence, and marriage as the prototype of all exchange. Yet he recognized the paradox that woman was not merely a sign, but also a producer of signs, which is to say, not only an object but also a subject. This alternation of women between object and subject runs throughout the myths we will consider here. J.-P. Vernant (1983, 133) has pointed to the contradictory nature of woman as both symbol of family continuity and circulating commodity:

> In marriage, in contrast to all other social activities, it is the woman who is the mobile social element, whose movement creates the link among different family groups, whereas the male remains tied to his own hearth and home. The ambiguity of the female status lies thus in the fact that the daughter of the house (more closely linked to the domestic sphere by virtue of her femininity than is a son) can nevertheless not fulfil herself as a woman in marriage without renouncing the hearth of which she is in charge.

Another consequence of this mobility is that the daughter who leaves her natal home to enter into that of her husband becomes a wife who is always an outsider, potentially a kind of double agent. Moreover, the integrity of the lineage she enters depends on her fidelity to her husband, and this fidelity is seen as closely linked to her role as guardian of the household possessions.[2] Not only a possession herself, she is often a custodian of possessions as well.

In Hesiod's treatment of women and marriage, anxiety about women's relationship to the household goods is very much in the forefront. In this context, it is worth noting that in the *Works and Days*, it was from a large storage jar (*pithos*) of the sort used to store grain, rather than a box, that Pandora, the archaic Greek prototypical woman, released evils into the world of men.[3] While later versions attribute her act to a stereotypical, and destructive, female curiosity, Hesiod does not provide a motivation. Pandora's attribute of the jar and her release of its baneful contents in the *Works and Days* connects the origin of women to concerns about the use and control of scarce resources (Detienne 1963; Sussman 1984; Petropoulos 1994). That her jar contains evils, including famine, rather than sustenance, goes hand in hand with Hesiod's repeated insistence that women consume household resources rather than contributing to them. Hope alone remains trapped inside, a detail that has remained puzzling to most interpreters: is hope an evil that has not been released, or a good thing withheld from (or available to) men? As several scholars have shown, the theme of the retention or release of the jar's ambiguous contents also points to a related anxiety about reproduction (Vernant 1980; Zeitlin 1995, 1996).

The Greek myth of Pandora explains several features of the human condition: the origin of women, the institution of marriage, and the begetting of children, as well as the general harshness of men's lot on earth. Usually what is remembered is the first of these origins, but what I aim to show here is that all of these elements are tightly bound together in a relentless logic of misogyny, which obscures the actual and indispensable contributions of women to human existence. I will begin by examining the creation of woman as narrated in two archaic Greek poems that have come down to us under the name of Hesiod: the *Theogony* and the *Works and Days*.[4] In my treatment of these accounts I will argue that behind this negative version of women's contributions, beginning with the name Pandora itself, it is possible to identify traces of a more positive valuation that has been perhaps deliberately obscured.

As an interesting foil, I will compare this myth to one told by the Chambri people of Papua New Guinea, about a Golden Girl whose appearance also has consequences for the lives of men and for the institution of marriage. While Pandora and the Golden Girl both seem to be artifacts rather than organic human beings, their appearances lead to very different outcomes, which can best be explained by differences in the social organization of two very different cultures. Not surprisingly, gender relations hold the key to these differences.

I will close with some thoughts on the more nuanced valuation of women as both producers and exchangers found in other archaic Greek texts. As this brief survey will show, women's gifts and their role in exchange are by turns appreciated and distrusted, although rarely are they as completely elided as in the two Hesiodic versions.

WOMAN AS TREACHEROUS GIFT OF THE GODS

The very origin of woman is explained by the archaic poet Hesiod (seventh century BCE) as the result of a conflict between Zeus, father of the gods, and

Prometheus, the trickster god and friend of mortals. These two, well matched in wits if not in power, have quarreled over the allotments to men and gods in sacrifice, and over the control of fire. Prometheus has given the secret of fire to men, despite Zeus's desire to withhold it. In a retaliatory gesture aimed not directly at Prometheus but at his beloved mortals, Zeus creates a trap in the form of a lovely maiden. The woman, who is called Pandora ("All-Gifts") in the *Works and Days,* but who remains unnamed in the *Theogony,* brings not gifts but troubles to men. This she does explicitly by opening a jar full of evils, but also implicitly in that her arrival entangles them in the institution of marriage and the cycle of reproduction. The version in the *Theogony* (590–612) conflates the origin of women with the origin of marriage, and leaves one to wonder whether before her arrival all human beings were male. (I am not the first to observe the curious fact that the Hesiodic tradition does not feel it necessary to explain the creation of men.)

This alluring but dangerous creature, like many other ambiguous gifts in Greek myth, has been fashioned by the divine master craftsman, Hephaistos.[5] Although she is made of earth (*Theogony,* 571; *Works and Days,* 70), she is clearly a divine artifact, and further divine contributions—fine garments, golden necklaces, or a golden crown—turn her into something of a luxury object (Brown 1997). Pandora, the name she is given in the *Works and Days* (80–82), is glossed by the poet as a reference to the gifts given to her by all the gods and goddesses who created and adorned her:

> Without delay the renowned lame god fashioned from earth, through Zeus's will, the likeness of a shy maiden, and Athena, the gray-eyed goddess, clothed her and decked her out. Then the divine graces and queenly Persuasion gave her golden necklaces to wear, and the lovely-haired Seasons stood round her and crowned her with spring flowers. Pallas Athena adorned her body with every kind of jewel, and the Slayer of Argos—Hermes the guide— through the will of Zeus whose thunder roars placed in her breast lies, coaxing words, and a thievish nature. The gods' herald then gave her voice and called this woman Pandora because all of the gods who dwell on Olympos gave her a gift—a scourge for toiling men. (Athanassakis 2004, 71–82)

The name Pandora can, however, be interpreted in quite another way, one that makes her an active giver of benefits rather than a passive recipient. Her name can be read not only as the "All-Receiving," but also as the "All-Giving," an epithet that would more properly apply to the earth goddess Gaia than to a mortal woman.[6] In fact, Hesiod's explanation is unique, as this is the only place where the epithet *pandora/pandoros* or the related form *pandoteira* bears a passive meaning, that is, *receiving* gifts.[7] All other uses of these terms in Greek are clearly active, as in "all-bounteous, giver of all," epithets applied to the life-giving earth. In Hesiod's account, however, the newly created woman brings not plenty but scarcity. Her arrival introduces misery to men, in part because of her threatening and destructive fertility, which keeps them enslaved to agricultural labor to feed growing families (Detienne 1963; Sussman 1984; Petropoulos 1994).

The *Theogony* focuses less on her adornments and more on the arts and skills imparted to the first woman by the gods: Athena teaches her to weave and Hermes to lie and cheat. As previously noted, the Hesiodic tradition discounts even those feminine skills such as weaving that are culturally valued elsewhere in Greek culture (Lyons 2003; see also Zeitlin 1995 and 1996). In the *Odyssey* (7.109–111), for example, Athena imparts knowledge of weaving, along with good character, to the Phaeacian women. Hesiod's pairing of weaving and lying, on the other hand, suggests a more sinister association: textiles are part of the deceitful but attractive outer form that makes of Pandora a gift that is both treacherous and irresistible.

The *Theogony* emphasizes that with woman comes the ambiguous institution of marriage (589–612). The lines that follow reveal ambivalence about this institution. A man who does not marry will have a miserable old age and strangers will inherit his property. Hesiod allows for the possibility, however remote, of finding a good wife (608), but nonetheless insists that wives consume precious resources without making their own contribution to the household wealth. In most times and places in ancient Greece, especially among the poor, women played a large role in subsistence agriculture (Sussman 1984; Petropoulos 1994) as well as in textile production. Yet in Hesiod's account, the wife's role as producer is suppressed, hidden like the gifts of the earth or like hope trapped inside the lip of Pandora's jar.

Elsewhere in ancient Greek art and literature, beginning with the Homeric poems, which most scholars consider earlier than Hesiod, women of all classes are depicted at the loom, suggesting not only that their economic contribution was self-evident, but also that this association was central to gender ideology (Jenkins 1985; Barber 1994).[8] Textiles are the quintessential female product, and as such have a specific place not only in the domestic economy but in the symbolic order as well. Cloth is often contrasted with precious metal objects, which are the province of men. In this division, Greek culture is similar to many others in which wealth is seen as gendered, male wealth consisting of durable objects of metal or stone, while female wealth is more ephemeral, made of cloth, leaves, or other flexible materials that may be woven or plaited (Weiner and Schneider 1989).

The association of textiles with women can be seen in the phrase *erga gun-aikon,* "the works of women," which in archaic Greek almost always refers to the garments women weave, which are characterized as soft, shining, graceful, and beautiful.[9] Hesiod, on the other hand, couples the phrase *erga gunaikon* with the word *mermera,* "baneful, anxiety-producing" (*Theogony,* 603). For him, women's works are not textile contributions to household wealth but the source of undefined troubles, perhaps sexual in nature. The exact meaning of the phrase, however, is not obvious. Arthur (1982) has suggested that the reference is to the pressing nature of sexual desire that women stir up in men.[10] As with the very name of the first woman, the phrase *mermera erga* evokes a positive aspect of women's role, only to dismiss it. Not only is women's production devalued, but apparently so also is their role as sexual companions.

Why this should be so becomes clearer when we examine the Hesiodic attitude toward offspring. The *Works and Days* (372) recommends strictly limiting the number of offspring to one son to keep the inheritance intact. Women's reproductive potential is thus a double-edged sword. While several later authors also recommend leaving only a single heir, this advice seems ill-suited to an agrarian life, except in times of famine. The poet seems aware of the contradiction, for he follows up immediately with a conventional observation that having many children allows one to amass more wealth. His ambivalence on this point is part and parcel of the ambivalence about women, marriage, and reproduction that runs throughout the poem. One might venture to suggest that the unclear status of Hope, left in the jar, corresponds to the ambiguous status of the offspring in the woman's uterus. Are children merely a burden, or are they the hope for the future? And might that hope prove illusory? All of these questions are implicit in the equation of the pithos with the uterus (Vernant 1980 and 1989; Zeitlin 1996).

Despite a few grudging admissions of the usefulness of having numerous children, Hesiod's precepts obscure the value of woman as producer, casting her instead as a highly dubious object of exchange—in short, a bad bargain. Her childbearing potential does not strengthen the household but threatens to overwhelm it with unwanted progeny. Her potential for agricultural labor is denied; instead she lives off the labor of men. Rather than being a preserver of the household goods, she is a devourer. Even her *erga,* the paradigmatic work of women at the loom, are unraveled, transformed into a vague sexual threat. She stands—clothed in deceit but denuded of traditional female virtues—as a figure for the mystification of women's economic contribution. Created as revenge for Prometheus's deceitful exchange, she embodies the impossibility of reciprocity between husband and wife.

Although Hesiod has paradoxically placed the giving and receiving of gifts into a context of what Marshall Sahlins (1972) has called "negative reciprocity," this has been possible only through the suppression of the more positive possibilities also to be found in Greek culture. Before turning to these, however, I propose a cross-cultural detour to examine a myth from Papua New Guinea that may help to throw some features of the Greek case into relief.

PANDORA AND THE GOLDEN GIRL: MARRIAGE AND ITS DISCONTENTS IN GREECE AND NEW GUINEA

In Hesiod, Woman/Pandora was created by the gods as a punishment for men, and tricked out with charms, wiles, and a crown of gold. Among the few representations of this myth in visual art are several that show her emerging from the earth.[11] The myth of Pandora points to a golden age before women existed, and associates her coming with the arrival of all the ills of the human condition—plagues, poverty, and toil. As I have argued above, this myth operates within a program that explicitly denies the value of female contributions to many aspects of social life, including both production and reproduction.

It is therefore instructive to compare a myth told by the Chambri of Papua New Guinea that deals with many of the same issues, through the figure of the Golden Girl. My information about this myth is derived from the field-work of Errington and Gewirtz (1987). This woman, with skin the color of gold, is kept hidden in the earth, and the men who have found her visit her for sex instead of going to their own wives. In comparing these two myths, it will be worth considering possible explanations for both their similarities and their differences.

The Greek Pandora is a divine creation, who emerges into a world that had until this point seen no women, although female goddesses were legion (Lombardi 1994, 27).[12] Her advent marks the beginning of marriage and, by extension, of misery for men. By contrast, the Golden Girl emerges unexplained from the ground, into a world where marriage is already central to social organization. But for the Chambri, although the institution of marriage is accepted as a given, it is also the source of social inequalities. In marriage transactions, wife-takers are considered inferior to wife-givers. "Chambri wife-takers are regarded as owing their lives to those who have provided them with mothers, who are the sources of nurture and life."[13]

Part of the charm of the Golden Girl is that she seems temporarily to erase these social divisions. When she is discovered by the members of a certain men's house, they sleep with her and then hide her in a trough. They share her peacefully, thus temporarily reordering society along more egalitarian principles. Even more radically, the Golden Girl seems to stand outside all economic exchange, all production and reproduction. The situation is, however, untenable: human beings cannot escape exchange or reproduction. The wives become suspicious when their husbands stop visiting them, and they find the Golden Girl and kill her. A sequel myth suggests that the reconciliation of men and women afterwards was rather rocky. Although the husbands try to return to their wives, not all of them survive the attempt. Some of them are killed while others are driven off. As Errington and Gewertz note, the women construct a new community "in which they are able to pursue their own interests with complete disregard of the men. . . . There they continue to live happily and successfully without any men at all." (1987, 63).

Both of these female figures appear at the intersection of nature and culture. Each is simultaneously a living being and a artifact. Pandora is created by the gods (or by Hephaistos alone) and loaded up with gifts and adornments to make her more irresistible to men (Brown 1997). Among these gifts is the gold crown. The Golden Girl's origins are never explained, but she is described has having skin of gold, and the men hide her in a trough, as gold is hidden in the earth. Like Pandora, she is both woman and precious object. Unlike Pandora, however, her arrival seems to have no economic consequences, either negative or positive, beyond the disruption of the existing system of marriage exchange.

Errington and Gewertz note that there is a historical element to this feature of the myth: the detail of the trough is multivalent, and can be partly connected to the rise of gold-mining among the Chambri: "The goldenness of the girl is appreciated as valuable; the men hide her in a trough used by miners."[14] It has similarly been suggested that Hesiod's tale of Pandora reflects changes in the economic situation—perhaps a period of drought—that make women's contribution of offspring more problematic than it had formerly been.[15] Furthermore, the representation of woman as a precious artifact suggests commodification and could be ascribed (in the Greek case) to worries about the expense of dowering daughters. None of these concerns is made explicit in either mythic account.[16] Whether or not the extreme misogyny of the Hesiodic myth was motivated by a time of economic change or crisis—which it is impossible to know—such anxieties about women's economic role can be found throughout Greek literature.

Another interesting feature of these myths is the tendency to reduce *women* to the universalizing singular *woman*. Hesiod's origin of women begins with the creation of a single woman, and makes no attempt to explain how women come to represent approximately half the population (possibly fewer in a society that practiced infanticide and exposure, and did not feed female children as well as male children).[17] The Chambri myth effects this concentration of female identity somewhat less completely, but it does so nonetheless. The Golden Girl supplants all other women, and the men stop visiting them. For a time, it is as if the Golden Girl is the only woman. This changes when the wives come back into the story only to discover the hidden girl and do away with her. Here again we see the differences in the two myths. The Golden Girl, who represents a regressive fantasy of a life without the institution of marriage, cannot continue to exist. The appearance of Pandora, however negatively she is represented, nonetheless inaugurates the present social arrangement, which of necessity includes marriage and offspring. In this way, she represents, if not an actual improvement in the lot of men, an inevitable historical progression.

In the Greek myth, the adorned woman of miraculous origin ends a fantasy of an existence without marriage. In the Papuan one, she introduces a period in which the fantasy of a world without marriage can be played out only to be ultimately rejected. For the period in which the secret of the Golden Girl is contained, the men "regain" the pleasures of a non-hierarchical world in which there is no distinction between wife-takers and wife-givers. In the actual society of the Chambri, wife-takers are considered inferior to wife-givers, and only the abrogation of the institution of marriage can interrupt this source of social inequality and unease. While preserving the precious resource of the Golden Girl for themselves, they nonetheless are able to share harmoniously with the other members of their men's house.

> Because [the Golden Girl] did not have to—indeed, could not—be exchanged, she established no distinctions among the men. . . . [Instead she unifies them] "by terminating the relationships they had with their wives, and, thus, with their affines and agnates. She is all the men need, and they would have been happy to remain together—undifferentiated as affines, agnates and members of different generations—if only their wives would have allowed it." (Errington and Gewertz 1987, 59–60)

That this is an untenable fantasy is clear from the consequences: the murderous anger aroused in the women and the men's desire to reconcile with their wives and return to their former married state. Society cannot survive if men no longer sleep with their wives or have children with them. The fantasy that all the men can share one woman peacefully points not so much to a wish for polyandry as for the desire to interrupt the inexorable logic of marriage exchange.[18] Like other, more explicitly incestuous fantasies, such a fantasy would ultimately lead to the destruction of society, because the network of relationships created by marriage exchanges would fall into disrepair.

Another impossible feature of this story is that the golden woman, having been commodified—to the extent that she is associated with gold ore dug out of the earth—circulates only within an extremely limited circle of related men. Her removal from the earth and exposure to the light leads to her destruction and the end of this very limited form of circulation. With her death, the men must attempt to return to their marriages, that is, to the larger world of circulation and inequality.

A world without marriage means different things to Hesiod and the Chambri. For Hesiod, it means leaving behind the cares associated with children and the ambiguous, even dubious, contribution of women to the subsistence economy. As I have noted above, it is very likely that women's contributions in the archaic period were far less ambiguous and better recognized than Hesiod would have us believe, but the poet's misogyny and general cantankerousness (whether or not deepened by economic hardship) join to paint as bleak a picture as possible of women's value to society, as well as every other aspect of rural life. For the Chambri, marriage means involving oneself in the hierarchical struggle that places wife-takers below wife-givers. Escape from this system can be compared to the dream of an escape from exchange that some other societies see as part of a utopian vision of a world without marriage (Lévi-Strauss 1969, 496–97). Hesiod has little to say about sex but he drops a few dark hints about the troublesome works (*mermera erga*) of women, possibly, as mentioned earlier, a reference to the desire they provoke. By contrast, the Chambri myth assumes the desirability of women and provides sexual satisfaction for the men who have essentially abandoned their marriages, through shared union with the Golden Girl. If all men can marry the same woman, all social differences can be blissfully erased.

There is another feature that connects these two myths. The Chambri men's house is referred to as a "belly" and has female associations. The rounded part of a vase or jar is called a belly in ancient Greek as in English, and the *pithos* that Pandora brings with her has been compared to a woman's uterus, and its contents to a fetus (Vernant 1980; Arthur 1983; Zeitlin 1995; Brown 1997, 27).

Given the negativity of Hesiod's attitude toward childbearing, the fetus can be seen as one more evil contained in Pandora's jar. Once again, the Chambri myth emphasizes sharing, while the Greek myth emphasizes the opposite: the idea is to keep, not to let out; what is contained is marked as negative. In Papua, the men's house is conceptualized as female, but it is the source of good things.

Each of these myths offers a cautionary message, but the messages are quite different. The Greek myth emphasizes the danger of gullibility or incautiousness. Epimetheus ("Afterthought"), the dim brother of Prometheus ("Forethought"), who stupidly accepts Zeus's gift of the woman on behalf of man despite his brother's warnings, shows what happens when one doesn't listen to good advice, as does Pandora's famous opening of the jar.[19] The overall "moral" burden of the myth, however, is more accurately described as a theodicy. In explaining why the gods have allotted lives of toil and disease for men, it functions as an injunction to accept the inevitable. The Chambri myth is a regressive fantasy of an imagined utopian state innocent of marriage, while the Greek myth represents a progression, necessary even if not desirable, to "the way we live now." What is more, the moral of the Chambri myth stresses the necessity of men and women continuing to live in a state of complementarity. This is signaled at the end of the Chambri myth, when the Golden Girl has been discovered and killed by the men's neglected wives, and the men are left to attempt reconciliation.

The myth of Pandora is an example of what Malinowski called a "charter myth," and the institution it charters is that of marriage, with all its attendant evils. The tale of the Chambri is clearly of a different sort, although it leads to a similar conclusion. This cautionary tale warns of what might happen were men to deviate from the institution of marriage as it has already been established. In this way it reinforces social institutions rather than explicitly offering a charter for their origins. The end result is much the same: marriage is inescapable. At the same time, the Papuan sequel myth clearly alludes to the difficulties that men and women experience in getting along, just as the Pandora myth does. Unlike the Greek myth, however, the Chambri myth does so not from an explicitly male perspective but from one that takes into account the positions of both women and men. In the words of Errington and Gewertz (1987, 64), "the interests of both men and women can be adequately served only if there is sufficient compromise so that the strategies of one sex do not completely exclude those of the other."

Yet certain questions inevitably arise in connection with both myths. Why are women associated with precious objects? Why are they associated with the earth? Why the tendency to reduce all women to a single essentialized figure of "Woman"? At the same time, this unique woman has a different cultural value, since in the Greek case, she represents the beginning of the established order, while for the Chambri, she represents a deviation from it. At least a partial answer can be found in the fact that the two societies are diametrically opposed in their gender organization and ideology: the Chambri are egalitarian while the Greeks are male-dominated and misogynist. For this reason, in the former case the artificial, commodified woman is a threat to marriage and the established order, and in the latter she *is* marriage. In the Greek case, she brings misfortune—resented but necessary—to men, while in the Papuan, she brings misfortune to a society made up of both men and women, causing an imbalance that must be redressed.

The Greek myth emphasizes the perniciousness of the created female, associating her with a precious but potentially dangerous metal (Brown 1997). Her association with earth might seem less paradoxical if we consider that not only gold but also monsters emerge from the earth. This terrestrial origin is assigned in Hesiod exclusively to women, whereas in other versions of the creation of human beings, in ancient Greece and elsewhere, men and women share the same earthly fabric.[20] As observed above, the existence of men does not seem to require any explanation.

While both egalitarian and male-dominated societies recognize a degree of conflict between men and women, the egalitarian Chambri tell a story that ends up validating marriage while showing its *interruption* as the source of social ills. The Hesiodic myth, emerging from a patriarchal society, insists on *marriage itself* as the source of ills, even if it is necessary to fly in the face of the evidence in order to do so.

OTHER WAYS OF VALUING A WOMAN

The extreme pessimism of the Hesiodic view of women is echoed in other works of archaic Greek literature, most notably the seventh-century BCE poem by Semonides of Amorgos that compares types of women to various animals (*Fragment, 7*). These works are evidence of a strong misogynist strain that runs throughout ancient Greek culture. Nonetheless, there is a second tendency, one based in part on a notion of a gendered division of labor, which grants women a role—circumscribed but also valued—in the family and in human society as a whole.

This tendency can be found in some measure in both the *Iliad* and the *Odyssey*. The Homeric epics were based on older, orally transmitted material, but took their current written form sometime between the eighth and the seventh centuries BCE. Most scholars believe the *Iliad* to be somewhat older than the *Odyssey*, and both to be prior to the Hesiodic corpus. The amount of time that may have passed between the composition of these works is probably not enough, however, to account for such great social changes, so it is safer to attribute the different valuation of women in these works to differences in the social and economic context, as well as to geographic and generic differences.

The valuation of women in Homer, although generally more positive than that of Hesiod, can never be completely disentangled from the role of exchange object (Brown 1997, 46). Nonetheless, the Homeric view allows room for a more positive assessment of women's worth. A brief survey of the treatment of women in the Homeric epics will show how this is possible. A chain of exchanges of women runs through the story of the Trojan War (Lyons 2012). It begins with the stealing or seduction of Helen by Paris, continues through the sacrifice of Iphigeneia and the fight between the heroes Agamemnon and Achilles over the female captives Chryseis and Briseis, and finally ends with the sacrifice of the Trojan princess Polyxene to the angry spirit of the dead Achilles. While most of these events occur outside the dramatic time of the *Iliad,* the theme of the exchange of women among men is still central to that poem.

Women are treated as property to be passed from hand to hand, but they are also clearly valued. Not only the captives around whom begins the quarrel between Agamemnon and Achilles, but other often nameless women are mentioned both as exchange objects with a specific value (given in number of cattle) and as skilled producers of textiles. Agamemnon and Achilles seem genuinely attached to their two spear-captives. Helen herself, the cause of the war, is said by the old men of Troy to be worth all the trouble she has brought them. And she is also shown to be a producer, working at her loom on a weaving that depicts events from the war. While weaving is the archetypal women's work, the epic poet shows her to be in some way his equal, as she also creates an epic narrative in cloth.

In the *Odyssey,* while there are slave women whose value or purchase price is expressed in terms of so many head of cattle, there are also women clearly treasured for their own qualities. Why else, after all, would Odysseus choose to return home to his mortal wife instead of living forever with a goddess, as Kalypso offers him a chance to do? The nurse Eurykleia was purchased by Odysseus's father, Laertes, for twenty head of oxen (*Odyssey,* 1.431), but despite this he did not touch her out of respect for his wife.[21] In this example, two very different kinds of valuation, affective and economic, come face to face.

Unlike in the *Iliad,* women in the *Odyssey* both give and receive gifts. These gifts are sometimes completely unremarkable and unproblematic, especially when women give textiles, as when Arete gives clothing to Odysseus (7.109ff.). By contrast, Helen's gift of a robe to Telemachos (*Odyssey* 15.125–8) is a bit more ambiguous. She says it is to be kept for his future wife, but her own unreliability as a wife casts a shadow over the gift.

Precious metal objects given to women are more problematic. In book 18, Penelope is offered a golden necklace by one of the suitors, and another offers a garment with golden clasps. The disguised Odysseus watches, content to see his clever wife increasing the household wealth at the suitors' expense, but a few brief allusions elsewhere in the poem hint that a woman may be induced to betray her husband or son in exchange for a golden bauble.[22] Thus the details of the suitors' gifts have one meaning to the self-confident Odysseus and another to the audience, who may recognize the ambiguity of the situation. It is interesting that he does not raise an eyebrow at the gifts, when he has been warned by Agamemnon in the Underworld not to return home openly, in case Penelope should prove as faithless as his own murderous wife, Clytemnestra: "Land your ship / in secret on your island; give no warning. / The day of faithful wives is gone forever."[23]

These gifts can be broken down rather neatly into two categories: gifts of cloth given by women to men, generally with no evil outcome; and gifts of metal given by men to women with potentially disastrous results. The *Odyssey* places the more positive textile exchanges in the foreground of the narrative, as befits the happy ending and the generally positive valuation of women throughout most of the poem.[24] At the same time, passing allusions to peripheral female characters such as Eriphyle and Asterope, who are induced by bribes (also called *dora*) of golden objects to betray their men, suggests lingering anxiety about women as participants in exchange.[25] This latter tendency will become pronounced later in Greek literature. In the tragic dramas of the classical period (fifth and fourth centuries BCE), even women's gifts of cloth will become deadly, as in Sophokles's *Trachiniai* and Euripides's *Medea*, where these gifts become delivery systems for destructive poisons.[26]

For all that she is troublesome, Pandora is also inevitable. She represents a necessary rupture with a former life, an impossible golden age existing outside social networks of exchange, a life without production or reproduction. She is created by Zeus in anger over Prometheus's trick of stealing fire for mortals, and with it (according to Plato's *Protagoras*), the arts of Athena and Hephaistos—weaving and metal-working, respectively.[27] These two arts are then used against mortals in order to make woman irresistible. Apparently mortals cannot have production without reproduction, cannot have technology without also having sexual dimorphism and the division of labor. Even if this marked gendered division of labor is systematically written out of Hesiod's account, it sneaks back into the picture in the form of the *technai* (skills or crafts) of the gods Hephaistos and Athena.

What Pandora takes with one hand, she gives back with the other. Man loses his freedom from toil, but gains thereby access to a new world not only of social interaction but also of creativity and invention. Made of clay and decorated with gold, she is composed of the very raw materials on which that creativity is to be expended. Without the gift of woman (and the gifts of women), man cannot go forward, cannot fully experience what it is to be human. With her, he must progress, even if the journey is sometimes arduous and painful. Unlike the Golden Girl of the Chambri, this new creation represents not a temporary interruption in the usual conditions of social life, but an entrance into human life itself. Through the opening of the jar, with its extremely ambiguous results—even the pessimism of Hesiod cannot fully disguise this—come not only the evils of mortal existence but all of its possibilities as well.[28]

NOTES

Epigraph is from Hesiod's *Works and Days* in Evelyn-White 1964, line 356.

1. The work of J.-P. Vernant (1914–2007), with its elegant and profound interpretations of ancient Greek myth, illustrates this point brilliantly. Without in any way attempting to hide under his aegis the shortcomings of my own readings, I dedicate this article to his memory. One of his last publications was *Pandore, la première femme* (2006).

2. Odysseus in the Underworld inquires of Teiresias whether his wife still respects the marriage bed and keeps his things safe: *Odyssey* 1.178–79; 19.525–27.

3. The transition from jar to box was documented by Erwin and Dora Panofsky (1962). For the homology of Pandora and the jar, specifically through the association of the belly of the jar and the womb, see Sissa (1990, 154–55).

4. See Lamberton (1988) for the idea that these poems derive from an originally fluid corpus transmitted orally, like the Homeric poems.

5. Other divine gifts made by Hephaistos include the necklace of Harmonia (and later Eriphyle) and the arms of Achilles.

6. Not only was Pandora made of earth, but a deeper association with Gaia may perhaps be indicated by several images in which the figure of Pandora is shown emerging from the ground; see note 11.

7. *Pandoteiros/a* has an agent ending common in Greek, making it unambiguously active. (The *-tor/-ter/-teiros* ending indicates one who performs an action.)

8. A similar association of virtuous women with spinning wool can be found in Roman culture. See D'Ambra (2007, 94).

9. At *Iliad* 6.289–90 this phrase refers to the weaving of captive Sidonian women; at *Odyssey* 7.96–97, to the weaving of the Phaeacian women, and at *Odyssey* 10.222–23 to Kirke's weaving.

10. We may find support for Arthur's interpretation at line 66 of the *Works and Days,* which refers to the "cruel longing and limb-wearying cares" with which Aphrodite endows Pandora. The possibility that women's own desire could be threatening is clear from lines 586–87, where we learn that in the summer, at the time of the Dog Star, "women are most wanton, but men are at their weakest."

11. For example, a white ground cup by the Tarquinia Painter, c. 470–460, British Museum D 4, where she is labeled "Anesidora," and a red-figure crater by the Niobid Painter c. 460, British Museum E 467. These images are discussed in detail by Lissarrague (2001).

12. It is worth emphasizing that while goddesses are female, they are not *women,* a word properly reserved for mortals. See Loraux (1992).

13. Errington and Gewertz (1987, 26). As they further explain, "[E]ach Chambri man by the fact of his birth incurs an ontological debt. . . . Since wife-givers have provided life, wife-takers remain perpetually indebted to them" (30).

14. "Yet, these historically contingent experiences are given cultural meaning within a story which is fundamentally about male-female relationships." Errington and Gewertz (1987, 58); Gewertz (1985).

15. Sussman (1984, 83–88). But for the limits of an appeal to contemporary economic conditions, see Zeitlin (1995, 52) and Brown (1997, 39n69).

16. On the false problem of dowry versus bride-wealth in Homeric epic, see Brown (1997, 41) and Morris (1986, 105ff).

17. See Amartya Sen (1990) on the demographic problem of "missing women." Many of the same causes, such as smaller food rations for girls, have also been documented for ancient Greece.

18. See Lévi-Strauss (1969, 496–97) on similar fantasies of escape from the obligations of marriage exchange among the Andaman Islanders of India.

19. It must be admitted that the text we have only implies but says nothing explicit about a prohibition against opening the jar. The theme of Pandora's curiosity, while popularly assumed to be her motive for opening the jar, is also not found in Hesiod, but only in later elaborations. Brown equates her action of opening the jar with that of Epimetheus (her husband-to-be) when he accepts the gift of the woman: "both husband and wife are prompted by an unwise impulse to involve themselves in something they falsely believe will be to their advantage" (1997, 30).

20. The creation of humankind from earth is found—to limit ourselves temporally and geographically—in Genesis; in many myths of the ancient Near East; and also in Plato's *Protagoras* (320dff.), where, however, fire is mixed in.

21. See Brown (1997, 44), on the significance of this exceptionally high price.

22. Eriphyle is mentioned in *Odyssey* 15.247, and Astyoche in *Odyssey* 11.521.

23. *Odyssey* 11.455–56 (Fitzgerald 1963).

24. The brooch given by Penelope to Odysseus (*Odyssey* 19.256–57) is a rare example of a gift of metal from a woman to a man. In this case it is a harmless one, however, because it is between spouses.

25. This is explored more fully in Lyons (2003) and Lyons (2012).

26. In the *Trachiniai,* Deianeira sends a cloak to her straying husband Herakles, having imbued it with what she believes is a love potion, but which turns out to be a poison that burns into his flesh. Euripides's Medea uses a poisoned cloak and crown to kill the princess for whom her husband, Jason, has abandoned her.

27. The gift of technology is only implicit in Hesiod, but it becomes explicit in Plato's *Protagoras* 321c–e: "already the appointed day had come, when man too was to emerge from the earth into the daylight. Prometheus, being at a loss to provide any means of salvation for man, stole from Hephaestus and Athena the gift of skill in the arts, together with fire." (Translation: Guthrie, in Hamilton and Cairns, 1961).

28. This chapter reprises some parts of Lyons (2003) but with a significant change of emphasis. I owe many thanks to Morny Joy for her helpful comments.

Arthur, Marylin [Marilyn Katz]. 1981. "The Divided World of Iliad VI." In *Reflections of Women in Antiquity,* ed. Helene P. Foley. New York: Gordon and Breach. 19–44.

———. 1982. "Cultural Strategies in Hesiod's Theogony: Law, Family, Society." *Arethusa* 15: 63–82.

———. 1983. "The Dream of a World without Women: Poetics and the Circles of Order in the Theogony Prooemium." *Arethusa* 16: 97–116.

———. 1984. "Early Greece: The Origins of the Western Attitude toward Women." In *Women in the Ancient World: The Arethusa Papers,* ed. J. Peradotto and J. P. Sullivan. Albany: State University of New York Press. 7–58.

Athanassakis, Apostolos N., trans. 2004. *Hesiod: Theogony, Works and Days, and Shield of Heracles.* Baltimore: Johns Hopkins University Press.

Barber, E. J. W. 1991. *Prehistoric Textiles: The Development of Cloth in the Neolithic and Bronze Ages with Special Reference to the Aegean.* Princeton, NJ: Princeton University Press.

———. 1992. "The Peplos of Athena." In *Goddess and Polis: The Panathenaic Festival in Ancient Athens,* ed. J. Neils. Princeton, NJ: Princeton University Press. 103–17.

———. 1994. *Women's Work: The First 20,000 Years; Women, Cloth, and Society in Early Times.* New York: W. W. Norton.

Bourdieu, Pierre. 1970. "The Berber House, or the World Reversed." *Social Science Information* 9: 151–70.

Brown, A. S. 1997. "Aphrodite and the Pandora Complex." *Classical Quarterly* 47: 26–47.

D'Ambra, Eve. 2007. *Roman Women.* Cambridge: Cambridge University Press.

Detienne, Marcel. 1963. *Crise agraire et attitude religieuse chez Hésiode.* Brussels: Latomus.

Errington, Frederick, and Deborah Gewertz. 1987. *Cultural Alternatives and a Feminist Anthropology.* Cambridge: Cambridge University Press.

Evelyn-White, H. G., ed. and trans. 1964. *Hesiod, the Homeric Hymns, and Homerica.* Cambridge, MA: Harvard University Press.

Fitzgerald, Robert, trans. 1963. *Odyssey.* Garden City, NY: Anchor Press.

Friedl, Ernestine. 1967. "The Position of Women: Appearance and Reality." *Anthropological Quarterly* 40: 97–108.

———. 1975. *Women and Men: An Anthropologist's View.* New York: Holt, Rinehart and Winston.

Gewertz, Deborah. 1985. "The Golden Age Revisited: A History of the Chambri between 1905–1927." In *History and Ethnohistory in New Guinea,* ed. E. Schieffelin and D. Gewertz. Sydney: Oceania Publications.

Hamilton, Edith, and Huntington Cairns, eds. 1961. *The Collected Dialogues of Plato.* Princeton, NJ: Princeton University Press.

Hurcombe, Linda. 2000. "Time, Skill and Craft Specialization as Gender Relations." In *Gender and Material Culture in Archaeological Perspective,* ed. M. Donald and L. Hurcombe. New York: St. Martin's Press. 88–109.

Hurwit, Jeffrey M. 1995. "Beautiful Evil: Pandora and the Athena Parthenos." *American Journal of Archeology* 99: 171–86.

Jenkins, I. D. 1985. "The Ambiguity of Greek Textiles." *Arethusa* 18: 109–32.

Lamberton, Robert. 1988. *Hesiod.* New Haven, CT: Yale University Press.

Lévi-Strauss, Claude. 1969. *The Elementary Structures of Kinship.* Boston: Beacon Press.

Lissarrague, François. 2001. "La fabrique de Pandora: Naissance d'images." In *Eve et Pandora: la création de la première femme,* ed. Jean-Claude Schmitt. Paris: Gallimard. 39–67.

Lombardi, Tiziana. 1994. "Alcune Considerazioni sul Mito di Pandora." *Quaderni Urbinati di Cultura Classica,* n.s., 46: 23–34.

Loraux, Nicole. 1978. "Sur la race des femmes et quelques-unes de ses tribus." *Arethusa* 11: 43–87.

———. 1992. "What Is a Goddess?" In *A History of Women.* Vol. 1, *From Ancient Goddesses to Christian Saints,* ed. P. Schmitt Pantel. Trans. A. Goldhammer. Cambridge, MA: Harvard University Press. 11–44.

Lyons, Deborah. 2003. "Dangerous Gifts: Ideologies of Marriage and Exchange in Ancient Greece." *Classical Antiquity* 22 (1): 93–134. Reprinted in *Women and Property in Ancient Near Eastern 17and Mediterranean Societies,* ed. D. Lyons and R. Westbrook. Washington, D.C: Center for Hellenic Studies, 2005. http://chs.harvard .edu/wa/pageR?tn=ArticleWrapper&bdc=12&mn=1219

———. 2012. *Dangerous Gifts: Ideologies of Gender and Exchange in Ancient Greece.* Austin: University of Texas Press.

Marquardt, Patricia A. 1982. "Hesiod's Ambiguous View of Women." *Classical Philology* 77: 283–91.

Mauss, Marcel. 1990 [1950]. *The Gift: The Form and Reason for Exchange in Archaic Societies.* Trans. W. D. Halls. New York: Routledge.

Morris, Ian. 1986. "The Use and Abuse of Homer." *Classical Antiquity* 5: 81–138.

Panofsky, Dora, and Erwin Panofsky. 1962. *Pandora's Box: The Changing Aspects of a Mythical Symbol.* New York: Bollingen Foundation.

Papadopoulou-Belmehdi, Ionna. 1994. "Greek Weaving or the Feminine in Antithesis." *Diogenes* 167: 39–56.

Pedrick, Victoria. 1988. "The Hospitality of Noble Women in the Odyssey." *Helios* 15: 85–101.

Petropoulos, J. C. B. 1994. *Heat and Lust: Hesiod's Midsummer Festival Scene Revisited.* Lanham, MD: Rowman and Littlefield.

Sahlins, Marshall. 1972. *Stone Age Economics.* New York: Aldine de Gruyter.

Saintillan, David. 1996. "Du festin à l'échange: Les grâces de Pandore." In *Le métier du mythe: Lectures d'Hésiode,* ed. F. Blaise, P. Judet de la Combe, and P. Rousseau.. [Villeneuve d'Ascq]: Presses universitaires du Septentrion. 315–48.

Sen, Amartya. 1990. "More Than 100 Million Women Are Missing." *New York Review of Books,* December 20, 61–66.

Sissa, Giulia. 1990. *Greek Virginity.* Trans. Arthur Goldhammer. Cambridge, MA: Harvard University Press.

Sussman, Linda S. 1984. "Workers and Drones; Labor, Idleness and Gender Definition in Hesiod's Beehive." In *Women in the Ancient World: The Arethusa Papers,* ed. J. Peradotto and J. P. Sullivan. Albany: State University of New York Press. 79–93.

Vernant, J.-P. 1980. *Myth and Society in Ancient Greece.* Trans. J. Lloyd. London: Methuen.

———. 1983. "Hestia-Hermes: The Religious Expression of Space and Movement in Ancient Greece." In *Myth and Thought among the Greeks.* London: Routledge and Kegan Paul. 127–75.

Vernant, J.-P. 1989 [1979]. "At Man's Table: Hesiod's Foundation Myth of Sacrifice." In *The Cuisine of Sacrifice among the Greeks,* ed. M. Detienne and J.-P. Vernant. Trans. P. Wissing. Chicago: University of Chicago Press. 21–86.

———. 2005. *Pandora, la première femme.* Paris: Editions Bayard.

Weiner, Annette. 1974. *Women of Value, Men of Renown: New Perspectives in Trobriand Exchange.* Austin: University of Texas Press.

———. 1992. *Inalienable Possessions: The Paradox of Keeping While Getting.* Berkeley: University of California Press.

Weiner, Annette, and Jane Schneider, eds. 1989. *Cloth and Human Experience.* Washington, DC: Smithsonian Institution Press.

West, M. L. 1966. *Hesiod's Theogony.* Oxford, UK: Clarendon.

———. 1978. *Hesiod's Works and Days.* Oxford, UK: Clarendon.

Zeitlin, Froma. 1995. "The Economics of Hesiod's Pandora." In *Pandora: Women in Classical Greece,* ed. E. D. Reeder. Princeton, NJ: Princeton University Press. 49–56.

———. 1996. *Playing the Other: Gender and Society in Classical Greek Literature.* Chicago: University of Chicago Press.

TWO

Nietzsche, the Gift, and the Taken for Granted

Lorraine Markotic

Without a doubt, a good number of Nietzsche's writings are not only sexist, but misogynist. Unlike many philosophers who write about "man," taking women either to be subsumed under this term or not, but in any case of no particular interest in themselves, Nietzsche has much to say about women. Unfortunately, much of this much that he has to say is either virulently nasty or simply silly. Fortunately, Nietzsche has other things to say as well. In addition to his rather grim and dim comments, he also makes statements about women that indict the society that limits and constrains them. For Nietzsche was sufficiently both a social philosopher and an analyst of the presence of power in interhuman relations to realize that women frequently act in a certain way because this is what men want, and what society and culture demand. He often states this fairly clearly.

On the one hand, then, we have Nietzsche's sexist and misogynist comments and, on the other, his incisive critique of patriarchy. Beyond this, there are numerous writings on women that are simply ambiguous (not that many of his writings are unambiguous, but some are more obviously hermeneutically demanding). Nietzsche's aphoristic style contributes to this, and Nietzsche himself worried that his writings would be misinterpreted, insisting that individual aphorisms not be isolated from broader thematic concerns. Just as philosophers gradually came to understand Nietzsche's works not as eclectic collections of opinions and observations, but as intertwined explorations of philosophical ideas, so too his comments on women—even ones that seemed plainly derogatory—began to be considered in relation to his other critiques and concepts. For example, a comment on women's superficiality was no longer simply examined as a prejudicial remark, or considered in terms of men's interest in women's appearance, but also investigated in relation to Nietzsche's critique of notions of philosophical "depth" and his admiration for the ancient Greek interest in surface. In other words, Nietzsche's statements on women came to be regarded as part of a constellation of concepts (to borrow a term from Adorno). Philosophers began to consider not only what Nietzsche wrote about women, but the concept of "woman" in Nietzsche and what was configured with this concept.

Such an approach is clearly evident in Derrida's well-known *Spurs: Nietzsche's Styles,* which looks at the concept of "woman" in relation to conceptions of truth in Nietzsche. Derrida finds in Nietzsche three types of woman representing three notions of truth. The first involves a traditional notion of woman as falsehood, as excluded from philosophy and truth (considered to exist), the second is an inversion in which woman represents the subtle and elusive nature of truth (regardless of whether she believes in it). In the third notion, however, woman goes beyond the first two positions (representing undecidablity—neither an essentialist notion of truth nor a reaction to it), and it is she who affirms herself. Derrida refers to her as "a dissimulatress, an artist, a dionysiac" (97). Now, attractive as such an image of woman is, the representation of woman as "free spirit," as incongruous and contradictory, is ultimately another cliché; indeed, it is an archetype if not a stereotype. Moreover, because such a dancing woman[1] is inspiring, she fits all too well into an idea of woman as muse, a position Nietzsche readily saw for women—even when it was they who affirmed themselves. Hence, without even addressing Nietzsche's fraught and often bizarre relationships with individual women (his mother, his sister, Lou Andreas-Salomé, Cosima Wagner), one can safely say that Nietzsche had a complex and conflicted relationship to the *concept* of "woman."

Moreover, it is not even enough to look at the concept of woman in Nietzsche's work, and it was an important step when commentators began to consider whether there could be said to be a (non-essentialist) concept of the "feminine" in Nietzsche's work.[2] For many of the concepts that Nietzsche develops are ones that would traditionally be associated with a notion of the "feminine" (though Nietzsche himself would hardly have used this term). Nietzsche's critique of objectivity and reason, his emphasis on the Dionysian, his interest in metaphor and language, his consideration of questions of style, and his attention to the body seem more compatible with a "feminine" than a "masculine" philosophy. It is along these lines that I would like to proceed in relation to the concept of the gift. I do not intend to link Nietzsche's writings on the gift to his writings on women. Rather I intend to show that Nietzsche's unusual elaboration of the gift can be regarded as "feminine"; and, furthermore, that it contains elements that could even be considered feminist. Alan Schrift (2001) has convincingly shown that Nietzsche's concept of generosity can be said to involve a "feminine economy" of giving (even though, again, Nietzsche would not have termed it such). Here I would like to show that Nietzsche's formulation of what is involved in a gift—giving and receiving, generosity and gratitude—entails a "feminine" notion of the gift.

Let me begin by looking at what Nietzsche writes about the gift and giving. Nietzsche's insistence on the gift and his endorsement of giving is most explicitly addressed in *Thus Spoke Zarathustra*. In the section "On the Gift-Giving Virtue," Zarathustra says: "Tell me: how did gold attain the highest value? Because it is uncommon and useless and gleaming and gentle in its splendor; it always gives itself. Only as the image of the highest virtue did gold attain the highest value" ("On the Gift-Giving Virtue" §1).[3] Zarathustra gives almost unrelentingly; his giving is rooted in power and joy. Zarathustra gives because he is abundant and overflowing. Zarathustra's giving is often compared to the sun, a kind of overflowing of light and warmth. But the problem with this solar metaphor, in my view, is that we generally presume upon the sun's light and warmth, at least in western culture. An image of giving as overflowing abundance, therefore, encourages the receiver to take for granted what is being given. I believe this is one of the most problematic aspects of the gift: instead of being recognized as a gift, it comes to be expected and is taken for granted. This is a concern to which I shall return later on.

Despite Nietzsche's keen encouragement of gift-giving, he recognizes its complexity. His conception of giving is far removed from naïve notions of Christian charity or secular philanthropy; he is well aware that there are forms of giving or apparent generosity whereby the giver simply hopes to gain something—or even a lot—in return. He also realizes that people may give merely in order to appear generous, to gain recognition, to be admired, to think of themselves as superior, or simply to feel good about themselves. He even observes that some people are charitable out of a desire for possessions! Such people "doctor" (that is, "set up") those they want to help—make them into "their deserving project," we might say today:

Among helpful and charitable people one almost regularly encounters that clumsy ruse which first doctors the person to be helped—as if, for example, he "deserved" help, required just *their* help, and would prove to be profoundly grateful for all help, faithful and submissive. With these fancies they dispose of the needy as of possessions, being charitable and helpful people from a desire for possessions. One finds them jealous if one crosses or anticipates them when they want to help. (BGE §194)

Nietzsche is astutely aware that people may be generous for all kinds of self-interested reasons. And he even observes that generosity may be a coping mechanism. A short aphorism titled "Generosity" runs as follows: "With the rich, generosity is often just a type of shyness" (GS §199, 2001). Here generosity may be a way of connecting with people or forging social relations when one is timid. Without a doubt, generosity is impelled by exceedingly diverse motives.

Moreover, even if one genuinely wishes to be of assistance in the face of someone's suffering, Nietzsche explains that this is far from a straightforward matter. The assumption that one can jump in and help is not only presumptuous but diminishes the person experiencing misfortune. It identifies her or his needs as plain and perceptible. Nietzsche is especially critical of benefactors who jump in immediately, of those who "believe they have helped best when they have helped most quickly!" (GS §338, 2001). He writes:

> What we most deeply and most personally suffer from is incomprehensible and inaccessible to nearly everyone else; here we are hidden from our nearest, even if we eat from the same pot. But whenever we are *noticed* to be suffering, our suffering is superficially construed; it is the essence of the feeling of compassion that it *strips* the suffering of what is truly personal: our "benefactors" diminish our worth and our will more than our enemies do. In most cases of beneficence toward those in distress there is something offensive in the intellectual frivolity with which the one who feels compassion plays the role of fate: he knows nothing of the whole inner sequence and interconnection that spells misfortune for *me* or for *you*! (GS §338)

One never knows the intricacies of another person's life. The assumption that an individual who is suffering can be aided in an obvious, efficacious way is naïve and often insulting. It is an epistemological error to assume that one knows an individual well enough to identify and implement a remedy. Nietzsche has an almost Freudian sense that simple, practical solutions to another's suffering belie the complexity of the individual's psychic life as well as their social and familial background. He is here quite withering toward those who "jump in" to help with what he derisively calls "*the religion of snug cosiness*" (GS §338, 2001; emphasis in original). Clearly, certain forms of "helping" and some apparently generous actions are simply pseudo-generosity or even a form of domination and control.

Yet notwithstanding his astute critique of such forms of generosity, Nietzsche ultimately esteems and advocates giving, and also magnanimity. Indeed, he very much admires magnanimity, believing that it distinguishes those he calls noble beings from more ordinary people, and that it is a characteristic of great thinkers (D §459). Nietzsche has no respect for those who go after the weak; he believes that one's adversaries should at least be one's equals, if not stronger than oneself. Hence, he admires magnanimity at the same time as he is aware that it is something that is possible only when one has power over others; and he often discusses it in the context of the victorious and the defeated. For example, when Nietzsche refers to those humans who he hopes will pave the way for another, better type of existence, he depicts them as follows: "human beings whose cheerfulness, patience, modesty and contempt for great vanities is just as distinctive as their magnanimity in victory and patience with the small vanities of the defeated" (GS §283, 2001). Elsewhere, Nietzsche lists magnanimity toward the defeated as one of four cardinal virtues (along with being honest with oneself and friends, brave toward enemies, and polite—always) (D §556, "The Good Four"). He is also aware that when one is struggling, one has little time for magnanimity; it is only when one feels that one has achieved something great that one is likely to be gracious: "A human being who strives for something great considers everyone he meets on his way either as a means or as a delay and obstacle— or as a temporary resting place. His characteristic high-grade *graciousness* toward his fellow men becomes possible only once he has attained his height and rules" (BGE §273).

It should be clear, then, that just as Nietzsche is not naïve about generosity, so too is he not naïve concerning magnanimity. His understanding of both concepts is subtle and sophisticated. In an insightful aphorism titled "Magnanimity and Related Things," he even suggests that magnanimity is simply another form of egoism. He writes:

> The magnanimous person—at least the type of magnanimous person who has always made the strongest impression—strikes me as a person with a most extreme thirst for vengeance, who sees satisfaction nearby and drinks it down *already in imagination* so fully, thoroughly and to the last drop that a tremendous, quick nausea follows this quick excess, and he now rises "above himself," as they say, and forgives his enemy, indeed blesses and honours him. . . . Magnanimity has the same degree of egoism as revenge, only egoism of a different quality. (GS §49, 2001)

To propose that magnanimity involves egoism, however, is not to suggest that it is simply a form of self-interest. This is very important. A large number of Nietzsche's writings are concerned with unmasking allegedly selfless motives and showing the self-interest that underlies them; the goal of many of Nietzsche's aphorisms would seem to be to expose our illusions and self-delusions about our "virtuous" behavior or our "altruistic" actions. It is crucial to note, however, that Nietzsche is not suggesting that human beings generally, or even predominantly, act out of expediency. His insight into human psychology is far too nuanced for such a view. Indeed, he considers such a view not only limited, but a sign of one's own limited nature. He stresses that those whose outlook and actions are instrumental have difficulty even fathoming magnanimity.

> For common natures all noble, magnanimous feelings appear to be inexpedient and therefore initially incredible: they give a wink when they hear of such things and seem to want to say, "Surely there must be some advantage involved; one cannot see through every wall"—they are suspicious of the noble person as if he were furtively seeking his advantage. If they become all too clearly convinced of the absence of selfish intentions and gains, they view the noble person as a kind of fool: they despise him in his pleasure and laugh at the sparkle in his eye. (GS §3, 2001)

Nietzsche points out that persons who act out of crude self-interest have trouble understanding the giving of oneself that certain activities might involve; for example, they have difficulty grasping how someone could "risk health and honour for the sake of a passion for knowledge" (GS §3, 2001). In spite of his unrelenting attack on altruism and self-sacrifice, and his vehement critique of the Christian notion of charity, Nietzsche does not consider human actions to be motivated only or even primarily by instrumental rationality.

Throughout his writings, Nietzsche equates what he calls slave-morality with utility. This is discussed in *The Gay Science* (GS §3, 2001), is explicitly stated in *Beyond Good and Evil* (BGE §260), and is a persistent theme of *The Genealogy of Morals*. Nietzsche observes that in a utilitarian climate, giving and generosity will be considered suspect or regarded as foolish; indeed, such actions may even come to be a cause for shame and, more radically, for repression:

> There are occurrences of such a delicate nature that one does well to cover them up with some rudeness to conceal them; there are actions of love and extravagant generosity after which nothing is more advisable than to take a stick and give any eyewitness a sound thrashing: that would muddle his memory. Some know how to muddle and abuse their own memory in order to have their revenge at least against this only witness: shame is inventive. (BGE §40)

Here "extravagant generosity" induces shame. There could be many reasons for this. One might feel that one has given more than one can afford, that one has given up too much. One might feel that one's extravagant generosity will be perceived as a weakness. A man might feel that giving is something associated with women. Or one might feel ashamed to have given to someone who takes the gift for granted, barely noticing it. Whatever the case may be, one feels a need to forget and to hide one's actions, even from oneself. Perhaps our individualistic society makes great generosity seem bizarre. Nietzsche suggests that our culture is not really comfortable with generosity (and certainly not with extravagance). Some things are best kept to oneself, or even from oneself, and extravagant generosity seems to be one of them.

The above passage is quite striking, I think. Of course, as with many of Nietzsche's aphorisms, one might wonder to what extent Nietzsche is criticizing the sociopsychological phenomenon he detects and depicts. The aphorism as a whole, however, is concerned with masks, and Nietzsche suggests that there is much that is best concealed from social scrutiny and hasty interpretation. He understands that one might want to hide, but *not* that one should be ashamed of, extravagant generosity. Ultimately, Nietzsche advocates giving and generosity, and criticizes a culture that would condemn it.

This is something Alan Schrift explores in his innovative article "Logics of the Gift in Cixous and Nietzsche: Can We Still Be Generous?" Schrift argues that there is an economy of generosity in Nietzsche's works comparable to the one advocated by Hélène Cixous. He elaborates Cixous's critique of the notions of the self and intersubjectivity that underlie the acquisition of property, modes of appropriation, and expectations of return. According to Schrift, Cixous sees these as impelled less by a wish to appropriate than by a "fear of loss; the fear of losing what is already possessed," (117) which she ties to the "masculine." Against possessive individualism[4] and the assumption of scarcity that discourage a masculine economy from giving, Cixous advocates an economy of generosity. Schrift argues that one can find a similar economy of expenditure in Nietzsche although Nietzsche does not, needless to say, regard it as feminine (rather more as masculine; 119). Zarathustra stands in relation to his followers as a "giver of gifts," Schrift notes, and when Zarathustra first comes down from his cave to rejoin humanity, "he is over-full and needs to locate those to whom he can bring the gift of his teaching" (114). He is "committed to giving even beyond what he possesses," "is never impoverished by this need to give," and does not "ever reconsider his judgment that the gift-giving virtue is the highest" (115). Moreover, Nietzsche's writings, especially *On the Genealogy of Morals,* allow us to observe how the instinct for revenge is overcome and replaced with a spirit of generosity. A recurring image in Nietzsche, Schrift writes, is the "image of strength as the ability to actively forget and forgive the debts one is owed, to endure petty injury without reacting, to withhold punishment" (115). In summary, Schrift sees Nietzsche as presenting a nobler, higher economy, "grounded in excess strength sufficient to squander its resources if it so chooses" (116).

Schrift advocates a politics of generosity, but one of the most important points he raises, in my view, is that generosity will not always be welcomed. Referring to Zarathustra's insistence that gift-giving is an art (Z, "The Voluntary Beggar"), Schrift states that "great care and skill are required if the recipients of one's generosity are to avoid feeling indebted" (115). He notes Cixous's reference to the uneasiness men have in a situation where they do feel obligated: "If you are a man, Cixous observes, nothing is more dangerous than to be obligated to another's generosity: 'for the moment you receive something you are effectively "open" to the other, and if you are a man you have only one wish'—to annul that openness by returning the gift as quickly as possible" (117). Aside from the essentialist tone of this statement—which the body of Cixous's work undercuts and which Schrift himself addresses— the resistance to receiving is an exceedingly important point, I think.

This resistance, indeed enmity, to receiving, is evident in an interesting passage in Gary Shapiro's *Alcyone: Nietzsche on Gifts, Noise, and Women.* At the very beginning of *Thus Spoke Zarathustra,* when Zarathustra comes down from the mountain he meets a hermit whom he tells that he is bringing humanity a gift. The hermit advises Zarathustra to give humanity alms, but Zarathustra says he is not poor enough for that. Shapiro interprets as follows:

> When Zarathustra replies to the hermit, "I give no alms. For that I am not poor enough," we can take him to be commenting on such a completely asymmetric relationship of giver and receiver. When one gives alms, for which one expects no return whatsoever, one humiliates the objects of one's charity by placing them in a situation that emphasizes their impotence and incapacity. Zarathustra's remark says, in effect, that the need to establish such an asymmetry is itself a form of poverty, for one who was rich, strong, and overflowing would take delight in the contest of circulation and gift exchange. (29)

Now I had always assumed that when Zarathustra says he is not poor enough to give alms, he is referring to the fact that he brings *ideas,* that he intends to give something more valuable than material objects. Indeed, I think the book goes on to suggest that Zarathustra's gifts are his notion of the suprahuman and his doctrine of the eternal recurrence. What I find interesting, however, is, first, Shapiro's assumption that Zarathustra desires a return for his gift and, second, his assertion that when one gives and expects no return whatsoever, "one humiliates the objects of one's charity."

As noted, Nietzsche has suggested that extravagant generosity might lead to shame, but without a doubt in western culture one is much more likely to feel ashamed or embarrassed if one receives. Shapiro reinforces this view when he states that it is humiliating to receive a gift one cannot return. Plainly, there is a strong, and I think fairly prevalent, feeling that it is preferable not to be the object of another's generosity, not to be "subjected to" it. Following Cixous, I would regard this as a traditionally male perspective, although I think it is one that has become widespread in western society. If we had a choice, I think most of us—both women and men—would prefer not to be on the receiving end of things; we would rather be the ones who are giving and generous and magnanimous. But Nietzsche himself suggests that there is actually something miserly, something unmagnanimous(!), in this feeling or position: "It is so unmagnanimous always to play the bestower and giver and to show one's face when doing so!" (D §464). In my view, Nietzsche assumes neither that there need be a "contest of circulation and gift exchange" nor that receiving without being able to give anything in return necessarily involves humiliation.

Moreover, some recent theories of the gift have attempted to extract the gift from economies of exchange, have considered its distinctiveness to lie precisely in its *not* circulating. Centrally important for thinking about the concept of the gift is, of course, Marcel Mauss's groundbreaking work *The Gift*, published in 1950. Mauss presents a notion of the gift intended to encourage us to think about how circumscribed gift-giving is in western capitalist societies and how linked it is to notions of possession and acquisition. Referring to a number of different societies that he calls archaic, Mauss focuses on the potlatch as the event that most obviously challenges patterns of accumulation in western societies. These potlatches involve extreme giving away (and sometimes even destroying) of nearly all that one owns, to the extent that one may impoverish oneself. Potlatches entail complex relations of status, implication, obligation, and responsibility for restitution. But as Jacques Derrida points out, although Mauss's topic is "the gift," his text addresses exchange, obligation, and debt—almost everything, bar "the gift."

Derrida begins his work *Given Time* by articulating the "impossibility" of the gift. He writes that the gift, even if it cannot help but evoke an economic relation or economic value, must be that which "interrupts economy," which "in suspending economic calculation, no longer gives rise to exchange" (7). Unlike Shapiro, Derrida proclaims that the concept of the gift must "defy reciprocity or symmetry" (7). Unlike debt or obligation, the gift must not circulate, must not be exchanged, must remain "aneconomic" (7). Derrida writes:

> For there to be a gift, there must be no reciprocity, return, exchange, coun-
> tergift, or debt. If the other *gives* me *back* or *owes* me or has to give me back
> what I give him or her, there will not have been a gift, whether this restitu-
> tion is immediate or whether it is programmed by a complex calculation of a
> long-term deferral or difference. (12; Derrida's italics)

This becomes apparent, Derrida points out, if the receiver immediately gives back something; in such a case, it is difficult to think of there having been a gift. It is also difficult to think of there having been a gift if the receiver feels that he or she has contracted a debt, if the receiver feels in any way obligated to the giver. In this sense, one could say that it is necessary that the receiver "not *recognize* the gift as gift" (13; Derrida's italics). When the receiver recognizes the gift, he or she "gives back, in the place, let us say, of the thing itself, a symbolic equivalent." (13). In other words, by recognizing the gift as gift, by acknowledging it as freely given, one gives back a kind of symbolic currency to the giver and, in a sense, this annuls the gift. Derrida even states that the *intentional meaning* suffices for the "simple *recognition* of the gift *as* gift, *as such,* to annul the gift as gift even before *recognition* becomes *gratitude.* The simple identification of the gift seems to destroy it" (14; Derrida's italics). Moreover, it is not only the receiver but also the giver who must not recognize the gift. Otherwise, Derrida writes, he begins "as soon as he intends to give, to pay himself with a symbolic recognition, to praise himself, to approve of himself, to gratify himself, to congratulate himself, to give back to himself symbolically the value of what he thinks he has given or what he is preparing to give" (14). In other words, even anonymous gifts and gifts that are turned down do not elude exchange insofar as they involve symbolic approval on the part of the giver. Derrida concludes: "There is no more gift as soon as the other *receives*— and even if she refuses the gift that she has perceived or recognized as gift" (14; Derrida's italics). This is the "impossibility or the double bind of the gift" (16).

Hence, after arguing that the gift cannot be recognized and remain a gift, Derrida suggests that perhaps the event of the gift must contain a notion of forgetting. Not only must the receiver forget the gift, but so too the giver. The gift must not be retained as a memory from which the giver draws symbolic sustenance and affirmation. Furthermore, Derrida insists that this must be an absolute, instantaneous forgetting, more extreme even than the psycho-analytic notion of repression. For displacing an event into the unconscious is, of course, a way of preserving the event—as is evident in the manifestation of symptoms.[5] Derrida is referring to more radical forgetting.[6]

In fact, there is a particular aphorism in Nietzsche's works that does describe a radically forgotten gift. In this aphorism, Nietzsche could be said to be depicting an instance of a Derridean gift that is not "perceived or recognised as gift." Yet this aphorism depicts an immensely problematic situation, involving the relationship between men and women. Let us look at what Nietzsche writes:

> Woman, conscious of man's feelings concerning women, assists his efforts at idealization by adorning herself, walking beautifully, dancing, expressing delicate thoughts: in the same way, she practices modesty, reserve, distance—realizing instinctively that in this way the idealizing capacity of the man will grow. (—Given the tremendous subtlety of woman's instinct, modesty remains by no means conscious hypocrisy: she divines that it is precisely and actual naïve modesty that most seduces a man and impels him to overestimate her. Therefore woman is naïve—from the subtlety of her instinct, which advises her of the utility of innocence. A deliberate *closing of one's eyes to oneself*—Wherever dissembling produces a stronger effect when it is unconscious, it *becomes* unconscious.) (WP §806)

Here we have an instance of a gift that is forgotten. The woman does not give up an object, or even her time or her energy; she gives up herself. The man does not notice, and the woman forgets what she has done. Derrida's ideal of a gift that is forgotten, one that avoids entering an economy of exchange, leaves us with *The Stepford Wives,* but initiated by the women.

Now Nietzsche's aphorism seems to be suggesting that the forgetting of the intention behind the act occurs over time (Derrida refers to an instantaneous forgetting), and Nietzsche may even be speaking phylogenetically rather than ontogenetically, postulating that woman's embodiment of man's desire occurs over generations. So one could perhaps argue that this is not an instance of a gift, but simply a case of self-effacement produced by patriarchal culture: that the transformation stems from expediency, not from any desire to give, and is far from a gift event. Nevertheless, I think this aphorism comes closer than any other example to Derrida's invocation of a gift that is forgotten—and that it is indicative of problems in Derrida's conceptualization of the gift. For the woman who changes in accordance with the desire of the man forgets that she has done so and expects no acknowledgment from him for embodying his desire, just as the man does not acknowledge or even notice the change.[7]

Although the aphorism is an extreme one—a giving up of the self—I think it is indicative of a disturbing aspect of Derrida's analysis of the concept of the gift and perhaps of recent analyses of the gift generally. Derrida believes that the danger that threatens the gift, the hovering peril that threatens to annul it, is that it become absconded into an economy of exchange. For Derrida, what invalidates the gift is its participation in a symbolic, sacrificial, or economic structure. He writes: "From the moment the gift would appear as gift, as such, as what it is, in its phenomenon, its sense and its essence, it would be engaged in a symbolic, sacrificial, or economic structure that would annul the gift in the ritual circle of the debt" (23). In my view, however, what also annuls the gift is exactly for it *not* to appear as such, as gift, in other words, *for it to be taken for granted.* What might be clearly regarded as a gift in one context is no longer a gift when it is expected by the receiver and considered to be nothing out of the ordinary by the giver. Plainly, there are social and cultural contexts in which "giving" by one group of persons and "receiving" by another is expected and socially entrenched. This annulment of the gift is the more insidious one, I think. In any case, I consider it at least as unsettling that a gift might not be recognized, or even noticed, as that it might be marred by entering an economy of exchange.

In my view, then, Derrida's horizon of a gift that is immediately forgotten is all too compatible with giving that is taken for granted, especially giving by women. For historically, women were supposed to "give" to others; their giving was expected, often not even regarded as giving, but considered "natural" (immediately forgotten, in a sense). For example, women were traditionally expected to give their time and energy in caring for others, especially the ill or the elderly, and even today women are more likely to be the caregivers—both physically and emotionally—for friends and family. Without a doubt, the line between giving and expected self-sacrifice is never a clear one. But in my view, the problem is not that women give to others or care for others; the problem begins when this giving is taken for granted. When it is assumed rather than appreciated.

For this reason, I would like to turn to the notion of gratitude. Acknowledging and expressing thanks for what one has been given—even or especially if it is something that could be presumed upon—undermines its taken-for-granted quality. While the concept of the gift and the notion of giving have been increasingly explored by philosophers (Derrida, Marion, Levinas, Bataille), Nietzsche not only examines giving and receiving, but also addresses the notion of gratitude. This notion is not something he constantly discusses, but it is an idea that permeates his work. And it is an important concept for those who might feel less troubled by gifts that enter economies of exchange than by gifts that remain invisible as gifts because they are taken for granted. Here, then, I would like to consider Nietzsche's ideas on receiving, and his attention to the concept of gratitude.

Just as Nietzsche does not consider generosity feminine, so he does not consider the idea of gratitude a "feminine" notion. Nonetheless, I consider gratitude both a concept that can be considered "feminine" and one that is important for feminists. First, traditionally women received gifts and were grateful for them because they themselves had little wealth and purchasing power. Men had more difficulty feeling gratitude, and instead felt obligated and uncomfortable when they were given something, as Cixous notes. They often wanted to "pay back" what they received as quickly as possible. To be the "receiver" in a certain sense put men in the position of women, of those who are less powerful and who are dependent on the generosity and good graces of others. Often when men received (especially from women) they denied that the gift was "any big deal"; perhaps it was simply what they "deserved" and could take for granted. The second reason, then (as I have already argued), that gratitude is an important concept for feminism is that women's gifts are far less likely than men's to be appreciated, or possibly even noticed. Historically, femininity was often conflated into motherhood, and women were expected to be self-sacrificing not only in relation to their children, but in relation to others around them. It is because women's giving of their time, their energy, and themselves not only often goes unappreciated, but is often *not even recognized as a gift* that gratitude is a crucial concept for feminism.

In an aphorism titled "Learning How to Pay Homage," Nietzsche writes:

> Anyone who breaks new paths and has led many people onto new paths discovers with amazement how clumsy and poor those many are at expressing their gratitude; indeed, how seldom gratitude *is able* to express itself at all. It is as though whenever gratitude wants to speak, something gets caught in her throat so that she just clears her throat and falls silent clearing her throat.

Here I would like to note the interesting fact that two different translators of Nietzsche's *The Gay Science*, Walter Kaufmann and Josefine Nauckhoff, both decided to render gratitude as female. While the German noun *Dankbarkeit* takes a feminine article (as do most words with *-keit* endings), *die Dankbarkeit* could simply be translated as "gratitude" without necessarily being personified. I would like to suggest that our resistance to gratitude is linked to the fact that it is regarded as a female trait. But let me continue the aphorism:

The way in which a thinker comes to sense the effects of his thoughts and their reorganizing and unsettling power is almost a comedy; it seems at times as if those who have been affected basically feel insulted and can only express what they take to be their threatened independence through a welter of incivilities. Entire generations are needed to invent merely a polite convention for thanks . . . (GS §100, 2001 [Nauckhoff])

As with most of Nietzsche's keen insight into psychological phenomena, his discernment actually concerns sociopsychological phenomena. Our discomfort with gratitude is indubitably not simply an individual but a cultural malaise. We have difficulty expressing or perhaps even feeling gratitude—especially toward others' ideas—because this seems to undermine our sense of self-sufficiency—a traditionally masculine notion that has been, and still is, highly valued in western society. To receive from another might be taken to imply that we needed something that we were unable to obtain ourselves: this threatens our independence (as Nietzsche notes). It suggests dependence or at least interdependence—a position that masculinist culture denigrates (not something Nietzsche notes). Moreover, being open to and receiving from another, and acknowledging that one has been transformed by another's ideas, involves relinquishing notions of wholeness and completeness. Just as Cixous suggests that acquisition is impelled less by a wish to appropriate than by a fear of losing what one already has, I think not wanting to receive is linked less to a wish to become autonomous than a fear of losing one's (alleged) independence, self-sufficiency, and completeness. (And this fear may itself be rooted in the fact that independence, self-sufficiency, and completeness are always, in part, artificial and illusory constructs.)

Let me return to *Zarathustra*. In Zarathustra's case, the problem is less that his gifts are taken for granted than that they are rejected or misunderstood. Zarathustra's gift is rejected by the people in the marketplace, who mock Zarathustra when he speaks of the suprahuman, saying they would prefer the "last" human instead. And Zarathustra's notion of the eternal recurrence is not grasped by those who seem to embrace it, but simplified and turned into a little rhyme. *Thus Spoke Zarathustra* reminds us that gifts may be repudiated or misconstrued. Yet this is not to say that Nietzsche wishes that his ideas simply be acknowledged and adopted by others. In the very section elaborating on the gift, "On the Gift-Giving Virtue," Nietzsche explicitly addresses the issue of discipleship. Zarathustra insists that his disciples attempt to find their own way. He says such things to them as the following: "Verily, I counsel you: go away from me and resist Zarathustra"; "One repays a teacher badly if one always remains nothing but a pupil"; and

"Now I bid you to lose me and find yourselves" ("On the Gift-Giving Virtue" §3).

Nietzsche values independence: independent thinking and independent actions. And while his works frequently seem fraught with contradictions, on this at least they are exceptionally clear. As already noted, Nietzsche links independence and self-sufficiency with the ability to give, characterizing noble natures as having "a self-sufficiency that overflows and gives to humans and things" (GS §55, 1974). But for Nietzsche independence and self-sufficiency involve not only being able to give, *but also being able to receive, and being able to acknowledge that one has received.* Nietzsche sees it as a weakness when one is so tied to a notion of self-sufficiency that one cannot receive or admit that one has received and, moreover, feel grateful. For the problem of possessive individualism is not only the problem of possessiveness—the tendency of western culture to encourage individuals to hoard—but also the problem of individualism—an individualism that tends to delude itself about its self-sufficiency and what it acquires on its own. Nietzsche states: "Nothing is self-sufficient, neither ourselves nor things."[8] Nietzsche's insistence on gratitude suggests, to the contrary, that it is a failing to take something for granted, to not notice that it was what one needed or wanted. This is almost a feminist perspective, I think (although Nietzsche would probably roll over in his grave at the thought). For feminists have long pointed out the illusory aspect to masculine notions of autonomy and self-reliance: we rely on and receive from one another, especially from other women, much more than our individualist society likes to concede. Schrift's "Logics of the Gift in Cixous and Nietzsche" connects Nietzsche's notion of giving impelled by generosity, abundance, and overflow with Cixous's alternative "feminine" form of giving founded in generosity, sharing, and the building of community. Similarly, I would suggest that drawing on Nietzsche one might develop an alternative "feminine" notion of gratitude (regardless of the sex involved), linked to receptivity, interdependence, and insufficiency (the last need not be a negative trait in my view).

It is worth noting that in Nietzsche's aphorism "Learning How to Pay Homage," quoted at length above, there is a tone of superiority in relation to the person who has "led" people onto "new paths." This is certainly problematic. But Nietzsche's writings in general (in spite of their often polemical tone) indicate what we can and have learned from earlier thinkers and times. As a thoroughgoing genealogist, Nietzsche consistently stresses that our ideas emerge from elsewhere (than our conscious selves), and he emphasizes that we should acknowledge and be grateful for what we have learned. He includes himself here. For example, despite his condemnation of Christianity, especially his repeated attack on its suppression of human drives, Nietzsche does not hesitate to acknowledge that Christian discipline and repression "*educated* the spirit," (BGE §188; Nietzsche's italics) and that with Christian value judgments, for the first time "the sex drive sublimated itself into love" (BGE §189). In spite of his virulent hostility toward Christianity, Nietzsche notes that it had certain positive effects. Additionally, while the phrase "God is dead" is attributed to Nietzsche, Nietzsche himself does not think this is something he has discovered, but rather a cultural event he describes. In his view, it opens new horizons and is something for which we should be grateful. In an aphorism titled "How to Understand Our Cheerfulness," he writes: "Indeed, at hearing the news that 'the old god is dead,' we philosophers and 'free spirits' feel illuminated by a new dawn; our heart overflows with *gratitude,* amazement, forebodings, expectation—" (GS §343, 2001; italics added).

Of course, gratitude, like generosity and magnanimity, is a complex concept, and it should be obvious that Nietzsche would not unilaterally praise gratitude. He is certainly aware that it can become sycophantic. In an aphorism titled "Grateful," he writes: "One grain of gratitude and piety too much:—and one suffers from it as from a vice and, for all one's honesty and independence, falls prey to a bad conscience" (D §293). And in another aphorism, "Fame," he writes: "When the gratitude of many towards one throws away all shame, fame arises" (GS §171, 2001).

But Nietzsche was a classical philologist, and one of the many things he admired about the ancient Greeks was their grateful attitude toward life. In *Beyond Good and Evil,* he writes: "What is amazing about the religiosity of the ancient Greeks is the enormous abundance of gratitude it exudes: it is a very noble type of human that confronts nature and life in *this* way" (BGE §49; emphasis in original). Now, ancient Greek society was, of course, extremely male-dominated. Nevertheless, just as it is important that Nietzsche draw attention to the Dionysian aspects of ancient Greek culture (despite scholars' emphasis on Greek rationality), so it is important that Nietzsche underscore the ancient Greeks' attitude of gratitude (which scholars are also inclined to neglect). The gratitude of the ancient Greeks is a recurrent theme in *The Birth of Tragedy* and is, in part, the basis of Nietzsche's infamous critique of Socrates. In an aphorism in *The Gay Science* titled "The Dying Socrates," Nietzsche explicitly objects to Socrates's ungrateful attitude toward life. He interprets Socrates's dying words as suggesting that life is a disease from which he will be glad to be cured. Nietzsche's hostility to Socrates—a figure esteemed, indeed revered, in western philosophy and culture—stems from his view that Socrates's attitude toward life was indicative of a baleful turn in Greek society. Hence, Nietzsche ends the aphorism with "O friends! We must overcome even the Greeks!" (GS §340, 2001).

As is apparent in Nietzsche's often-quoted phrase "What doesn't kill you makes you stronger," Nietzsche encourages his readers to consider adversity a challenge rather than a burden. He writes: "A loss is a loss for barely an hour; somehow it also brings us a *gift* from heaven—new strength, for example, or at least a new opportunity for strength!" (GS §326, 2001; italics added). Indeed, it is Emerson's ability to be grateful that contributes to Nietzsche's admiration for this thinker whom one would not necessarily associate with Nietzsche. Nietzsche praises Emerson, for "always finding reasons for being contented and even grateful" (TI, "Expeditions of an Untimely Man," §13). This does not mean, however, that Nietzsche fosters naïve optimism, or even any kind of optimism as it turns out. In *The Birth of Tragedy*, Nietzsche is consistent in his critique of optimist illusions and self-delusion and in his emphasis on, and esteem for, pessimism. He does, however, consider there to be different types of pessimism. There is the religio-moral pessimism that suffers resentfully, is hostile to life, and needs a solution to the riddle of existence. And there is the pessimism of the ancient Greeks, a pessimism that has faced the horror and absurdity of existence, that draws strength from this knowledge and suffering, and creates in a spirit of joy and gratitude: "Those imposing artists who let a *harmony* sound forth from every conflict are those who bestow upon things their own power and self-redemption; they express their innermost experience in the symbolism of every work of art they produce—their creativity is gratitude for their existence" (WP §852).

Obviously, a grateful attitude toward life itself will not prevent a society, or indeed the individuals in that society, from taking for granted what they receive from others. Ancient Greek citizens not only had much unacknowledged assistance from women, but they also, as we know, relied upon slaves. Unfortunately, Nietzsche does not address the fact that gratitude is unlikely to be acknowledged or even experienced in relation to certain social groups. Neither does he address the fact that gratitude is probably in part disparaged in western society because it is considered a "feminine" notion. Nevertheless, Nietzsche emphasizes gratitude as a feeling that it is important both to experience and to acknowledge. In this way, he indirectly suggests that we should not take for granted what we receive.

In conclusion, I would like to suggest that rather than seeing gratitude as opposed to giving, one can consider it a form of giving insofar as it involves giving acknowledgment. It seems to me that a feminist concept of giving would be extensive and generous enough to include giving thanks. For thanks is a kind of generosity. It is also a kind of strength. If we regard it as such, Nietzsche suggests, we shall be less resistant to acknowledging and appreciating what we receive.

Clearly, it is important that we be aware that giving, generosity, and magnanimity are undervalued in western culture, and it is equally important that they be encouraged. But we must be careful not to foster giving and generosity in a manner that disparages receiving. Just as extravagant generosity should not—of course—be a cause for shame, neither should receiving (including substantial and significant receiving). Although we have begun to reflect on the complexity and sensitivity required to be a gracious giver, we need to think more about the complexity of—and also our resistance to—being a gracious and grateful receiver. A substantial gift should not lead to denial or the gift's being taken for granted out of fear that one will consequently relinquish an independence, self-sufficiency, and completeness that one never wholly possessed in the first place. Keeping in mind, then, that gratitude is—like giving, generosity, and magnanimity—a complex concept, and keeping in mind that one should be careful not to express "one grain" of gratitude too much as Nietzsche says, we should nonetheless not be so attached to the idea of self-reliance that we are unable to recognize and acknowledge and feel grateful for what we have received. Is there anyone who has ever truly pulled themselves up by their own bootstraps? Or have they always had a helping hand they just didn't seem to notice?

NOTES

1. In "Choreographies" (Derrida 1982), an interview with Derrida, the Dionysian woman is allied with the "maverick dancer" educed from Emma Goldman's well-known remark: "If I can't dance, I don't want to be part of your revolution."

2. As Caroline Picart notes, however, the concepts of "woman" and "the feminine" cannot always be distinguished, especially in Nietzsche's later writings. Picart makes the interesting argument that Nietzsche's conceptions of "woman" and "the feminine" change throughout his works, and that in those following *Zarathustra,* Nietzsche increasingly attempts to silence both the "feminine" and "woman" (25). Without a doubt, the attempt to consider the notion of a "feminine" in Nietzsche's work was important, and Graybeal's *Language and "The Feminine" in Nietzsche and Heidegger* (1990), Burghart's edited collection *Nietzsche and the Feminine* (1994), and Oliver's *Womanizing Nietzsche: Philosophy's Relation to the "Feminine"* (1995) were important books for English-language reception.

3. Quotations from Nietzsche's works are cited by aphorism number or by section title and number so that the reader may consult any translation or the original German. Abbreviations of texts are as follows:

BT: *The Birth of Tragedy*
BGE: *Beyond Good and Evil*
D: *Daybreak*
GS: *The Gay Science*
GM: *On the Genealogy of Morals*

Z: *Thus Spoke Zarathustra*
TI: *Twilight of the Idols*
WP: *The Will to Power*

4. As Schrift notes, this term was explored by C. B. MacPherson in *The Political Theory of Possessive Individualism: Hobbes to Locke* (Oxford: Oxford University Press, 1962).

5. Derrida indicates his awareness that there may of course be an unconscious economy of giving or receiving.

6. But, at the same time, Derrida states that this forgetting is not nothing, and he links this forgetting to Heidegger's analysis of the forgetting of Being. This is not something I shall be able to go into here.

7. One might perhaps wonder whether the intention that is forgotten is repressed; after all, Nietzsche does use the word "unconscious." But I do not think he is using the term in its psychoanalytic sense; the forgetting involved here is not a repression stemming from conflictual desires.

8. *Sämtliche Werke: Kritische Studienausgabe 12,* ed. G. Colli and M. Montinari (Berlin: Walter de Gruyter, 1967), 307. This passage is quoted in Hatab, 55.

REFERENCES

Burghart, Peter J. 1994. *Nietzsche and the Feminine.* Charlottesville: University Press of Virginia.
Derrida, Jacques. 1979. *Spurs: Nietzsche's Styles.* Trans. Barbara Harlow. Chicago: University of Chicago Press.
———. 1982. "Choreographies." Interview with Christie McDonald. *Diacritics* 12 (2): 66–76.
———. 1992. *Given Time: I. Counterfeit Money.* Trans. Peggy Kamuf. Chicago: University of Chicago Press.
Graybeal. Jean. 1990. *Language and "The Feminine" in Nietzsche and Heidegger.* Bloomington: Indiana University Press.
Hatab, Lawrence J. 2005. *Nietzsche's Life Sentence: Coming to Terms with Eternal Recurrence.* New York: Routledge.
MacPherson, C. B. 1962. *The Political Theory of Possessive Individualism: Hobbes to Locke.* Oxford: Oxford University Press.
Mauss, Marcel. 2000. *The Gift: The Form and Reason for Exchange in Archaic Societies.* Trans. W. D. Halls. Foreword by Mary Douglas. London: Routledge.
Nietzsche, Friedrich. 1966. *Beyond Good and Evil: Prelude to a Philosophy of the Future.* Trans. Walter Kaufmann. New York: Vintage.
———. 1967a. *The Birth of Tragedy.* Trans. Walter Kaufmann. New York: Vintage.
———. 1967b. *On the Genealogy of Morals.* Trans. Walter Kaufmann. New York: Vintage.
———. 1967c. *The Will to Power.* Ed. Walter Kaufmann. Trans Walter Kaufmann and R. J. Hollingdale. New York: Random House.
———. 1968. *Twilight of the Idols.* In *Twilight of the Idols/The Anti-Christ.* Trans. with introduction and commentary by R. J. Hollingdale. Harmondsworth, UK: Penguin.

———. 1974. *The Gay Science.* Trans. Walter Kaufmann. New York: Vintage.

———. 1976. *Thus Spoke Zarathustra.* In *The Portable Nietzsche,* ed. and trans. Walter Kaufmann. Harmondsworth, UK: Penguin.

———. 1997. *Daybreak: Thoughts on the Prejudices of Morality.* Ed. Maudemarie Clark and Brian Leiter. Trans. R. J. Hollingdale. Cambridge: Cambridge University Press.

———. 2001. *The Gay Science.* Trans. Josefine Nauckhoff. Cambridge: Cambridge University Press.

Oliver, Kelly. 1995. *Womanizing Nietzsche: Philosophy's Relation to the "Feminine."* New York: Routledge.

Picart, Caroline Joan S. 1999. *Resentment and the "Feminine" in Nietzsche's Politico-Aesthetics.* University Park: Penn State University Press.

Schrift, Alan D. 2001. "Logics of the Gift in Cixous and Nietzsche: Can We Still Be Generous?" *Angelaki* 6 (2): 113–23.

Shapiro, Gary. 1991. *Alcyone: Nietzsche on Gifts, Noise, and Women.* Albany: State University of New York Press.

THREE

"Everything Comes Back to It": Woman as the Gift in Derrida

Nancy J. Holland

I mostly speak, and this has been true for a long time, of sexual differences, rather than of just one difference—dual and oppositional—which, along with phallocentrism, with what I also dub carnophallogocentrism, is in fact a structural feature of philosophical discourse that has been dominant in the tradition. Deconstruction goes by that route in the very first place. Everything comes back to it. Before any feminist politicization (and even though I have often associated myself with that, on certain conditions) it is important to recognize this powerful phallogocentric basis that conditions more or less the whole of our cultural inheritance.

—JACQUES DERRIDA, "CHOREOGRAPHIES"

I may have told this story another time, in another place, perhaps even in another way, but I want to tell it again here, in speaking of women and the gift.

I met Sarah Kofman when I was a graduate student, and encountered her perhaps twice after that. Then, one day many years ago, the tear sheets from one of her articles arrived in the mail with only a scribbled note, now illegible from the passage of time. I tried to determine why she should send this bit of writing to me, but found no obvious answer and filed it away. Sometime later I learned, quite indirectly, of her death. And sometime after that, I learned, again quite indirectly, that she died a suicide. With each new layer of understanding, that article, that gift, became something very different.

But it was not the first gift she had given me. Much earlier, when we first met in the late 1970s, she assured me that I was not wrong in seeing that already each time Derrida spoke of *différance,* of writing, and of much else, he spoke always and also of Woman. From that validation came my career as a philosopher. So, much belatedly, here is my gift to her.

That a gift is never purely a gift is already clear in "Plato's Pharmacy" (1968). There Derrida quotes Marcel Mauss, in a footnote: "the etymologists are right in comparing the *potio*, 'Poison,' series with *gift, gift* ['gift,' which means 'present' in English, means 'poison' or 'married' in other Germanic languages.— Trans.]" (Derrida 1981, 131). The reference to marriage is not gratuitous. The discussion of the *pharmakon* in "Plato's Pharmacy" is woven throughout with two central figures: writing, the main theme in Derrida's earliest work, and Woman/women. Derrida recounts Socrates's explanation that "it was while she was playing with Pharmacia that the boreal wind caught Orithyia up and blew her into the abyss," adding that "Pharmacia (*Pharmakeia*) is also a common noun signifying the administration of the *pharmakon*, the drug: the medicine and/or poison" (1981, 69–70). In Derrida's text, writing, Woman, and the *pharmakon* (as well as its cognates, the *pharmakeus*, scapegoat, and the sacrificial *pharmakos*) all disrupt the phallocentrism of Plato's dialogue and hence of the tradition it inaugurates. And this configuration of undecidables along with (among others) the gift, and more recently hospitality, democracy, and forgiveness, mark, if they do not define, the five decades of Derrida's critical reading of that tradition.

As those decades pass, the centrality of Woman to the understanding of this undecidability becomes clearer. Ten years after "Plato's Pharmacy," in relation to Nietzsche, Derrida says that "[t]he question of woman suspends the decidable opposition of true and non-true and inaugurates the epochal regime of quotation marks which is to be enforced for every concept belonging to the system of philosophical decidability" (1987, 83, 85). Like writing, Woman is poison even at the same time as she renders the alternation between cure and poison, between true and non-true, undecidable. Hence, she is always both dangerous and impossible, like the gift that Woman also is.

> Either, at times, woman is woman because she gives, *because she gives* herself, while the man for his part takes, possesses, indeed takes possession. Or else, at other times, she is woman because, in giving, she is in fact *giving herself for*, is simulating, and consequently assuring the possessive mastery for her own self. (1987, 87; his emphasis)

As the spoken word passes through a distorting mirror in Plato to become the dangerous written word, for Nietzsche Woman disrupts male mastery by being both and at once man's true possession and an illusion, a poison (*gift*) that mirrors his self-possession.

The "feminist politicization" of this discourse becomes explicit in "Choreographies," Derrida's 1981 interview with Christie V. McDonald (1997). Again, the link between women and the gift is clear, and tied to the impossibility of the gift, if not of women per se. In the context of Heidegger's thought, McDonald asks whether "the question of sexual difference is not a regional one" (1997, 24), that is, subordinate to ontological difference, to the *es gibt* linked to the German *gift* (poison again, as Mauss warned us).

> The question proceeds, so to speak, from the end; it proceeds from the point where the thought of the gift [*le don*] and that of "propriation" disturbs without simply reversing the order of ontology, the authority of the question "what is it," the subordination of regional ontologies to one fundamental ontology. I am moving much too rapidly, but how can I do otherwise here? From this point, which is not a point, one wonders whether this extremely difficult, perhaps impossible idea of the gift can still maintain an essential relationship to sexual difference. One wonders whether sexual difference, femininity for example—however irreducible it may be—does not remain derived from and subordinated to either the question of destination, or the thought of the gift. (1997, 30–31)

Not that women can be thought only from the gift, note, but that a femininity that may also be irreducible might only be thought in such a way once sexual difference, here in the singular, enters into the Heideggerian question.

THE GIFT OF TIME

The question of Heidegger and sexual difference is highlighted in a series of articles published between 1983 and 1993 under the title "*Geschlecht*," an untranslatable German word that means at once, and among other things, gender, lineage, race, and species. These texts are intertwined in time and theme with two others published in the early 1990s: *Given Time* (1992) and *The Gift of Death* (1995), closely related texts both of which are devoted to the impossible gift.[1] *Given Time* explicitly repeats the underlying argument of "*Geschlecht* I" (as well as of much of Derrida's other work), in parentheses (quickly followed by another reference to Mauss): "note that we say between men, apparently *between men,* both in the sense of humanity and of masculinity, and of a humanity better represented, as always in this exemplarist logic, by the example of men than by that of women" (1992, 115; his emphasis). The privileged example of the spoken word in Plato is here repeated in the privileged example of men. This move in Heidegger is characterized in "*Geschlecht*

I" (echoing "Choreographies") as "confirming all the most traditional philoso-phemes, repeating them with the force of a new rigour" (1992, 68).

Given Time also outlines the paradoxical logic of the anthropology of gift exchange: "For there to be a gift, there must be no reciprocity, return, exchange, countergift, or debt." Derrida notes, however, that "[w]e know that as good, it can also be bad, poisonous (*Gift, gift*), and this from the moment the gift puts the other in debt." He wants to depart "in a peremptory and dis-tinct fashion, from this tradition" and say that "[t]he donee owes it *to himself* even not to give back, he *ought* not owe . . . and the donor ought not to count on restitution." It follows "at the limit, that he not *recognize* the gift as gift" because "the simple phenomenon of the gift annuls it as gift, transforming the apparition into a phantom and the operation into a simulacrum." Derrida ends by saying, "Consequently, if there is no gift, there is no gift, but if there is gift held or beheld *as* gift by the other, once again there is no gift; in any case the gift does not *exist* and does not *present* itself" (1992, 12–15; his emphasis).[2] The gift as (non-)gift initiates a cycle of exchange.

In "*Geschlecht* II" Derrida links Heidegger, gift, and poison in the context of sexual difference:

Nothing is less assured than the distinction between *giving* and *taking,* at once in the Indo-European languages we speak . . . and in the experience of an economy—symbolic or imaginary, conscious or unconscious, all these values remaining precisely to be reelaborated from the precariousness of that opposition of the gift and of the grip, of the gift that presents and the gift that grips or holds or takes back, of the gift that does good and of the gift that does bad, of the present [*cadeau*] and of the poison (*gift/Gift* or φάρμακον, etc.). (1987, 176; his emphasis)

In the last "*Geschlecht*" article, however, Derrida explores Heidegger's con-cept of the friend in terms of a different impossibility of the gift.

Φιλία [for Heidegger] is in short the other's proper, the gift to the other of what is to the other its very own proper or properness. And what this is due it. But this due escapes no doubt the dimension of the contracted debt. . . . It is necessary to pose the question and to respond if, why, and how such a gift, the gift itself is possible or necessary: the gift of what one does not have as the only gift possible. (1993, 195)

Or are these two impossible gifts the same?

How can one give what one does not have to a friend who cannot see it *as* a gift without returning it to the (hermeneutic) circle/cycle of an exchange without (sexual) difference/*différance*?

One might give, for instance, a friendship that does not exist until that moment when it is seen, not as a gift, but as something that exists in the "between two" discussed in "*Geschlecht.*"

One might give time. Derrida reminds us that

> the structure of this impossible *gift* is also that of Being—that gives itself to be thought on the condition of being nothing (no present-being, no being-present)—and of time which . . . is always defined [by the tradition] in the paradoxia or rather the aporia of what is without being, of what is never present or what is only scarcely and dimly. (1992, 27; his emphasis)

Mauss, he notes later, says that "'[t]ime' . . . is needed to perform any counter-service" in a cycle of exchange (1992, 39).

By the same logic, one might also give words—for Derrida, never one's own. Such giving can be seen as the source of *logos,* of language—"one must also remember first of all that language is as well a phenomenon of gift-counter-gift, of giving-taking—and of exchange" (1992, 81).

Or one might give counterfeit money, a wealth one does not have that might be for the recipient a poisoned gift and hence not a gift, as in the story by Baudelaire at the heart of *Given Time.*

One might give birth.[3]

> The question of the gift should therefore seek its place before any relation to the subject, before any conscious or unconscious relation to self of the subject. . . . There where there is subject and object, the gift would be excluded. A subject will never give an object to another subject. But the subject and the object are arrested effects of the gift, arrests of the gift. At the zero or infinite speed of the circle. (1992, 24)

Or death (*donner la mort*)—"the question of the gift will never be separated from that of mourning" (1992, 129n).

Or give a woman in marriage, another "between two," another *philia,* another cycle of exchange. As Derrida reminds us with regard to the erasure of sexual difference in Heidegger, "This 'between two' as rapport (*Bezug*) drawn into relationship (*trait*) with both birth and death belongs to the very

Being of *Dasein*, 'before' any biological determination, for instance" (2001, 66). Biology would be outside this exchange "between two," just as women are outside the anthropological understanding of marriage as sister exchange. One gives a wife as what one does not have because she is owed from before one's birth, and one receives her as a gift poisoned not only with that debt, but also with her own subject/self outside the circle of gift and debt. Derrida says in *Given Time*, "You will very quickly suspect that, if woman seems to be absent from this narrative, her exclusion could well be organizing the scene and marking its tempo like a clock" (1992, 103).

THE GIFT OF SILENCE

Thus, for Kierkegaard at least, Sarah and Abraham's necessary and impossible silence before her organize the tragic scene of the sacrifice of Isaac. In *The Gift of Death* Derrida asks:

> Would the logic of sacrificial responsibility within the implacable universality of the law, of its law, be altered, inflected, attenuated, or displaced, if a woman were to intervene in some consequential manner? Does the system of this sacrificial responsibility and of the double "gift of death" imply at its very basis an exclusion or sacrifice of woman? (1995, 76)

Woman is both sacrificial gift and the poison that risks the rupture of the circle of exchange, here between men and god(s). Derrida organizes this text around "the relations among sacrifice, suicide, and the economy of the gift" (1995, 10), all linked explicitly to Christianity:

> The gift made to me by God as he holds me in his gaze and in his hand while remaining inaccessible to me, the terribly dissymmetrical gift of the *mysterium tremendum* only allows me to respond and only rouses me to the responsibility it gives me by making a gift of death [*en donnant la mort*], giving the secret of death, a new experience of death. (1995, 33)

Christianity, like the gift as gift, is impossible for Derrida because it requires one "to answer for what one does, says, gives; but it also requires that, being good and through goodness, one forget or efface the origin of what one gives," that is, the Self (1995, 51). It shares the paradoxical structure of friendship, of democracy, of Woman.

And not only Christianity. This text is interwoven with more recent works by Derrida through the questions that link Abraham to the other religions of the Book. "The reading, interpretation, and tradition of the sacrifice of Isaac are themselves sites of bloody, holocaustic sacrifice. Isaac's sacrifice continues every day. Countless machines of death wage a war that has no front" (1995, 70). Already in "Choreographies" Derrida links women and the theme of globalization that marks the last decade of his work: "we cannot separate world-wide feminism from a certain fundamental Europeanization of world culture" (1997, 29).

Thus a unified thematic emerges that clearly illuminates how, for Derrida, every philosopheme of our tradition is irrevocably interwoven with a phallocentrism predicated on the exclusion of Woman/women that traces back to Plato and beyond. An (impossible) feminism "before any feminist politicization."

A TAINTED GIFT?

But . . .

Derrida himself warns us that "with the gift there is always a 'but'" (1992, 62). Women and the gift, if not explicitly sacrifice and suicide, return in "*Fichus*," the address he gave on receiving the Theodor W. Adorno Prize on the not-irrelevant date of September 22, 2001. In this bilingual (French-German) address, he notes that *fichu* as a noun means a woman's scarf, but as an adjective it can mean what is "bad, lost, condemned." His dying father, he reports, said to him one day "I'm *fichu*" (2005, 173), so death is not far here.

The focus of the Adorno Prize address is a dream that Walter Benjamin relates in a letter to Gretel Adorno from a detention camp. In this dream, the letter *d* is written on a piece of fabric, *fichu*. Derrida notes that this *d* might, among other things, refer to the name "Dora" that was shared by Benjamin's first wife and his sister. Derrida goes on to say that Dora "in Greek can mean skin that has been scorched, scratched, or worked over" (2005, 176), also *fichu*. His translator, Rachel Bowlby, however, adds a note: "The more usual etymology is from *doron,* gift; Adorno's own name, Theo*dor,* from the same root, means 'gift of the gods'" (2005, 203), Why this blindness on Derrida's part to the obvious in the name of the Woman/women? Why always in his work such blindness, mixed with such blinding insight?

In *Memoirs of the Blind* (1993), Derrida links blindness in men with weeping women. A sexual difference/*différance* of loss. One thinks of Oedipus and Jocasta, but Derrida also refers to that other great scene from the life of Isaac, the scene organized not by his absent mother, but by his all-too-present wife:

Rebecca takes advantage of her husband's blindness in order to substitute one son for another, that is, Jacob, the favorite younger son, for Esau, at the moment of the testamentary blessing. A nagging and interminable question: how does one sacrifice a son? (1993, 23)

Derrida sometimes loses sight of the fact that the sacrifice of the son is a paradox that exists only within a system shaped by the sacrifice of the daughter, through marriage or death—in either case, by Woman as gift, as necessary poison. That Derrida always lingers on the edge, shadows the limits of the system created by that sacrifice, is as much a key to understanding his work as the ways in which he illuminates its phallogocentrism.[4]

Which leads us to forgiveness, yet another undecidable, like women, "that requires us to think the *possible* (the *possibility* of forgiveness, but also of the gift, of hospitality—and by definition the list is not exhaustive; it is that of all the *unconditionals*) *as the impossible*" (2005, 79). An infinite and impossible work of mourning. As always.

NOTES

Epigraph is from "Choreographies," Derrida 2005, 154.

1. The foreword to *Given Time* notes that it is based on a seminar originally given in 1977–78, that is, prior to both "*Geschlecht*" and "Choreographies"; the translator's preface to *The Gift of Death* notes that it was originally published in a collection of papers from the Gift of Ethics conference in 1990, at which Derrida actually delivered a section of *Given Time,* then not yet published.

2. Compare "O my friends, there is no friend," the Aristotelian text at the core of *The Politics of Friendship* (Aristotle 1997).

3. For a more complete discussion of this (im)possibility, see Holland (2001a).

4. I have argued this more fully elsewhere, for instance, in Holland (2000), (2001a), (2001b), and (2005).

REFERENCES

Aristotle. 1997. *The Politics of Friendship.* Trans. George Collins. New York: Verso.
Derrida, Jacques. 1981. *Dissemination.* Trans. Barbara Johnson. Chicago: University of Chicago Press.
———. 1987. "*Geschlecht* II: Heidegger's Hand." Trans. John P. Leavey Jr. In *Deconstruction and Philosophy,* ed. John Sallis. Chicago: University of Chicago Press. 161–96.
———. 1992. *Given Time: I. Counterfeit Money.* Trans. Peggy Kamuf. Chicago: University of Chicago Press.
———. 1993. *Memoirs of the Blind.* Trans. Pascale-Anne Brault and Michael Naas. Chicago: University of Chicago Press.
———. 1993. "Heidegger's Ear: Philopolemology (*Geschlecht* IV)." Trans. John P.

Leavey Jr. In *Reading Heidegger: Commemorations,* ed. John Sallis. Bloomington: Indiana University Press. 163–218.

———. 1995. *The Gift of Death.* Trans. David Willis. Chicago: University of Chicago Press.

———. 2001. "*Geschlecht:* Sexual Difference, Ontological Difference." Trans. unattributed. In *Feminist Interpretations of Martin Heidegger,* ed. Nancy J. Holland and Patricia Huntington. University Park: Penn State University Press. 53–72.

———. 2005. *Paper Machine.* Trans. Rachel Bowlby. Stanford, CA: Stanford University Press.

Derrida, Jacques, and Christie V. McDonald. 1997. "Choreographies." In *Feminist Interpretations of Jacques Derrida,* ed. Nancy J. Holland. University Park: Penn State University Press.

Holland, Nancy. 1986. "The Treble Clef/t: Jacques Derrida and the Female Voice." In *Philosophy and Culture,* vol. 2, ed. Venant Cauchy. Proceedings of the XVIIth World Congress of Philosophy, 1983. Montreal: Editions du Beffroi/Editions Montmorency.

———. 2000. "In This Text Where I Never Am: Discourses of Desire in Derrida." In *Continental Philosophy VII: Philosophy and the Discourse of Desire,* ed. Hugh Silverman. New York: Routledge. 159–70.

———. 2001a. "'With Arms Wide Open': *Of Hospitality* and the Most Intimate Stranger." *Philosophy Today* 45 (5) (SPEP Supplement 2001): 133–37.

———. 2001b. "The Death of the Other/Father: A Feminist Reading of Derrida's Hauntology." *Hypatia* 16 (1): 64–71.

———. 2005. "Derrida's Wake." *Radical Philosophy Review* 8 (2): 131–42.

Irigaray, Luce. 1985. *This Sex Which Is Not One.* Trans. Catherine Porter. Ithaca, NY: Cornell University Press.

Rubin, Gayle. [1975] 1997. "The Traffic in Women." In *The Second Wave: A Reader in Feminist Theory,* ed. Linda Nicholson. New York: Routledge. 27–62.

FOUR

Melancholia, Forgiveness, and the Logic of *The Gift*

Kathleen O'Grady

INTRODUCTION: *MAPULA*

There is a line in Marcel Mauss's renowned essay *The Gift* that never fails to interrupt that simple repetitious rhythm of one mind engaged with another in the act of reading; I am talking here of the easy tick-tock movement of the head, from left to right and back again, like the pendulous bulb that gives to time its measure. The passage in question resists this motion, demands pause, and a measure of its own. Each time I finish reading the phrase, I invariably return to its beginning to read it over once again, and again, as if repetition in rupture will somehow make sense of itself.

The line reads as follows: "Now in our view one of the most important acts noted . . . and one which throws a strong light on sexual relationships, is the *mapula*, the sequence of payments by a husband to his wife as a kind of salary for sexual services" (Mauss 1967, 71). Mauss here is simply referring to Malinowski's work on the Trobriands, and of the system of gift exchange that functions as the substratum of their economy. So, why does this straight-forward sentence, a passing observation that is not returned to again in the book, jar the fluid, forward motion of my reading? It may be because this is one of very few references made by Mauss to an economy of the gift that *includes women,* who are typically the objects of gift-giving and not the recipients (though it is true that Mauss does not actually include in his reference the gifts received by the women for their "sexual favors"). It could also be because this is the only reference where Mauss discusses the active participation of women in the giving of gifts, that is, as donees, and not just as objects or recipients. Then there is Mauss's ambiguous yet sweeping reference to the power of this information to "throw a strong light on sexual relationships" generally. But the phrase itself, which implicitly frames so much of the contemporary literature on gift-giving, rests precariously on a presupposition. In

101

Mauss's sentence, women are the objects of desire, since they give as their gift "sexual services." Women are positioned in the sentence as the recipients of desire. The husband must give something other, something the wife needs— but does not "desire"—as a payment for his desires. Yet for Mauss's statement to have meaning of any kind, one must accept that his observation is contingent upon the assumption that *women are without desire(s)*, that they must gift their bodies to the desires of men, but they themselves do not desire.

The power of Mauss's phrase to threaten the forward passage of my reading is derived from *a lack*; the sentence receives its force from an *absence*; from the omission of woman's desire from the text. In fact, it could be said that this absence marks the whole of *The Gift*, that the very economy of the gift is predicated on this absence. In this chapter I would like to examine the way in which Julia Kristeva returns desire to the configuration of the female subject generally and, in a delightful inversion of Mauss, predicates the logic of "the gift" itself on *woman's desire*. I will demonstrate this through an examination of Kristeva's *Black Sun*, an exposition on female melancholia, and her aesthetic-theology of "forgiveness."

MELANCHOLIA AND THE REFUSAL OF "THE GIFT"

Julia Kristeva's *Black Sun, Tales of Love*, and *Powers of Horror* can be considered together as a trilogy, with each text taking as its object a different dynamic of subjective formation. While in *Tales of Love* Kristeva pursues representations of agape throughout the ages, and in *Powers of Horror* she unravels the operations of abjection; in *Black Sun* Kristeva undertakes a genealogy of melancholia by investigating its manifestations in different cultures, from various historical times, as well as the particular form it takes in her individual psychoanalytic patients. She locates melancholia at the juncture of physiology and psychology, at the crossroads of both cultural and corporeal forces. It is from her analysis of melancholia, in addition to her two texts on love and horror, that she challenges both the Freudian and the Lacanian Oedipal understanding of language acquisition, and aligns the logic of "the gift"—in her reading, always a gift of language—with woman's desire.

As a point of departure, Kristeva returns once again to Freud's essay "Mourning and Melancholia." Here Freud suggests that a comparison between these two states can function to highlight the more complex psychic manifestations of the melancholic. Mourning, a "natural" condition that is commonly initiated by the death of a loved one (or the loss of an ideal), evinces similar psychic characteristics to melancholia. A complete lethargy overtakes the individual, psychomotor ability is rapidly reduced, replaced by an insurmountable physiological fatigue and psychic exhaustion. The individual rejects the activity of the world outside and may refuse food and company and suffer from extreme insomnia. Neither the melancholic nor the mourner is capable of loving another in place of the lost love.

Yet melancholia, unlike mourning, is typified by an extreme hatred of the self. The melancholic's repugnance does not come from a concern with physical appearance, social acceptability, or intellectual ability, but from a heightened sense of moral inadequacy. As Freud states, "In mourning it is the world which has become poor and empty; in melancholia it is the ego itself" (Freud 1957, 246). The melancholic, unlike the person in mourning, anticipates punishment for her unethical behavior and seems to encourage, rather than conceal, public exposure of her faults.

Just as the manifestations of melancholia appear to overlap with those of mourning, the event that generates each condition also shares similarities. The melancholic, like the mourner, has also suffered a great loss. But while they both share a process of bereavement, the melancholic is left bewildered by the *cause* of her condition; the mourning party has a conscious understanding of what has been lost, but the melancholic does not consciously comprehend her loss. Freud, and Lacan, following his model, recognize this as an "object loss" that cannot be surrendered by the individual and so is maintained at the expense of the ego, leaving it empty, "like an open wound" (Freud 1957, 253). A narcissistic identification with the loved one is the way in which the melancholic is able to hold fast to the loved one despite being rejected or abandoned by that individual. But, as both Kurt Abraham and Melanie Klein have also noted, the melancholic's relation to that other is marked by ambivalence—love and aggression—which combine to channel libidinal energies at the ego itself, instead of at a new (loved) object (Kristeva 1989, 11). The melancholic's moralistic judgments constitute a hidden aggression that, though directed at the self, is more accurately aimed at the loved other who has deserted her.

But while Freud and Lacan theorize melancholia within a kind of object relations field—that is, they place it after the Oedipal stage of development, when the child has already achieved an individual identity and becomes a speaking subject and the mother its first object—Kristeva places the origins of melancholia at an earlier stage: the pre-Oedipal. Her descriptions of the melancholic do not so much reject the Freudian model as augment his understanding.

Kristeva's melancholic, in contrast to Freud's, is marked foremost by a complete *atheism,* not just the denominational proclivity of one who has been stripped of religious conviction, but a kind of *semiotic atheism,* a condition where all faith and values are undone, all signs emptied of their significance, when the promise for meaning of *any kind* has been revoked. Kristeva's analysis of melancholia is primarily as a *linguistic* disorder. The most distinct manifestation of melancholia in Kristevan theory is the extreme asymbolia of the afflicted subject, the failure of language to communicate or convey meaning. The possibility for signification in language is lost; all signs are seen as empty and barren. At the same time the remaining speech of the melancholic has a flat, monotonous pitch and is uttered without inflection or intonation. All affect—the rhythms, pulsions, flows, and energy charges of linguistic construction, what Kristeva calls "semiotic language"—is stripped from the melancholic's language use. It is as if she does not herself believe the words that she is uttering.

And yet Kristeva's atheistic melancholic is also a kind of *mystic*. Though separated from linguistic functions, she is immersed in an affective bond that links her physical being to the shadow of an archaic Other. This sublime Other promises the melancholic union, that is, absolute meaning, something that language can never offer. At the same time, however, the separation between the sublime Other and the melancholic is intensified since there is only an "insistence without presence," a shadow that beckons, but, like all shadows, can never be brought to light.

It is not peripheral that Kristeva situates Nerval's "black sun" at the base of her understanding of melancholia. The black sun represents the other side of Platonic light, which provides rationality, representation, and meaning.[1] The Platonic sun brings *separation and definition,* and, as Plato writes, it "not only makes the things we see visible, but also *brings them into existence*" and gives them "being" (Plato 1961; my emphasis). The melancholic refuses the Platonic sun and situates herself directly to face the black sun, the lure of all that surpasses meaning, linear logic, and denotative signification; it is her "glass, darkly." The black sun beckons for a subjective fusion with the melancholic, but does not grant this melding of borders, making of the melancholic a prisoner of a promise, the inhabitant of an empty plane.

Yet the melancholic as mystic, Kristeva notes, is not without some kind of joy. Her devotion to the affective reverberations of the sublime Other grants her something beyond that which words are able to capture and fix in place, a clarity of vision that confirms the lack of meaning in anything outside of the black sun itself. To this she devotes her body, the site itself of these affects, and she is self-righteous in her mute understanding.

Kristevan psychoanalytic theory aligns the asymbolia of the melancholic with a yearning for the pre-Oedipal, archaic mother. Melancholia consists of a wistful looking back toward the prelinguistic state, to the unity that

existed between the mother-child before any separation or subjective formation took place. Kristeva's melancholy person does not mourn for an object
as such, but for "*la Chose*," the unsignifiable, both a place and a pre-object
that cannot be articulated, but that the melancholic endeavors to (re)inhabit.
Accompanying this longing for the archaic mother is a strong hostility, a
belief that one has been unjustly "deprived of an unnameable, supreme good"
(Kristeva 1989, 13). This "Other" is so fundamental to the melancholic, so
closely aligned with the subject (and this is particularly true for women who
have a more immediate identification with the mother), that the aggression
becomes internalized and focused on the self. The depression that the melancholic experiences is in actuality a protracted hatred for this Other that she
feels has forsaken her.

Kristeva does not deny that melancholia may emerge from external conditions, the loss of a loved one, for example, or from physiological, "neu-
ronal," and/or "endocrinal" causes, but it always, and chronic melancholia
particularly, reaches back toward the process that every subject undergoes to
become a speaking subject, a subject of and in language; that is, the subject's
movement away from the archaic mother. At its foundation Kristevan melancholia is caused by a denial of the *necessary separation* between the subject
and the archaic mother.

But melancholia is not a rejection of the Oedipal process—the separation
that founds subjectivity—since the melancholic is able to function appro-
priately and appear normal to others in the everyday, symbolic world; this
would not be possible if Oedipalization were rejected. And as Kristeva has
noted elsewhere, if the motivation for subjectivity were to be solely located in
the Oedipal realm, it would function to deny the archaic mother any role in
language acquisition (and place the dynamic of the language contract solely
in the realm of the Law of the Father). What Kristeva wants to uncover is
the movement that makes possible the play, the ambiguity and elasticity,
of linguistic signification, and the renewal of language itself within its own
practice. At the same time, she hopes to map the structurations of the subject to this dynamic dialogic play of (semiotic-symbolic) language. Kristeva
must, therefore, simultaneously locate the motivation for separation from the
archaic mother prior to the definitive separation that occurs in the Oedipal
stage and uncover an early foundation for language acquisition.

It is for *a gift* that Kristeva searches, something to diffuse this Oedipal trap
that Freud and Lacan have left behind. What she wishes to locate in the pre-
Oedipal is a logic that will enable the subject to move from the mother-child
dyad, of its own accord, and without abjecting the mother, *a gift* that will
grant the subject something to satisfy itself in place of the mother.

Kristeva returns to Freud in order to move beyond him; she finds in his "Ego and the Id" an undeveloped reference to a third party, an archaic "father," which Freud names "the father in individual prehistory." This so-called pre-Oedipal "father" is not an anthropomorphic, sexed figure. In fact, the term is misleading since the "archaic father" does not denote an "entity" outside of the mother at all. What Kristeva discovers, or should I say the *absence that she uncovers*, is the *desire* that *the mother* has for someone *outside* of the mother-child dyad. This desire becomes the third term, the "archaic father," and provides a tertiary logic to the hitherto dyadic formation of the pre-Oedipal realm. While the child understands itself only in its relation to the mother (since it is not yet distinct, as a subject, from the mother), the mother does not define herself *only* in relation to the child. The mother has desires that extend beyond those of the child, desires for someone other than the child itself. The desire conveyed by the mother for someone other is expressed in and through language, a discourse that brings difference to the previously undifferentiated mother-child entity. This desire—*a gift of love*— is itself what motivates the child toward the "speaking other," the object of the mother's desire.

Mauss's text on the gift is centered on an economy of exchange. The gift is given in confident expectation of what is to be received. Cixous and Clément call this economy the "law of return" as opposed to a law of "equal return"— more is always anticipated than what is given. The recipient of the gift is burdened by the receipt of the gift—it has been "put on his back," as the Tlingit say (Mauss 1967, 105)—for there is the duty to return a gift in excess of the gift received, reciprocity being presupposed. Strathern refers to this process as "enchainment" since it creates a condition of social relations based on obligation and duty, one person "enchained" to the other, with gift exchange being the means to facilitate this potentially exploitative bond (Strathern 1988, 161). The gift then becomes a type of commodification, since it unveils a relation between persons that rests on production, consumption, and accumulation, and creates a climate of reciprocal dependence. Mauss indicates that there is no gift that is independent from this economy of exchange; no "pure," "genuine," or "free" gifting is ever possible.

But the gift economy that Mauss delineates is precisely what Kristeva wishes to undo. What she proposes in its place is the possibility for a *pure gift*, the gift of the mother's desire, which founds the first moments of subjectivity and brings the subject to language. The mother's desire for another constitutes a "true" gift, in the Kristevan frame, being both "disinterested" and "forgetful." The child is neither the object nor the recipient of the desire, yet remains its indirect beneficiary. The desire functions as a kind of accidental overflowing that provides mobility for the child from homogeneity toward heterogeneity through language. The mother's desire, then, is not a gift in and of itself; that is, it is not something given directly *to the child*, but *gifts itself anyway in its very excess* to the child and thus marks the beginnings of separation from the archaic mother. In Kristeva's schema there is no predetermined response or reciprocation that enchains the subject of this gift to the speaking other, since the gift itself is "unencumbered"; the gift, in its purity (outside of the logic of return), simply affords an *openness to the other*. It does not close, make "present," or grant "being" but opens up. And it is this openness to the other which Kristeva believes constitutes the lining of our being.[2]

At the same time, this gift, which Kristeva also calls "agape" and so gives it a theological resonance, remains outside of the logic of time.[3] The pure gift is never "present" as such to the child, nor "presented" to her, but nevertheless the same gift promises a future "present/presence" to the subject in and through the language which conveys the mother's desire. It is a "depropriation," rather than an appropriation, a giving that is beyond closure, and has no end in sight (Cixous and Clément 1975, 87). The child has no desire to possess the gift, but reaches toward it in a movement away from sameness to difference. Kristeva's gift is not calculating, does not calculate. It is simply *woman's desire*. Kristeva's archaic father permits the subject to exceed her own limits, to enter into that space *between* the mother-child dyad and the speaking other; this space *between* is nothing else but the realm of language.

Ultimately, melancholia is defined by Kristeva as *a refusal of the gift* of the pre-Oedipal father. It is an attempt to reject the *mother's desire* for anything beyond the subject herself. A melancholic subject recoils from the third party and longs for, but cannot retrieve, the archaic mother. The symbiosis between the mother and child cannot be reinstated and so the subject is left abandoned and isolated: orphaned from both archaic mother and father. The external support for identification (from the archaic father, who also enables the ability of the language function) is refused, and so the ego is left in a meaningless state, outside of linguistic and imaginary practice (Kritzman 1991, 144). Not able to return to the unity with the archaic mother, yet denying the third party that brings the subject to language, the melancholic hovers over a void that threatens to engulf her.

Again, Kristeva returns to a *theological* term (though her passage to it has been through literature) to offer a kind of opening, a retreat, *but never a remedy,* for the melancholic subject. *Forgiveness,* Kristeva believes, can restore the melancholic subject to the gift of the archaic father, and bring her back again to the realm of language, the only place where "*la Chose*" can be retrieved.

Kristeva's analysis of melancholia situates itself on an irony. By revoking the gift (of the mother's desire) the melancholic refuses *the only means available* of recovering that archaic pre-object for which she hungers. Though "*la Chose*" is not recoverable, nor signifiable as such, Kristeva posits that it can nevertheless be *reclaimed* through the libidinal drives represented in the pulsions and flows of language, the phonetic and referential multiplicity that disturbs the linear, denotative quality of signification. Poetic creation allows for the renewal of the subject in the linguistic act, joins it again to "*la Chose*," but as it is represented in affective linguistic formations.

But what can it mean for the melancholic to forgive? Forgiveness, in the Kristevan definition, is an *opening up of the self to the gift*, an acceptance of the speaking other that the mother's desire draws forth. Do not be mistaken: forgiveness is not a counter-gift to the mother's desire. Rather, it is *the complete acceptance of this gift*, the embracing of the lining of love that the archaic father brings to language (Kristeva 1989, 216). This is a risky venture, to be sure, one that demands admitting the tenuous foundation of subjectivity—and *joying in it*. This is an imaginary process that is only possible *by giving* [*par donner*], for-giving.

What Kristeva unfolds is not so much a method, but an aim: to transform the defining symptom of the melancholic (asymbolia) and the painful, physical affects that the melancholic bears back to the realm of signification once again. Kristeva advocates the harnessing of melancholia itself in language as the only means to be free from it. For-giving transports the love and hostility that the melancholic feels for the archaic mother to a realm where it can be relativized and dissipated, recharged, and then dispersed. The melancholic's suffering is not eradicated, but becomes the foundation for the linguistic transaction. By naming the suffering, the melanchlic returns *meaning* to it once again, while at the same time tirelessly interrogating this same meaning: "Forgiveness, as a gesture of assertion and inscription of meaning, carries within itself, as a lining, erosion of meaning, melancholia, and abjection. By including them it displaces them; by absorbing them it transforms them" (Kristeva 1989, 206). The melancholic does not have to give up the suffering to which she has become attached, but can sublimate it.

Defining Kristevan forgiveness poses great difficulty. We cannot simply ask "*What* is given in forgiveness?" since that would be to return to Mauss, to the economy of exchange and the law of return. For forgiveness, as the gift itself, is not a *thing* given. The gift offers a fortuitous opening—and forgiveness? Forgiveness is not a giving away; it is not a giving in; it is not a giving up. Forgiveness is the impossible yet perpetual process, performed in and through language, of reaching toward and embracing this space opened up by the mother's desire. There is no duty or obligation to forgive; the self is not sacrificed to the gift. In fact, to sacrifice the self would be to refuse the gift. For, in the end, forgiveness is the gift that every subject gives to *her-self*—the gift of subjectivity itself: of being, in process, *par-donner*, by giving, for-giving.

NOTES

Thanks to Janet Martin Soskice, Morny Joy, and Dawne McCance for their helpful comments on an early draft of this essay.

1. See Nye (1987, 664–86) for an excellent analysis of Kristeva's rejection of the Platonic notion of subjectivity.

2. Kristeva's construct of the gift, however, does not function through the logic of "sacrifice," as does Derrida's *The Gift of Death* (1995), which makes the offering of Isaac the central and untainted gift of the western world. Neither is Kristeva's "gift" bound by the circular logic of return that characterizes Derrida's *Glas* (1990).

3. As Philippa Berry has noted, the feminine gender of agape leads Kristeva logically to refer to the "gift of God as elle" (Berry 1995, 233).

REFERENCES

Berry, Philippa, 1995. "Kristeva's Feminist Refiguring of the Gift." *Paragraph* 18 (3): 223–40.

Cixous, Hélène, and Catherine Clément. 1975. *The Newly Born Woman.* Trans. Betsy Wing. Minneapolis: University of Minnesota Press.

Derrida, Jacques. 1979. *Spurs/Éperons.* Trans. Barbara Harlow. Chicago: University of Chicago Press.

———. 1990. *Glas.* Trans. John P. Leavey Jr. and Richard Rand. Lincoln: University of Nebraska Press.

———. 1992. *Given Time: 1. Counterfeit Money.* Trans. Peggy Kamuf. Chicago: University of Chicago Press.

———. 1995. *The Gift of Death.* Trans. David Wills. Chicago: University of Chicago Press.

Freud, Sigmund. 1957. "Mourning and Melancholia." In *The Standard Edition of the Complete Psychological Works of Sigmund Freud.* Vol. 14. Ed. and trans. James Strachey. London: Hogarth Press. 243–58.

Heidegger, Martin. 1972. *On Time and Being.* Trans. Joan Stambaugh. New York: Harper & Row.

Hyde, Lewis. 1979. *The Gift: Imagination and the Erotic Life of Property.* New York: Vintage.

Irigaray, Luce. 1985. "Women on the Market." In *This Sex Which Is Not One.* Trans. Catherine Porter. Ithaca, NY: Cornell University Press.

———. 1991. *Marine Lover of Friedrich Nietzsche.* Trans. Gillian C. Gill. New York: Columbia University Press.

Kristeva, Julia. 1982. *Powers of Horror: An Essay on Abjection.* Trans. Leon Roudiez. New York: Columbia University Press.

———. 1987. *Tales of Love*. Trans. Leon Roudiez. New York: Columbia University Press.

———. 1989. *Black Sun: Depression and Melancholia*. Trans. Leon Roudiez. New York: Columbia University Press.

Kritzman, Lawrence D. 1991. "Melancholia Becomes the Subject: Kristeva's Invisible 'Thing' and the Making of Culture." *Paragraph* 14 (2): 144–50.

Lévi-Strauss, Claude. 1969. *The Elementary Structures of Kinship*. Boston: Beacon Press.

Mauss, Marcel. 1967. *The Gift: Forms and Functions of Exchange in Archaic Societies.* Trans. Ian Cunnison. New York: W. W. Norton.

Nye, Andrea. 1987. "Woman Clothed with the Sun: Julia Kristeva and the Escape from/to Language." *Signs: Journal of Women and Culture in Society* 12 (4): 664–86.

Plato. 1961. *Collected Dialogues*. Ed. Edith Hamilton and Huntington Cairns. Princeton, NJ: Princeton University Press.

Strathern, Marilyn. 1988. *The Gender of the Gift: Problems with Women and Problems with Society in Melanesia.* Berkeley: University of California Press.

FIVE

Gift of Being, Gift of Self

Mariana Ortega

It's not enough
deciding to open.

You must plunge your fingers
Into your navel, with your two hands
split open,
spill out the lizards and horned toads
the orchids and the sunflowers,
turn the maze inside out.
Shake it. . . .

—GLORIA ANZALDÚA, "LETTING GO"

From Mauss, to Lévi-Strauss, to Derrida, the gift is presented, presents itself; it is eluded or it eludes us. Not a nicely wrapped box to be opened so as to find a clear, obvious, beautiful content. Questions of meanings, intentions, obligations, come to mind. The gift, connected to sociality and obligation (Mauss 1990) or to purity and impossibility (Derrida 1992), does not only represent the possibility for what some consider a purer, more "authentic," perhaps more noble economy than the market exchange engendered by modern capitalism; it can also point to excess and power (Bataille 1988)—but it can also be a gift of disclosure, of understanding, a gift of being (Heidegger 1972).

How impressive and also puzzling it is to see how the concept of the gift has morphed, transformed into a dizzying intellectual notion—from an anthropological understanding of tribal cultures with kinships and social groups to a philosophical and theological understanding that supposedly language itself cannot capture so that, in the end, we find ourselves trying to write about what cannot be written, trying to understand the ineffable, attempting to capture what will not allow itself to be fenced in—and somehow I start missing the point of the importance of the gift and missing the gift itself.

In this reflection on the gift, I do not wish to analyze how Mauss's understanding of this notion has changed, how Derrida and Irigaray have interpreted it, how Bataille ultimately connects it with irrationality. Is there something more fundamental to the gift than that which can be analyzed by way of philosophical thinking? This is the question that interests me. While reading Heidegger's own musings on this complicated and slippery concept, I somehow got a glimpse of the importance of the gift, why we need to continue to think of it and to try to understand it, perhaps to experience it, despite its connection to a sometimes elitist, over-intellectual discourse. I wonder about the importance and even the morality of a discourse that only a handful of intellectuals can access and understand. And yet, what is extraordinary and ordinary about the gift is that it is for all of us. Paradoxically, reading Heidegger's words, which are indeed available only to a handful, gave me a glimpse into the elusive notion of the gift.

In his lecture "On Time and Being," in which he wrestles with trying to explain something that he believes is not so easily explainable with language, the notion of the gift as well as the experience of the gift, Heidegger states:

> If man were not the constant receiver of the gift given by the "It gives presence," if that which is extended in the gift did not reach man, then not only would Being remain concealed in the absence of this gift, not only closed off, but man would remain excluded from the scope of: It gives Being. Man would not be man. (Heidegger 1972, 12)

My first reaction to these words was to think that for Heidegger only men get to be reached by the gift and thus get to be who they are. It is already hard to move on, to consider what this Heideggerian idea of the gift has to do with me. Yet, I continued reading the Heideggerian text as I have done with so many other philosophical texts that are written by men, about men, and to men, texts in which the simple word "man" is to denote the whole of mankind. Perhaps there is still something worth learning in these texts— although I am certain that whatever it is has to be revised so as to be inclusive of women, of the feminine—and not just the white, Anglo, European feminine as even feminist texts are bound to emphasize.

What did I sense, then, as I read these strange words about the gift by a philosopher who is notorious for having failed at understanding the connection between thought and the moral life but whose work might still offer us something. I caught a glimpse of the fact that perhaps the gift, which in the Heideggerian context is no longer the gift but "It gives," matters because it is precisely what makes us who we are. We are the receivers of this giving which opens up a world to us. For Heidegger, this giving is part of an explanation of a philosophy which moves from an attempt to reach a fundamental ontology, as his early work on *Dasein,* to a philosophy that wishes to move beyond metaphysics and reconsider being as *Ereignis,* as an event or appropriation which holds an intertwining of time and being. For me, it is a reminder that I have been offered an opening through which I can experience a world, with all its glory and disappointment, with all its various possibilities of projection as well as being-toward-death (Heidegger 1962).

At the most basic level, it is the grasping, the experiencing of that opening, that matters. If we want to follow Heidegger, we would want to know more— the relationship between "It gives" and time, the relationship between time and being—but what I care about is that there is this giving that encompasses the gift, me, and time, that I am the constant receiver of this gift, that I have a life to live despite its certain end. Of course, here I do not simply mean that life is a gift in the sense that an object may be a gift and that I should thus be grateful to whoever or whatever has offered it. Not all lives can be seen or should be seen as gifts or all gifts be thought of as good gifts. The point is that the very opening of "It gives" is an opening toward possibilities, a dynamic process in which possibilities are taken, denied, ignored, created, where worlds are disclosed—it is precisely who we are.

The gift, then, is not like a material object which I may offer to another so that I may be given yet another gift. It is not an offering that increases my chances at being considered a better person or that facilitates my travel to the transcendent. It is not merely a sign of our social contract with others, or a sign of purity or excess. I do not desire to understand the gift in its purity or in its excess as we are bound to think of it if we follow Derrida or Bataille. I do not even ask who or what is represented by Heidegger's *"Es gibt"* ["It gives"]. I do not ask if God or the divine is behind "It gives" or the gift. Still I appreciate Heidegger's reminder of the relationship of between *Ereignis* and the words of the poet, the one that paints with words, words that according to Heidegger unconceal what is (Heidegger 1971, 74).

Here I am reminded not of Rilke, Heidegger's poetic hero, through whose words Heidegger explains the relevance of poetic thinking for an understanding of dwelling (Heidegger 1971), but of Gloria Anzaldúa's *"Tlilli, Tlapalli: The Path of the Red and Black Ink"* (Anzaldúa 1987, 65), in which Anzaldúa explains the production of a work of art, whether in words, paint, or gestures, thus moving beyond the spell of the written. Yet she sticks with words, and her words, her stories, are "acts encapsulated in time, 'enacted' every time they are spoken aloud or read silently" (67). Of the object created Anzaldúa writes:

> When invoked in rite, the object/event is "present"; that is, "enacted," it is both a physical thing and the power that infuses it. It is metaphysical in that it "spins" its energies between gods and humans" and its task is to move the gods. This type of work dedicates itself to managing the universe and its energies. (67)

How close these words sound to the unification of earth and sky, divinities and mortals, which happens in the Heideggerian understanding of poetic thinking and writing (Heidegger 1971)! Anzaldúa, however, honors what she calls the mythological soil of this continent as she sees tyranny and ethnocentrism in European mythology and aesthetics (Anzaldúa 1987, 68).

What is fascinating in the works that Anzaldúa offers, in her words, is that she sees them as performances whenever they are read out loud or silently, performances of her own being as connected to time, to the world and to those who read them. They are also offerings, or as she puts it, they are "blood sacrifices":

> This is the sacrifice that the act of creation requires, a blood sacrifice. For only through the body, through the pulling of flesh, can the human soul be transformed. And for images, words, stories to have this transformative power, they must arise from the human body—flesh and bone—and from the Earth's body—stone, sky, liquid, soil. (75)

It is so interesting to see both Heidegger and Anzaldúa grasping for meaning, one prioritizing thinking, the poetic thinking that reveals the oneness between earth and sky, god and humans, the other following her flesh and blood, for Anzaldúa writes not just with ink but with her whole body and flesh, the flesh that Heidegger ignores, following its nightmares, aches, traumas, fears, desires, and yearnings. Her blood sacrifices are offerings, the gift that she provides her readers; they are openings, openings that disclose her and us—openings that allow ourselves to be who we are.

These offerings, what we may call a gracious gift, however, do not need to be intellectualized for the sake of academic discourse or dissected for their possibility of purity. What is important in them is the disclosure of a life and of a world that, although it may puzzle and confuse us, can also allow for the possibility of our own disclosure, even in all our difference. In them,

Anzaldúa gives herself and opens up a world for us, a world where we can find her and our own selves. What is fundamental about the gift, then, is that we are it and of it—giver, act of giving, gift—all intertwined in that movement that we call existence and that, regardless of its metaphysical, ontological, or transcendental significance, we have but to live.

REFERENCES

Anzaldúa, Gloria. 1987. *Borderlands / La Frontera: The New Mestiza*. San Francisco: Aunt Lute Books.

Bataille, Georges. 1988. *The Accursed Share*. New York: Zone Books.

Derrida, Jacques. 1992. *Given Time: 1. Counterfeit Money*. Trans. Peggy Kamuf. Chicago: University of Chicago Press.

Heidegger, Martin. 1962. *Being and Time*. Trans. John Macquarrie and Edward Robinson. New York: Harper & Row.

———. 1971. *Poetry, Language, and Thought*. Trans. Albert Hofstadter. New York: Harper & Row.

———. 1972. *On Time and Being*. New York: Harper & Row.

Lévi-Strauss, Claude. 1969. *The Elementary Structures of Kinship*. Trans. James Harle Bell, John Richard von Sturmer, and Rodney Needham. Boston: Beacon Press.

Mauss, Marcel. 1990. *The Gift: The Form and Reason for Exchange in Archaic Societies*. Trans. W. D. Halls. London: Routledge.

SIX

The Gift of Being, Gift of World(s): Irigaray on Heidegger

Maria Cimitile

*We can receive anything from love, for that is a way of receiving it from our-
selves; but not from any one who assumes to bestow.*

—RALPH WALDO EMERSON

Recently in theoretical circles, the concept of the gift has been frequently
thematized and taken up, especially in conversation with Marcel Mauss's
canonical text, *The Gift,* written in 1925. In this book, Mauss argues that the
gift is a symbol of social and economic hierarchy, elaborating on the workings of power that underlie the gift and gift-giving. Alternatively, one can
look to Ralph Waldo Emerson's view that a true gift is unnecessary, excessive, and, if true, a gift only of the self. Emerson derides the idea that a gift
is an exchange, saying that if this is so, then it is not a gift. I want to take up
these two views of the gift to frame the thought of Luce Irigaray and Martin
Heidegger. For both thinkers, the Maussian view of the economy of the gift
is a metaphysical apparatus, and even tautological. Both would agree with
the criticism that Mauss's thought is western-centric, even if each applies the
criticism within differing frameworks and for differing aims. If like Emerson
one considers the gift to be an overflowing, one comes close to each of our
thinkers' visions—a framing for a way out of metaphysics. The very idea of
the gift is for both thinkers a condition and an event, a propaedeutic and a
futural saving. How the gift comes about is where the two diverge. Irigaray
reveals and corrects Heidegger's origin of the gift. She places his notion of the
gift squarely within masculinist discourse, revealing it to be masquerading as
a neutral, apolitical transcendental condition.[1]

As I have argued elsewhere, I believe Irigaray's work to be in conversation with Heidegger's above all else (Cimitile 2006). Irigaray herself says, "[H]

is thought enlightened me at a certain level more than any other and it has done so in a way that awakened my vigilance, political as well as philosophical, rather than constraining me to submit to any program" (Irigaray 2001, 315). This is equally and especially true of *Sharing the World* (2008), one of her latest pieces to be published, as well as of *The Way of Love,* her 2002 text wherein she enters into dialogue with Heidegger in order to structure her positive philosophy of relationality. In these recent works, Irigaray lays bare the necessities of genuine relationality, and the covering over of its possibility. In her earlier works, Irigaray pays careful attention to the detail of the history of western thought through her close textual analysis, using the philosophical tools of canonical thinkers to deconstruct their own projects, with Heidegger no exception. Her conversation in *Sharing the World* is again with Heidegger, who taught us what a *Destruktion* entails for thinking itself and is a lesson that Irigaray learned well. While Irigaray does not give us a formal *Destruktion* in *Sharing the World,* her new work is arguably predicated upon the deconstructive projects in her earlier writings, and in her interlocutions with Heidegger. Specifically, I would maintain that one will not thoroughly understand *Sharing the World* without having made one's way through Irigaray's earlier *The Forgetting of Air in Martin Heidegger* (Irigaray [1983] 1999). In this book, Irigaray, with a rigorously detailed textual analysis, turns Heidegger on himself.[2] In *Sharing the World,* Irigaray also accomplishes this same task, but she focuses instead on how we might achieve the emergence of a communal world of difference.[3] Examining Heidegger's thought, she locates underlying structures that limit his understanding of "worldhood" to one perspective, effectively eradicating difference in general, and woman's identity in particular. In contrast, Irigaray strives to show how the other must be cherished in order for both self and other to flourish. Such a cherishing still requires the gift of self, but a self very different from that of Heidegger's *Dasein.*[4]

Heidegger's project, from *Being and Time* onward, is to uncover the structures of Being, an ontological investigation that begins with an attempt to situate Being outside of traditional ideas of subjectivity (hence his use of the term "Dasein," "there-is," rather than "human being") and then continues by exploring the event of Being in language (Heidegger 1962). Throughout his writings, Heidegger critically examines the consequences of a metaphysics that privileges presence as the locus of Being and forgets the movement of Being. His criticism, demonstrated through the interpretation of the history of western philosophy, takes a number of forms throughout his work—the existential, the technological, and that of language itself. If one follows Heidegger's writings, one realizes that his work is essential to help us think beyond hegemonic structures of discourse and power—which, as Irigaray teaches us, have rendered woman invisible, a non-identity, or, to invoke Lacan, non-existent.

Irigaray takes up Heidegger's project to reveal a further outcome of the being of presence and dichotomous thinking. This is the non-relational, which she believes lies at the core of western thought. Heidegger does not struggle with the effects that these metaphysical structures and worldview have had on woman/women. In fact, as is widely recognized by his critics, he does not address human relationality adequately, if at all. Rather he sees and struggles against the technological attempt at mastery, the deadening of thought and curiosity, and the counter-attempt of language, art, and poetry to resist this mastery. In contrast, *Sharing the World* is solely concerned with relationality. Irigaray points out Heidegger's mishandling of the matter as well as initiating a discussion that can surely be seen as enhancing Heidegger's attempt to reveal the happening or event of being.

When Heidegger turned from his incompleted project of *Being and Time,* namely, the meaning of Being in general through an analysis of Dasein and its temporality, to study time and being in general, he wrestled with Be-ing, allowing himself to be enveloped in it, trying to grasp and convey it. The use of the hyphen in Be-ing (a translation of the German *Seyn*) signifies Heidegger's further attempt to break out of the purely subjective. He then turns toward the event of Be-ing as a happening, event, appropriation—terms that are translations of the German term *Ereignis.* All of his struggles with the linguistic phrasing to speak about *Ereignis* as Be-ing reveal a path, an open field, an awareness, a non-teleological thinking, if and when possible. The event of Be-ing and Da-sein is a struggle, and we are reminded of Heidegger's call upon the middle voice, an active passivity.[5] It is this sense that Irigaray brings into play to convey how two worlds rather than one could be possible, and what that might look like. The gift or event of Be-ing in Heidegger's thought becomes in Irigaray's hands the gift of true humanity, where Irigaray's thought has been leading us all along. Irigaray's teasing out of Heidegger's thought provides a rich and nuanced dialogue between the two.[6]

I will draw our attention to the role of the gift by examining the play that Irigaray enacts in *Sharing the World* with Heidegger's *Being and Time* and his further development of language and the event of Be-ing, and show where Irigaray's critique opens the way for her own positive notion of the relationality of two to emerge. By focusing on Irigaray's engagement with Heidegger, rather than an overview of *Sharing the World,* I want to help us understand how Irigaray's assertion of two worlds is a wholly new contribution to philosophy, a point I think we can only understand in contrast to the thinker that underscores the very idea of the world in twentieth-century thought.

Heidegger believes humanity receives the gift of Be-ing; Irigaray shows that this gift is only man's, not woman's. For Irigaray, the full realization of humanity will only occur when it receives the gift of two fully realized subjectivities, of two worlds—male and female.

HEIDEGGER'S WORLD

Irigaray undertakes an interpretation of Heidegger's phenomenological structure of the horizon of temporality from *Being and Time* to show how it necessitates a world of oneness and precludes the possibility of a full realization of humanity. Her claim is that by situating worldhood out of and in Dasein, Heidegger has cut off the very essence of relationality where it should be foremost *the* ontological grounding. The question Heidegger poses for himself and his readers in *Being and Time* is the question of the meaning of Being. To fully find the answer to the meaning of Being, Heidegger will claim that time is the horizon upon which we grasp Being, that is, the context or meaning of Being is time. The path to this insight begins in Division I, where Heidegger gives an analysis of the Being of Dasein (the Being for whom Being is a question). Because Being is a question for Dasein, and Dasein alone, Heidegger believes we must explore the very structure of the Being of Dasein so that we may discover Being itself. Central to Irigaray's reading of Heidegger is his discussion of worldhood in Division I. Heidegger shows that our temporality necessitates our projects. And here we must hear both the verbal and nominal senses of the term "project"— projecting into the future (out of the past) as well as the connotation of one's own interests and work. Our projects arise out of our temporal horizon and constitute our world. In Division II, Heidegger explores the Being of Dasein in terms of its temporality and encounters the authenticity of Dasein. These two divisions were to be preambles to the discussion of Being in general. Through Dasein's own Being, Heidegger believes we can grasp Being itself. For Irigaray, this is Heidegger's fatal flaw. Understanding Being through Dasein necessarily limits us to a subjective account. Heidegger himself drew the same conclusion, though it is clear from the text of *Being and Time* that even in this earlier working out of Being he does not stipulate that Being is under the mastery of Dasein. Rather, the phenomenological method of *Being and Time* demands that only through Dasein can we gain an understanding of Being. Heidegger came to believe that the phenomenological method he posed was not sufficiently radical. Where Heidegger and Irigaray differ, however, with regard to the problems of Heidegger's project is Irigaray's insight that this perspective of Dasein derives from the singular perspective of the masculine world and is thus cut off from the relationality of the first world of the other, namely, that of the relation of mother and child. For Irigaray, Heidegger's world is then not grounded in the real. And Heidegger's failure to grasp this insight at any point in his work dooms his attempt at finding relationality in any context.

According to Irigaray, we must recognize that the first world for human beings is that of the other/mother. This would entail a different temporality than that of ecstatic temporality, which is the temporality of Dasein—a thrownness out of the past into the future that constitutes the world. Rather, the world of the other/mother that Irigaray asserts requires a temporality of difference:

> [T]he presence of the one to the other becomes the place where two temporalities are linked together. The future of each one is modified, and thus the relations between past and future, from which the temporal bridge is built. Death can no longer be what univocally determines my temporality. A cultivation of life, in which each one participates, leads us to another temporality in which the future will never be a simple achievement of my past. (2008, 79)

Irigaray wants to open a space for the other that is founded ontologically and thus she corrects Heidegger's claims rather than outright rejecting the idea that time (and space) are determinative for our Being and meaning. A temporality of difference arises out of the first world of relationality for the emergence of two different worlds, but two that are intertwined. It is only this immediate transcendental that provides for true difference with regard to any relationship. As Irigaray says, "the other cannot belong to my past" (2008, 80), for if so, the other would be appropriated by the one in his thrownness and lose identity. By asserting a temporal dimension that engages an-other temporal dimension, Irigaray suggests not merely a merging of two ecstatic temporalities, but rather that temporality itself is constituted by relationality, difference. Thus her claim above, that it is life, rather than Heidegger's hallmark, death, that governs our very Being. Life, the first and absolutely necessary material and imaginable condition of Dasein, is nothing other than the relationality of two beings in gestation and birth. It is impossible for the temporality of this condition, of this first world, to be singular (in contrast to death). Two identities share a single project but remain two. On the other hand, ecstatic temporality makes the other a being among other beings—a thing. There is no structure in it to recognize the other as independent from one's own projects, in his or her humanity. This is the danger of the hermeneutic situation in Heidegger's thought.

From Heidegger's perspective, there is a necessity to worldhood and its temporal formation by overcoming the subject/object dichotomy. Taking his cue from Kant's transcendental turn, Heidegger wants to show that we both step into and create meaning as the very core of our temporal being. The world is contextual, it forms us, and we in turn form it—always already. Our temporality necessitates our projects and our world; they are one and the same. Relationality for Heidegger finds its origin here, though he thinks of it in terms of how Dasein relates to the world and Being as a contextual milieu. It is a basic hermeneutic insight that accounts for culture and the relation of self and world, yet one that later caused worry for Heidegger and his interlocutors. It is futile to deny this claim of situatedness, yet a consequence of it is a closure that prevents us from experiencing Be-ing, as Heidegger tries to rectify in his later writings. It also does not leave room for a full account of being-with-others, a point that many have noticed—and which Irigaray deftly shows in her philosophy of relationality. Being-with (*Mit-sein*), the term Heidegger uses in *Being and Time* to signify the existence of other Dasein, is, according to Irigaray, a relation of sameness. Others coexist with me, equal to one another. As much as this may appeal to our western notion of egalitarianism, it is actually the locus of the inability to recognize the other, difference:

> Such an opinion . . . forgets that the other, like myself, has belonged to a maternal world proper to each of us. To assert that we are with one another in the same way and that the world is common to us amounts to cancelling this first existence that we have lived and that makes up part of our manner of perceiving the world and of situating ourselves in it. (Irigaray 2008, 107)

Heidegger's world in its hermeneutic character covers over the world of the mother, who Irigaray explains is always particular, never a universal category. The mother is an irreducible individual who structures our otherness. Asserting a commonality of the world denies this singularity and negates this first unique world. The irony is, of course, intended by Irigaray. Heidegger's thoroughgoing argument throughout his corpus centers on the "covering over" or concealing of Being, and his attempt to reveal this concealedness or forgetting, as well as the heart of Being. In his desire to reveal the concealedness of Being, a perverse parallel occurs. In Irigaray's reading, Heidegger covers over the material transcendental condition for Being—the first beginning, the gift of the mother.

The psychoanalytic drama of the forgetting and/or rejection of the mother stems from man's desire to acquire an identity apart from the mother, but results in the erasure of the mother and woman—as woman is elided with the natural world. In his desire to differentiate himself from the mother, man creates a world absent of his relation to her: "Because of his lack of recognition of the mother as a transcendence in whom he first has his origins, man projects the origin of his self onto the totality of the world, unless he extrapolates it from God" (Irigaray 2008, xiii). Invoking Heidegger's analysis of techne, Irigaray says, "Woman has become nature-earth-matter at the disposal of an activity of man" (2008, 82). Demonstrating how man uses woman as a piece of equipment for his desire, she shows that this renders woman subjectless, a thing. The appropriation of the female other in projecting one's world—one's project, desire—results in the projection of a world that is partial and biased, based on one subjectivity, and which therefore does not represent the full human experience:

> The error of Western philosophy in part lies there: having intended to carry on with human individuation starting from a single transcendence corresponding to the necessities of a masculine subject. In such a unique design toward the whole of existing beings, woman cannot discover her transcendental possibilities. And, because of a failure to recognize double human subjectivity, a part of his own possibilities remains veiled to man himself. (Irigaray 2008, xvi)

Heidegger's thought exemplifies and perpetuates this error. Irigaray directly engages Heidegger on this issue, accusing him of "forgetting," and "appropriating," the mother:

> It is the mother who first brings us into the world. . . . But the philosopher has not yet considered this. He pays no attention and even forgets this original determination of our way of being in the world. . . . And his apprehension of the world requires an a priori reversal: the relation with the other will be included in the relation with the world, and not the contrary. . . . The priority given to an idea of the world—even a concrete world—with respect to the relation with the other, the first other, exiles subjectivity from its being in a real world. It enters an anonymous, impersonal, indefinite world: a world of "one(s)," or "there is." (Irigaray 2008, 123–24)[7]

In making evident Heidegger's appropriation and forgetting of the mother, Irigaray shows that as the mother is subsumed into the world (rather than the reverse), the other so follows. Heidegger "forgets" the mother by subsuming her into his world, just as our epoch has forgotten Being. Irigaray's use of "appropriate" and "appropriation" signals Heidegger's use of *Ereignis* in his later work—a discussion I will take up shortly. She wants the reader to recognize that though *Ereignis* signifies the ultimate discovery for Heidegger, it means invisibility for woman. There is no structural recognition of absolute singularity or difference because its origin is covered over. "There-is," being-there (Dasein) becomes an anonymous One—projecting the world of the masculine as "World." The rejection of the mother results in the homogeneity of subjectivity.

THE SECOND BEGINNING: TWO WORLDS

Irigaray offers an antidote to Heidegger's abstractions by laying out how we might achieve the recognition of two worlds, two subjectivities of sexual difference that stem from the maternal world of the other. What is ontologically constitutive of each of us must be attended to in the relation with the other. Briefly, we have seen from Irigaray's perspective what occurs when the masculine world is projected as a neutral universal world, that is, when relationality is covered over. By attending to the other, one recognizes that the project of our own world must be limited so as to leave room for the other. And as Irigaray shows, this is only possible through a temporality grounded in the mother-child relation. The other is our transcendental ground of experience, that is, the mother: "The first world of the subject is an other. Whether it is still in her body or born but dependent upon her, the little human lives in a world of its mother" (Irigaray 2008, 105). From this first world of relationality, all otherness is possible. Welcoming the other entails making ourselves available from within, possible because, and only because, of our own otherness founded in the first world of the mother (Irigaray 2008, 18–19). Having experienced ourselves as other in birth and early life, we are never a self-enclosed being. In Heideggerian locution, we are always already other—which is to say, our temporal constitution is dual, other, consisting in difference. As such, the transcendental condition of difference is situated within. And as Irigaray says, "Only a return to a something still more original, to the woman in the mother, to an identity different from ours . . . allows us to prepare the space and the time in which it will be possible for us to enter into the presence of the other, with the other" (2008, 114). Here we notice Irigaray's direct confrontation with Heidegger, who seeks to disrupt the metaphysics of presence. He cannot do so, despite his desire, because he does not desire two, that is, he cannot grasp relationality.

In turning to how we move into recognition of the other from this recognition of our maternal origin, Irigaray draws on the metaphor of a threshold, which is both a limit and an opening: "Recognizing one's own limits, as well as the existence of the other as irreducible to one's own existence, and searching for the means of entering into relations with him, or her, will then substitute for appropriation" (2008, 2). The metaphor instructs us to be conscious of the difference between two by granting that there are two worlds that must be maintained, each limited but not closed. This conundrum of limitation produces a fluid energy:

> The opening to the other, the encounter with him, or her, and the return to oneself continually produce moving boundaries, which provide a border for energy and allow it to blossom according to a living order. There are, thus, no longer limits imposed from an outside, formally abstracted from the present, but a being-in-relation that requires, at every moment, a restrained flowering for each one. (Irigaray 2008, 57)

Being-in-relation maintains and creates a movement and becoming of two, overcoming a closed metaphysical abstraction detached from the material real. Heidegger's project is also an attempt at the overcoming of a metaphysics of closure in asserting Dasein's ecstatic temporality to be a self beyond itself. But reading Irigaray, it can be seen that Heidegger's ecstasis is an unconscious desire for transcendence marked by closure and sameness. Only by cherishing two can a permeable limit occur, dissolving metaphysical closure. Yet how is this permeable limit, a "restrained flowering," achieved?

Playing on the phrase *Ereignis,* the event of Be-ing, Irigaray teaches that the *event* of encountering the other as other requires that we know who we are, what our own journey is. If we neglect this, we lose ourselves in the other: "Only [limits] allow us to have access to the other by respecting ourselves. If we are not faithful to ourselves, approaching the other proves to be impossible. What we could then experience would only be appropriation" (2008, 8). Faithfulness to oneself prevents being consumed by the other, into his needs, desires, projects. Irigaray demands this of both man and woman, yet clearly she is concerned with traditional philosophical thought that has rendered woman invisible, what in her earlier work she referred to as the economy of the same. Standing within and remaining true to oneself, but a self marked by otherness, is her aim: "And each one in each one, each in oneself, but also other. How to deal with this other, her and even him, whom I have seemingly become? Which was only possible because I was different, because I could meet with, marry, carry in myself the other. On the condition that I remain myself" (2008, 35). By remaining attendant to the otherness within and without, we offer a space for both the one and the two to emerge.

The partnering of limitation and openness is not easy or simple. It circumvents traditional logic, which is precisely what is needed. It requires a meditative awareness and vulnerability in leaving the already configured world, such that Heidegger's worldhood gives. The space Irigaray speaks of is not known, not formed, not determined. It must arise out of a desire that does not consume so that life can flourish for each: "To cultivate attraction requires it not being harnessed or paralysed by already defined habits, norms . . . gestures and discourses. . . . The awakening of energy has to remain vigilant and attentive to its source, without letting it be reduced to the anonymity of a 'there is'" (Irigaray 2008, 73–74). Again, Heidegger's sense of being-there, Dasein, is in Irigaray's eyes a lifeless abstraction. To forestall this, desire must be allowed to reach out to, but not to obliterate, the other. The other must be recognized, not as a consumable object, but as a subject.

Finding authentically dual subjectivity requires that we approach the other with silence, characterized as both passive and active, as a means of acknowledgment of the other: "Relations between two different subjectivities cannot be set up starting from a shared common meaning, but rather from a silence, which each one agrees to respect in order to let the other be" (Irigaray 2008, 5). With a silent making-way and listening, the other will not be incorporated into a language that absorbs all into one world, one meaning. Irigaray is of course playing with Heideggerian concepts and language in her invocation of silence. Silence, too, is speaking, is language. And the role of language for Heidegger's middle and late writings cannot be overstated. As he famously states in his "Letter on Humanism":

> Language is the house of Being. In its home man dwells. Those who think and those who create with words are the guardians of this home. Their guardianship accomplishes the manifestation of Being insofar as they bring the manifestation to language and maintain it in language through their speech. . . . Thinking . . . lets itself be claimed by Being so that it can say the truth of Being. Thinking accomplishes this letting. (1993, 217–18)

Language is the locus of the emergence of Being, the site of its unconcealedness or truth. In his later work Heidegger strives to show that Being, now Being, is gift. It is not a metaphysical encompassing of all beings in Being—but rather the emergence or movement of Be-ing (*Ereignis*) that makes the Being of beings possible. It is the reason and showing of why there is anything at all. That is, language is *Ereignis,* the event or appropriation of Be-ing: "Language is the clearing-concealing advent of Being itself" (Heidegger 1993, 230). The "letting" that thinking accomplishes is not "consent" to the emergence of being in the sense of controlling it. Rather "letting" is twofold: humans let Being emerge by standing open to receive it. It is an active passivity that receives the gift of *Ereignis:* "[Appropriation (*Ereignis*)] can only be experienced as the abiding gift yielded by Saying" (Heidegger 1971, 127). The appropriation by Be-ing happens to humans because our Being is ek-static (standing-out). It is marked by an openness to Be-ing that occurs in thinking/language. In this we stand outside ourselves by allowing Be-ing to envelope—not simply envelope *us,* though it certainly does, but rather, appropriate us, so that Be-ing can emerge into the open region.

In this manner, Heidegger attempts to correct *Being and Time,* and offer *Ereignis* as a way out of the pitfalls of subjectivity. Dasein is only because of the gift of Be-ing. He explains, "The appropriating event is not the outcome (result) of something else, but the giving yield whose giving reach alone is what gives us such things as a 'there is,' a 'there is' of which even Being itself stands in need to come into its own presence" (1971, 127). Dasein "ek-sists" (stands-out) in Be-ing. We partake in Be-ing such that we can stand outside ourselves to experience Being as we dwell or tarry in language, if it offers this gift. This relationality to Be-ing is a relationality to the self, but an open self, and more significantly to Heidegger, a relationality that allows us to experience the emergence of Be-ing, beyond our ability and our desires to capture and master it. We experience this gift if and only if we are attentive and allow the rupture to envelope or appropriate us. As Heidegger states: "Language has been called 'the house of Being.' It is the keeper of being present, in that its coming to light remains entrusted to the appropriating show of Saying. Language is the house of Being because language, as Saying, is the mode of Appropriation" (1971, 135).

While the Saying of language is essential to the emergence of Be-ing, *Ereignis* or the gift of Being, it stands apart from subjectivity per se. In the *Beiträge* (1989), Heidegger explains the "way" of the question of the meaning of being, noting that it is a path of more and more originary saying—not a trajectory of correction or development.[8] This is significant to understanding Irigaray's position with regard to Heidegger on relationality. After Heidegger dismisses the idea that changes are historical, that is, come from outside the question, he says "the way itself becomes more and more essential, not as 'personal development,' but as the exertion of man—understood totally non-biographically—to bring be-ing itself within a being to its truth" (Heidegger 1999, 59). Heidegger's entire philosophical project is an attempt to find the relationality of Be-ing, and it is not in any way a taking account or "attunement" to subjectivities or particularities. Rather the attunement is to the gift of Be-ing, and only this makes the relation to or between particularities recognizable. Irigaray, on the other hand, continues to contend against Heidegger that the Saying of this attunement is removed from the real, and therefore has no hope of relationality. Rather Irigaray's focus is on the silence of Saying for silence is a Saying that envelops *us*. Irigaray's own use of silence is one of respect for the alterity that is at the origin of each subjectivity. Paralleling Heidegger, she draws on the approach of silence as giving space or a letting be that goes beyond the singular subject to a gift of space for two. This letting-be allows for the emergence of two worlds, not simply the abstraction of appropriating Be-ing. Ironically, the emergence of two worlds embodies those characteristics that Heidegger claims—a path, an open field, an awareness—but for Irigaray it is grounded in the real of alterity. Letting-be for Irigaray is the gift of allowing us to open ourselves to the other as the other is, in his or her being: "My existence—or ek-sisting—is also received from the other through a gesture where doing and letting do, being and letting be, activity and passivity intertwine" (Irigaray 2008, 77).

Irigaray's use of Heidegger's phrases "ek-sisting" and "letting-be" signals at once her borrowing of the action of the middle-voice (active passivity) that is so important for *Ereignis* in Heidegger's work. Her usage, however, involves a criticism of his inability to recognize the speaking of difference. Letting-be in Irigaray's hands both corrects the phenomenological trap in which Dasein resides and the gift of *Ereignis* of Heidegger's later work. As a result, in Irigaray's view, despite his attempt to move beyond the problems associated with Dasein's subjectivity and reveal the emergence of Be-ing in language as an event beyond human being, Heidegger remains enmeshed in a "covering up" that undermines his efforts. Irigaray postulates that while *Ereignis* is a gift of Be-ing, it is actually derived from the irreducibility of the mother. For Irigaray, language, the house of Being, is built upon the "forgetting" or concealing of the mother:

> [D]iscourse has been constituted with the aim of organizing the world into a significant whole at the disposal of the subject . . . [It] becomes the world in which the subject dwells, a world that both ties the subject to and separates the subject from the existing real. This doubling of the existing real in which the subject dwells substitutes itself for the mother who was the first home. . . . This fabricated house, which is supposedly safeguarding Being, as much prevents Being. (2008, 121–22)

So it is that in attempting to rid his thought of the confines of subjectivity and put in its place a relation to Be-ing itself, Heidegger flees from the very source of relationality that would allow for Being to emerge within humanity. Though Heidegger's own project is much different, Irigaray's point is that he has an unacknowledged source and, more significantly, his project is not grounded in the real.

Irigaray offers instead a language that is initiated by silence and that gives a time/space for the flourishing of self(s). The gift in Irigaray's text, then, is an unfolding of a self that is both open and grounded in the temporality of other:

> I must not forget the already-there that constitutes me, but neither must I forget the ecstasy of being-with-the-other, faithful to the moment of our coming, the one and the other, into presence. I have to take care of these two dimensions that are essential to the constitution of my temporality: remembering myself and remembering the other, caring about the two while letting them be in their difference(s). Which requires me not to hold the other through an appropriation that makes me unfaithful to each of us. (2008, 81–82)

Heidegger's understanding of *Ereignis* as appropriation causes unfaithfulness because it forgets difference in the abstraction of Be-ing. It covers over otherness, or being-with, in sameness. Heidegger does try to grasp the richness of Being as not limited to subjectivity. His framing of the gift of Be-ing is developed to show what is aside from metaphysics. This is because he fears subjectivity cannot escape metaphysics, and so he tries to turn away from it, reframe it. In contrast, Irigaray fears that a world without true subjectivity is one that is not fully human. She takes the opposite approach in searching for the richness of relatedness. This is because she fears that in Heidegger's version of the emergence of Be-ing, and with it worldhood, we remain in a projected world of masculine experience only. This world, in its being-toward-death, is lifeless and murderous, killing the feminine. For both subjectivities, it is only the gift of death. Irigaray sets forth to describe the emergence of two beings and worlds as resulting from relationality. The result, as distinct from Heidegger's world, is the gift of life.

If we are to understand Irigaray fully, then, the welcoming of the difference of another being requires an overflowing of the self. I use this phrase, "an overflowing of the self," to try to capture Irigaray's sense of centering oneself while simultaneously reaching out. It prevents a trampling of either self or other—be it a consumption of the One into the other, or Other. At the same time, it provides for the gift of life—both figuratively and literally. It is life as relation, as an emergence and assertion of two worlds. The event of the emergence of two worlds is, for Irigaray, a gift of self: "Was not the paradoxical result of our meeting to bring us back to ourselves? To gather together each in oneself thanks to an opening to the other as other, which requires holding onto oneself, and also thanks to the gesture of the other assenting to the one who I am. . . . Through such a gift, which each offers to the other as a result of recognizing him, or her, as other, we are both two and one" (2008, 50).

In concluding, we might now recall Emerson: "We can receive anything from love, for that is a way of receiving it from ourselves; but not from any one who assumes to bestow" (1899, 133). While the context of Emerson's thought is to distinguish true from false gifts, it perhaps provides an ideal testimony of Irigaray's philosophy of relationality. The gift of self—that of limitation and openness—flows outward to the other in desire and exists both as love of self and other. But it can only be received from one who respects the other in herself, and not from one who attempts to appropriate the other into his horizon.

NOTES

1. One could easily interpret Irigaray's early essay "Women on the Market" as a thorough criticism of the gift as establishing social and economic hierarchies (as Mauss's work claims) by elaborating the gendered dimension of that economy. Certainly, Alan Schrift's inclusion of the essay in his edited volume, *The Logic of the Gift,* relies on this, as alluded to in his introduction to the volume.

2. See Cimitile (2001, 66–74) for an account of how in her early essay, The Forgetting of Air, Irigaray adopts and critiques language in Heidegger's thought.

3. It is clear in *Sharing the World* that Irigaray has heard her critics. In this latest text she attempts to think difference beyond sex, mentioning at times the effects of globalization and accounting for difference between any two—not only between male and female. However, the difference of experience between the sexes remains essential to her ontological claims. It is sometimes difficult to read her remarks regarding otherness in forms beyond sex/gender as anything but nods to her critics as they do not seem fully incorporated at a theoretical level. In fact, many times Irigaray explicitly states the necessity of recognizing sexual difference for humanity to flourish. The scope of this essay does not allow for a detailed discussion of these points, however.

4. Irigaray consistently uses the lower case *o* in "other" to signify the material other, not the Other as an abstraction. She critically discusses the Other as transcendence of divinity, a non-relationality. The few times I use the capitalized "Other," it is with the intent of this transcendence.

5. This is most evident in his 1989 work *Beiträge zue Philosophie (Vom Ereignis),* where he attempts to wrestle with the event of Be-ing.

6. I give a fuller account of this relationship in my manuscript, as yet a work in progress, tentatively titled *Irigaray and Heidegger: The Movement of Being,* wherein I attempt to lay out Irigaray's many conversations with Heidegger framed by the overall work of her corpus, as well as a critique thereof. For an excellent focused article on the relationship between the two thinkers, see Ziarek (2000).

7. Interestingly, in this chapter of *Sharing the World* Irigaray begins to refer to Heidegger as "the philosopher," which is the term Aquinas used to refer to Aristotle. Perhaps this has no significance other than that Irigaray is making clear the tradition in which Heidegger remains mired regardless of figures. Aristotle is of course one of

Heidegger's main interlocutors, with some scholars claiming that *Being and Time* is a commentary on the *Nicomachean Ethics*.

8. This is significant to understanding Irigaray's position with regard to Heidegger on relationality. After Heidegger dismisses the idea that changes are historical, that is, that they come from outside the question, he says, "[T]he way itself becomes more and more essential, not as 'personal development,' but as the exertion of man—understood totally nonbiographically—to bring be-ing itself within a being to its truth" (Heidegger 1999, 59).

REFERENCES

Cimitile, Maria. 2001. "The Horror of Language: Irigaray and Heidegger." *Philosophy Today* 45 (5) (Spring): 66–74.

———. 2006. "Irigaray in Dialogue with Heidegger." In *Returning to Irigaray: Feminist Philosophy, Politics, and the Question of Unity*, ed. Maria Cimitile and Elaine Miller. Albany: State University of New York Press. 267–88.

Emerson, Ralph Waldo. 1844. *Essays: Second Series*. Reprint. Cambridge, MA: Houghton Mifflin, the Riverside Press.

Heidegger, Martin. 1962. *Being and Time*. Trans. J. Macquarrie and E. Robinson. New York: Harper & Row.

———. 1971. "The Way to Language." In *On the Way to Language*. Trans. Peter D. Hertz. New York: Harper & Row. 111–36.

———. 1989. *Beiträge zur Philosophie (Vom Ereignis)*. Ed. Friedrich-Wilhelm von Herrmann. Frankfurt am Main: Vittorio Klostermann.

———. 1993. "Letter on Humanism." In *Basic Writings*, ed. David Farrell Krell. Rev. ed. San Francisco: HarperSanFrancisco. 217–65.

———. 1999. *Contributions to Philosophy (From Enowning)*. Trans. Parvis Emad and Kenneth Maly. Bloomington: Indiana University Press. Originally published in 1989 as *Beiträge zur Philosophie (Vom Ereignis)*.

Irigaray, Luce. 1985. "Women on the Market." In *This Sex Which Is Not One*. Trans. Catherine Porter. Ithaca, NY: Cornell University Press.

———. 1999. *The Forgetting of Air in Martin Heidegger*. Trans. Mary Beth Mader. Austin: University of Texas Press. Originally published in 1983 as *l'oubli de l'air chez Martin Heidegger*. Paris: Editions de Minuit.

———. 2001. "From *The Forgetting of Air* to *To Be Two*." In *Feminist Interpretations of Martin Heidegger*, ed. Nancy Holland and Patricia Huntington. University Park: Penn State University Press. 309–15.

———. 2002. *The Way of Love*. Trans. Heidi Bostic and Stephen Pulháček. New York: Continuum.

———. 2008. *Sharing the World*. New York: Continuum.

Schrift, Alan, ed. 1997. *The Logic of the Gift: Toward an Ethic of Generosity*. New York: Routledge.

Ziarek, Krzysztof. 2000. "Proximities: Irigaray and Heidegger on Difference." *Continental Philosophy Review* 33: 133–58.

SEVEN

Graceful Gifts: Hélène Cixous and the Radical Gifts of Other Love

Sal Renshaw

I shall have a great deal to say about the whole deceptive problematic of the gift.
—HÉLÈNE CIXOUS, "THE LAUGH OF THE MEDUSA"

Giving requires no courage, but to receive love so much strength, so much patience, and so much generosity must be extended.
—HÉLÈNE CIXOUS, *THE BOOK OF PROMETHEA*

If Anglo-American criticism were anything to go by, one could be for-given for thinking that the summum bonum of Hélène Cixous's thinking on the gift was reached somewhere around the mid-1970s with the publication of her polemical essay "Sorties." Here she adopted what has arguably come to be identified as a Derridean formulation of the gift—though it owes con-siderably more to Marcel Mauss—in asserting that axiomatic principle that "really there is no 'free' gift"; that "you never give something for nothing" ("Sorties" 87). But following this assertion in "Sorties," and in true Cixousian fashion, she had no sooner made this claim than she took off in a different direction toward what appeared then to be another question altogether. This change in direction concerned the contribution that sexual difference might make to reflections on spending, and thus to the problematics of economies of the gift. So while it is true for both Hélène Cixous and Jacques Derrida that there may indeed be no "free" gifts, for Cixous there are nonetheless notable differences in ways of thinking about economies of giving. For Cixous, these differences can be meaningfully traced along the lines of sexual difference.

There are, she suggested, "feminine" and "masculine" economies of the gift, and all "the difference lies in the why and how of the gift, in the value that the gesture of giving affirms, causes to circulate" (Cixous [1975] 1986, 87).[1]

Feminine economies are distinguished by a refusal of closure, by a denial of the impulse to return the gift, to enter the circle of exchange.

> Elsewhere, she gives. She doesn't "know" what she's giving, she doesn't measure it; she gives, though, neither a counterfeit impression nor something she hasn't got. She gives more, with no assurance that she'll get back even some unexpected profit from what she puts out. She gives that there may be life, thought, transformation. This is an "economy" that can no longer be put in economic terms. (Cixous [1975] 1980, 264)

Masculine economies, on the other hand, rush to closure, rush to suture the wound that gifts inflict via their insistence on a kind of opening to the other.

> [N]othing is more dangerous than obligation. Obligation is submission to the enormous weight of the other's generosity, is being threatened by a blessing . . . and a blessing is always an evil when it comes from someone else. For the moment you receive something you are effectively "open" to the other, and if you are a man you have only one wish, and that is hastily to return the gift, to break the circuit of an exchange that could have no end. (Cixous [1976] 1981, 48)

So it is no simple matter for Cixous whether or not there are gifts to be given, gifts and giftings that are pure and absolute. She is with Derrida on that particular question. She too would affirm the notion that the moment the gift is recognized as such, it ceases to be a gift. Thus the gift per se is impossible. But as is also true of Derrida, even if consistently misunderstood, Cixous does not take this to be the end of the story, the denouement. Rather for her, as for him, perhaps it is better understood as the commencement, the beginning that begins by way of accepting the invitation of the impossible and takes off from there. Consider Derrida's clarification of his understanding of the gift, offered in a conversation/exchange with Jean-Luc Marion at the Villanova conference Religion and Postmodernism in 1997 and previously elucidated in his books *Given Time* ([1991] 1992) and *The Gift of Death* ([1992] 1995). It is nothing if not an affirmation of the beginnings of a conversation rather than the end, an opening and not a closure.

> The gift, I would claim, I would argue, as such cannot be known; as soon as you know it, you destroy it. So the gift as such is impossible. I insist on the "as such." I will explain why in a moment. The gift as such cannot be known, but it can be thought of. We can think what we cannot know. Perhaps

thinking is not the right word. But there is something in excess of knowledge. We have a relation to the gift beyond the circle, the economic circle, and beyond the theoretical and phenomenological determination. It is this thinking, this excess, which interests me. . . . I never said that there is no gift. No. I said the exact opposite. What are the conditions for us to say there is a gift, if we cannot determine it theoretically, phenomenologically? It is through the experience of the impossibility; that its possibility is possible as impossible. (Derrida 1999, 60)

In light of this affirmation of both the impossibility yet the necessity of the gift we must also recognize Cixous's very similar concern with the relationship between gifting and knowledge. This is because both thinkers seem to identify a certain kind of knowledge as the condition for the annulment of the very possibility of the gift from the outset.

How does one give? It starts in a very simple way: in order for a gift to be, *I* must not be the one to give. A gift has to be like grace, it has to fall from the sky. If there are traces of the origin of the *I* give, there is no gift—there is an I-give. Which also signifies: say "thank you," even if the other does not ask you to say it. As soon as we say thank you, we give back part or the whole of the gift. (Cixous in Conley 1984a, 159)

While this passage illuminates the issue of the subject who gives, as does the passage from Derrida, the problem it raises largely concerns the subject who "knows." Hence the "ideal" gift is a gift that arrives as pure gift, and in order to do that it must be like "grace falling from the sky." Such arrivals circumvent and potentially destabilize the inherent economies of exchange that typically attend on the giving/receiving binary. To know one gives, to understand oneself as the source of the gift, is inevitably to find oneself locked into the binary economics of receiving and exchanging. Paradoxically, as has already been noted, because the gift to another is in some respects an opening to that other, the gift of the knowing giver simultaneously affirms the subjectivity of the giver over the subjectivity of the other. In this way it enacts a kind of sublimated, Hegelian, dance of domination. The cycle of exchange is advanced even in the most gracious and humbling expression of acceptance—"thank you"—for the thank you comes to function itself as a gift. It therefore has the secondary consequence of rebalancing the dangerously destabilized relation between self and other that was inaugurated in the gesture of giving in the first place. Thus, as both Marcel Mauss and Jacques Derrida have identified, the gift, which is also *pharmakon,* potentially poison, is always, at least potentially, an expression of a kind of dangerous knowledge. The knowledge that I am in receipt of a gift from the other is an intrusion on my integrity as discrete, contained, autonomous. To know that I am the source and initiator of a gift to the other is in some sense to force myself upon them, and in so doing reveal to them the illusion of their autonomy. On this account, gifting, especially to the extent that both giving and receiving, and self and other, are constituted precisely in discrete categorical opposition to each other, begins to look violent as well as poisonous.

In light of this seeming impasse that the binary logic, by implicitly dominating the conversation about the gift, appears to place us in, it is worth returning to Cixous's question, "How then does one give?" This is because I think the question hints at one of Cixous's long-standing interests—rethinking the seeming inevitability of binary logic via the phenomenal. Her concern with the gift thus fits into a set of recurring Cixousian tropes, motifs, and explorations, all of which, I believe, circulate in one way or another around an underlying concern. This is her preoccupation with the conditions through which we can imagine, articulate, and incarnate an ethical relationship between subjectivities—a relation that can bear and even love, rather than appropriate or annihilate, difference. Her work on gifting and the conditions under which gifting can express a love for the other as other is unquestionably a continuation of this theme: How should we receive the gifts of radical otherness? Can we understand otherness as gift? And what of love as gift? What of an/other love? At the heart of this theme, at least in my reading of Cixous, has been a desire to source love and gifting in generosity, excess, and abundance, thus providing a reflection on the conditions of subjectivity that might make such loving/gifting possible. In this regard I have found her work to offer implicitly a significant critique of the more familiar tropes of sacrifice, selflessness, and suffering that have typically accompanied the discourses of love in the western tradition. It is, then, something of a surprise to turn to some of her more recent work on animals, work which explicitly continues her explorations of "other love" and the gift, and to find within it the consistent presence of the motif of sacrifice.

The remainder of this chapter will consider some of the ways in which Cixous has long reflected on giving, but it will do so specifically via an engagement with her recent work on animals. In particular I will be taking up the stories she tells of her first dog, Fips, and subsequently her cat, Thea, for they are clearly providing her with a new occasion to push her thinking on otherness beyond the boundaries of human subjectivities. These particular animal others also provide the opportunity to engage with what I think of as Cixous's unique contribution to the contemporary conversation on the gift. This is because each of them, having either explicitly arrived as a gift (Fips), or only later being understood to have been a gift all along (Thea), is presented to the reader as a challenge in receiving well. Cixous's reflections on receiving, then, make for an obvious complement to her concerns for the "why and the how" of giving. Together they offer quite a different emphasis on the more broadly construed conversation about the gift that has had such a presence in recent continental philosophy. I think her attention to the phenomenal experience of giving and receiving at least gestures in the direction of a way that is elsewhere to the binary knot of selves who give and others who receive. Graceful gifts, that is, gifts which are in some sense ungiven, by being graceful have an uncanny ability to arrive, if only for a moment, in the stories Cixous tells of love. Yet, as we will see, and despite what is an obvious concern with alterities which survive their encounters with difference, neither Fips nor Thea, both of whom are at one level the gifts in these stories, arrive unscathed. There is a disturbing presence of sacrifice and suffering in both stories. Consequently, it is worth reflecting on why, in particular when she turns to animals, we see something that looks like an affirmation of a form of love that Cixous has long opposed. Moreover, these animal others are also inseparable from certain kinds of divinity—the story of Fips is shot through with references to figures in both the Hebrew and Christian testaments. In addition, Thea (literally the Greek feminization of *theos*/god) is described by Cixous at various points as her "minuscule Messiah" and her "prophet quotidian." Clearly there is an intentional, wonderful, and suggestive categorical slippage in these stories as Cixous troubles and reveals the not-so-discrete borders around human, the animal, and the divine. One very meaningful effect of this troubling is a closer association between the animal and the divine. Yet it is hard to avoid also noting the simultaneous and seemingly contradictory presence of a kind of suffering that is borne mostly on the bodies of the animals in these stories. This is a kind of suffering that reminds us that the history of human relations with the sacred has consistently rested on the very real sacrifices of animals, and perhaps still does.

THE FIRST OTHER

Cixous says that animals have been "with her" since the beginning, that they have always been there in her writing.[2] Her childhood in 1940s Algeria clearly offered her a complex world of experiences of "animality" at both the literal and symbolic levels. All too often, as she narrates in more recent semiautobiographical work on that childhood in Algeria, she found herself on the "animal" side of the human/non-human opposition that operates so relentlessly in colonial regimes. An Algerian Jew of German heritage whose mother tongue was German but whose lived world was a linguistic mélange of French, Spanish, and Arabic, Cixous was raised in a culture that was tenaciously marked by binaries, most especially that of insiders and outsiders, those who belonged and those who didn't. Yet, as is the way with boundaries, they were at one and the same time maintained and transgressed. While her father lived—he was a doctor who, because of his political and ethical commitments, had chosen to work in the Arab quarter with the poorest of their "neighbors"—the family felt considerably less the racial boundaries marking them as Jewish, French, and other to the Arab world which surrounded them. After the death of her father, however, that boundary was so relentlessly policed that she describes the family's daily life in terms of assault, attack, hunting, even war.[3] This turn toward violence takes as one of its victims Cixous's "first animal," the family dog, Fips. I want to sketch in some detail the story Cixous has written about this "first animal" of her life and dreams. It is a story narrated in an essay entitled "Stigmata, or Job the Dog," and the religious allusions go well beyond the title. In this story, Cixous attributes to Fips a necessary sacrifice, followed by a resurrection, which not only inaugurated the writing of her own "book," the book of her life as writing, but was also the precondition for her subsequent capacity to accept as gift the arrival of her cat, Thea, her "minuscule messiah and prophet quotidian." "As for me, I am ready to give my life for my cat but it was necessary that Fips should first have given his life for me" (Cixous 1998, 186). Framing the essay, and setting the terms of the reflection in a religious context from the outset, is the first sentence: "It all begins with *Felix Culpa*. A happy fault, a blessed wound" (181). The reader is tantalized. Whose wound? Whose blessing is being signaled here? For whom will this be a happy fault? Regardless of the answer to this question, what is evident here is the overtly sacrificial Christian framework of this story,[4] as suffering is clearly constituted as the path to divinity.

Fips was literally a postwar gift of the father to the children, who themselves would have preferred a human sibling. From the outset, at least for the children, Hélène and her brother, Pierre, the dog's animality is precisely what they deny—but of course they are children: this is not to apportion blame. Fips won't comply with their desires to tuck him into the box/cradle they have made for this, their substitute sibling, who is also their own symbolic child. As Cixous says:

> Fips did not let himself be laid in the bed of all our cares. We fought for
> several hours or several days. We caught the little one, we laid him out,

we flattened him, we ironed him, we held him in place while we covered
him with the sheet, and immediately in a start he overcame the box. Our
advances were not understood and we did not understand that they were not
understood. (1998, 187)

The children want the dog of their imagination, they desire the human-dog.
The dog they are confronted with is all dog soul verily bursting at the seams,
and they fail to recognize the difference. Without realizing that they are the
instigators of their own suffering, they feel the sting of a rejection they themselves made inevitable for they do love Fips—indeed, they loved him before
he even arrived, so much was he a dog of their dreaming, a dog of their
imagination. But beyond this failure on the part of the children to recognize
the gift of the other as other and to love him in his difference, an even greater
seismic shift affecting Fips the "family dog," Fips the "babydog," takes place
when the father dies. With him dies the one who gave the dog, the one who
saw and loved the dog soul, the one who did love the dog as other. No idolatry here. "It was my father who was his father without images and without
ideas" (189). And so, with the father newly dead, the traumatized family and
children were then under the care of the German Jewish mother and grand-
mother for whom Fips was not merely not a babydog, Fips was barely a dog,
so far had he fallen from grace. With the death of the father, the human/
animal boundary was resolutely affirmed in the advice given the children:
"feelings for an animal are 'not recommended'" (189). Fips was resoundingly
and heartbreakingly rejected and excluded, no longer truly part of the family, no longer the "family dog." He was fed "dogfood" but was not loved. Fips
withered. No one noticed.

And then, beyond the border dispute policing the human/dog, human/
animal boundary which had seen Cixous and her family on the human side
of that opposition, an/other border war broke out. With the death of the
father there was no longer any protection for the family from the antipathies
of their Arab neighbors who then saw only Jew and French. It is remarkable
how malleable the human/animal boundary war turns out to be as it gets
played out again but on new turf. For who is it we hunt but the animal and
who has become the animal now but the family?

It was then that from outside the garden the hunt was unleashed against us.
Our Arab neighbors encircled us in a daily siege. So the hunt was unleashed.
The acrid war that had been held back until then in the face of my father the
doctor swoops down on the family. We live besieged as diminutive soldiers
inwardly undermined by a just and bitter sympathy for our Arab assailants.

We defend ourselves like inhabitants who are forbidden by everything to attack the enemy. They called my father "my brother." Dead with him was this privilege, this love. Now we were Jews. Now we were French. Now we were Jewfrench, the worst in their eyes. Now we were insulted and I often bit the dust mad with rage. At least we did battle. My brother and I. But the dog was hostage. And we did not let him fight. It would have been a carnage. It was a tragedy. (189)

When in the name of protecting Fips, he is chained and thus imprisoned in the garden, he then loses the last vestiges of his autonomy, his "animal" free-dom. Cixous has already noted that this freedom was consistently directed at a wonderful kind of exceeding of his dogness. No longer able to leap over the limits of his own dog self, the hail of rocks that daily besiege him quickly ini-tiate a descent into a kind of madness borne of abject solitude and powerless-ness. But the denouement of the story as Cixous tells it is yet to come. Now seemingly also betrayed and abandoned by those he was trying to protect, the impotent Fips's final categorical shift into animality came when he sank his teeth into Hélène's foot. This occurred when she accidentally stood on him as she rushed to answer the door. He misunderstood this as an unpro-voked and unintelligible attack from one who, despite everything, he loved.

I did not see my dog see me jump wild-eyed with feet together on the bruised ground. I did not see my dog see me come on to his tumefied body with the brutal stroke of the alien executioner. No doubt I drove him mad. It seemed to him that it was hate. It seemed to him that now I too. And that there was no crime nor any betrayal that his own family was foreign to. In his extreme abandonment, And you too. Et tu quoque. It seemed to him I was not his sister and I was his assassin. (191)

It was a relentless and deep bite and Fips was only removed from Hélène's foot by force of the beating he received from the washerwoman. Suffering then from an equal sense of incomprehension and betrayal, Hélène and Fips are indeed finally sister and brother in the symmetry of their experience of the other as threatening and violent.

Interestingly, for the adult Hélène who looks back on this story of love and betrayal, of gifts that never quite arrive and of families torn asunder by the violence of racism, Fips's animality, his dogness, takes on another resonance. To the extent that his dogness is a signifier of absolute otherness, it takes her to God, that ultimate signifier of unknowable gifting. She recognizes that beyond the bite was the wound which never quite healed—the stigmata that ultimately reminded her of the suffering of the one who would die for her, the one who would give his life for her. It also evoked her failure to rise to the commandment to love her neighbor. In that moment of agony, she did not take Fips in her arms. She did not console the other in his grief. Her goodwill "didn't turn towards him"; she refused to give, indeed, she refused to even see. And Fips's suffering beyond this penultimate incident takes on truly biblical proportions when, added to his conditions of imprisonment in a family that no longer treats him as a member of the family, he is physically assailed by ticks the size of chickpeas which eat him alive right up until his death.

> Job was that dog I am sure. The scourges were sent to him, god was well hidden, the father dead, the house ruined and now the plagues and the ulcers. And without being conscious of it I did not love the leper like myself. (192)

As is true of all of Cixous's writing, complexly woven references to archetypal tropes within both the Hebrew and Christian testaments are at work here. In this case, particularly, I would argue they apply to the second commandment to love one's neighbor. Fips is at once Job, the uncomprehending victim of God's seeming abandonment, and a saint, the suffering sacred Christian martyr who for the sake of unending love of God will endure the worst humanity has to offer and for-give. Hélène, on the other hand, is a shining example of the transgression of the Jewish codes of hospitality, and she is certainly no Samaritan. What can Fips understand, having defaulted to the position of thinking he is "just" a dog? Cixous defends herself against the call to give to the other, the call to compassion, to empathy, which itself in some sense demands that the other be recognized as deserving such.

> I stopped thinking, I stopped feeling. After all I could not take on to my back this chained-up cross that waited for me in the garden, his feverish eyes that searched for my fleeing eyes as soon as I set foot on the earth of the garden. (190)

In the end, I think the tragedy of this story of denied messiahs and sacrificed victims overwhelms the sacrality of the gift that Cixous claims Fips was later to become. To whatever extent the story does pose an invitation to consider the relationship between the sacred, gifts, and otherness, it does so, I think, as a story of failure. Some forty years later, in reflecting on the way Fips keeps reappearing in her dreams, Cixous says she was finally able to truly love him, "but not then, not there in the garden of war, not yet, but later" (193). This is an ending which has significant appeal, especially to the extent that it resurrects love. After reading of the relentlessness of Fips's suffering, we are grateful to feel even the possibility of love directed toward him. But it is hard not to also take note of how this love actually applies to the particularity of Fips. This is a love not of the dog, not of the animal other, but of the animal re-membered, the animal/dog of a human memory. Ironically, Fips began as a human/dog, a dog of dreams, a dog longed for and desired in the imagination of the children, and he remains to the end a dog of dreams, an ephemeral specter of a dog.

How should we understand the nature of the love Cixous expresses here when it can in no way be relational, when one half of the relation is long dead? I believe Cixous answers this question herself at the beginning of the essay—although it is a disturbing answer—when she says it was "necessary" for Fips to "give" his life for her, because it took that for her to be ready to "give" up her life for Thea—the cat to come (186). Constituted in this way, with the repeated emphasis on the subjectivity of "Cixous" herself, is a shocking and somewhat clichéd story of sacrificial love which runs counter to the earlier recognition within the story. This was that it was Cixous who failed to rise to the commandment to love the other as other. In other words, she failed to rise to what she imagined some thirty years previously in "Sorties" to be a feminine economy of love and gifting. To imply that it was necessary for Fips to die in order for her to learn much later the nature of a more just love of the other, is to find oneself within a masculine economy of love where "profiting" is the measure of value. To the extent that the value of Fips's suffering in life and his subsequent death are constituted as somehow redemptive because they serve human interests, this is a very old story of human-animal relations. This is a story which positions animals in the service of human divinity yet excludes them from it in their own right.

Between the two stories I am engaging with here, this one of Fips and the one I am about to tell of Thea, there are two stories of the gift of love, or two different economies ordering the self-other relation. One, as I have noted, is marked by a "masculine" need to foreclose on the other as other, to love only that which returns as profit to the self. In reality, this is to love what is actually oneself in the other. This is the kind of love the children have for Fips. This is the love of the babydog. It is also, some forty years later, I would suggest, the love of the remembering woman. I'll leave the last word on this kind of love to Cixous herself for she makes startlingly clear here the impossibility of a genuine love of the other as other.

The dog was there and it wasn't right. I wanted him to love me like this and not like that. (I would have liked him to obey me like a dog. But if they had told me I wanted a slave I would have responded indignantly that I only wanted the pure ideal dog I had heard of.) He loved me as an animal and far from my ideal. (188)

The "other" economy of love, the "feminine" one which is oriented toward keeping the other alive, is the story of the gift, albeit also a flawed and imperfect gift, that is told in the tale of Thea, to which I now turn.

THEA'S FIRST GIFT
The First Arrival

The cat did not begin its life with the woman as a gift. It began as an obligation, a demand for hospitality. As the story is narrated in a section drawn from Hélène Cixous's book *Messie* (1996), translated into English and published in 2006 under the title "The Cat's Arrival," there are really two arrivals. There is an initial encounter structured around the demands of hospitality and a second moment which is more like something that happens *to* both the woman and the cat, something more like an event. Between the first and second we also have two stories of hospitality, one in which the stranger, who is always also in some sense the other, is accommodated but never really "taken in." Then there is another in which the opposite occurs. In this second arrival of the cat/stranger/goddess—for we cannot forget that this as-yet-unnamed stranger will become, or will she have always been, Thea?—we find a demonstrably less sacrificial story of the gift. Indeed, this is a story that is much closer to the notion of the gift as grace than was told in the tale of Fips.

As a piece of literature, "The Cat's Arrival" defies easy classification. On the one hand, it is memoir and it really does in some fashion tell the story of Hélène Cixous's first cat. On the other hand, this is fiction and the characters, such as they are, are archetypes. In that sense, with characters like the woman, the man, the beloved, the dead Father, the mother, the cat, and so on, "The Cat's Arrival" invites us to consider the story as universal. The narrative, such as it can be called a narrative, is in large measure about the way in which the woman's unexpected and initially unwelcome relationship with the cat disrupts the apparently proper order of things. It does this by disrupting her relationships with everyone else in her life—her mother, her lover, her children, even the cook. Indeed, in the end, the very rhythms of everyday life are profoundly destabilized by what becomes this woman's passionate love with this animal other. But the story I want to tell here is the story of the events that inaugurated that transition to love. Thus, what interests me here is precisely the movement from the refusal to embrace that forms the initial part of the story. This is because what can be seen to be at work here is the structure of the two libidinal economies of gifting that Cixous speculated about so long ago in "Sorties" ([1975] 1986), "Medusa" ([1975] 1980), and "Castration" ([1976] 1981). There, they appeared as ideas and deep wishes; here we see them played out as aspects of an actual if somewhat unlikely negotiation between self and other.

The Beginning

The cat only just arrives. The odds were very significantly stacked against it and it accomplished this unlikely task only by slipping around the will of the woman, who couldn't have been more consciously aware of and managing the threat that the animal other represented. This is a threat identified at the outset as a matter of heart, yet despite the defenses, the cat manages to slip past the *guardiens du coeur*. If it had been a matter of obligation to the animal itself, it would never have happened. "The Cat's Arrival" begins:

> In the meantime the cat arrived. A cat happened to them. The arrival happened at the woman's house. Who would have thought such a thing possible? Thousands of times before someone she had known had asked her to look after a cat.
> —A cat? Certainly not!
> Nor a dog, nor any creature dreadful to her heart.
> Since the age of five she had been aware that she would never allow creatures terrible for the tenderness of the heart beneath her roof. (21)

But despite the force and the antiquity of this refusal, this religio-ethical failure of hospitality to the animal other, a failure which had solidified into a habit, something happens to the woman. It happens when "a person" finds a cat, but cannot immediately care for it because they are called overseas. The woman is asked to look after the cat and she finds she cannot refuse. But it is clear that in not refusing, her concern is not with the cat per se, it is with the person who found the cat. We are still in the world of human relations here. The person is the beneficiary of the woman's sense of obligation, not the cat. For the moment the human-animal boundary established at the outset is maintained.

> No cat could have arrived by her free will. Even if she had found a thin and wretched one in front of her door she would not have kept it for a single day. She hadn't found it. The person who had found a tiny, hardly-formed creature had been called overseas suddenly and had therefore asked this very reserved woman if she could possibly look after the animal for a couple of

days. The woman hadn't dared to refuse but had still insisted: two days only and not a single day more. (21)

Of course two days becomes ten, ten becomes twenty-one, and the woman fulfills her threat to the person who found the cat. On the twenty-first day, when they have still not returned from overseas, she takes the cat to her cousin's and she leaves her there. This moment marks the formal end of the first arrival of the cat. But during the transition from two to twenty-one days, the woman has not been entirely unaffected by the presence of this animal other. The cat has continually threatened to transgress the habits of the heart the woman has so clearly established and wants to maintain. So determined is she to keep the animal "out," she even externalizes those boundaries and that anxiety into the world. The cat cannot transgress the physical space of her bedroom. It must remain outside the door, though the reader is certainly left with the sense of soft paws tenaciously marking time on the threshold.

> In the meantime the woman defended herself, refusing to cede any ground to the animal. The beast would not set foot in the bedroom. The woman is within, the cat is without. (21)

The passage is structured around categories and borders: the woman, a bounded human subject, is inside; the "animal," having in a single sentence categorically ceded ground in becoming now a "beast," is outside. The lines are drawn; there will be no negotiation. But this beast/animal/cat is threatening to transgress borders, to enter the bedroom anyway and thus to enter the symbolic space of love, the space where the woman has drawn the line. While the categorical terms of this territorial conflict are clear—woman/inside, cat/outside—fragility pervades the atmosphere. Surely it is fear that fuels this refusal of the other, this refusal to risk intimacy. Is the risk that in being on the inside, the cat might also be inside? In letting the cat across this threshold of all thresholds, will the woman inadvertently have gone beyond duty and hospitality, will she have inadvertently surrendered herself to this other? Who will she be then? The passage ends thus, with a command: "Do not love me the woman ordered because I will never love you" (21).

The Second Arrival

The narrative structure of the arrivals is exceedingly economical. Time is brutally condensed and the reader is moved between the first and second arrival in the space of only few sentences.

Without hesitation, on the twenty-first day the woman took the animal to her cousin's and left it there. The cousin had a garden. It was a Saturday. What do you think happened? On Sunday morning the little one was back again. (21)

Immediately, the reader can see that the one who returns is already, for the woman, not the one who left. A transformation has begun. The "animal" was dropped off, but it was "the little one" who was resurrected on this Sunday morning.[5] In a scene which somewhat reconfigures the elements of the Fips story, but nonetheless remains hauntingly similar, the cat that returned had suffered considerably for the time she had spent in this garden which was no Eden, a garden to which she had been condemned by the person charged with protecting her. Having been a victim of a passing dog that had left her with an ear "slashed to ribbons" and an eye "the size of an egg," the cat chose this moment to transgress that seemingly inviolable boundary the woman had been so vigilantly defending. A moment of inattention a mere few hours later was all that it took for the gift that was Thea all along to finally arrive. "That Sunday evening the woman forgot to close a door. It is by way of that that Thea made her entry into the heart of this story" (21). That Sunday evening the woman found herself the unexpected recipient of a kiss/gift which she took to be an incomprehensible expression of gratitude by the cat. The passage is longer but is worth citing in full.

With one ear out of two and an eye the size of an egg the cat came to thank the hostess for having saved her from the hell into which she herself had thrown her.
You're thanking me!!?
Naturally.
With a firm tread the cat climbs onto the woman's lap, looks the woman in the eye with a clear and decided gaze and abruptly a kiss on the alarmed mouth. This done, she climbs back down to earth. The kissed woman was surprised and asked herself who could have taught the animal this way of thinking. That evening the woman did not dare to treat the cat like a half-wit. It was thus that the certainly-not came to be. She sided with the cat against the human class. Goodness resided with the little one who had never suspected the violent thoughts harboured by the woman beneath her show of hospitality.
The cat spent the night on the corner of the bed nearest the door. The woman could not hurt the one who placed her life in her hands without suspicion. (22)

Because this story of the beginning of an other love ends in the surrendering of the threshold of the bedroom we know that the transition from animal, to cat, to Thea has been accomplished and that all along this has been a story about the possibility of loving the absolute other. Beyond the kiss and what I think of as the woman's still mistaken understanding that the cat can be made sense of in human terms, the boundaries between cat and human, although shaken, nonetheless remain—hence her thinking that the cat's behavior flows from a way of "thinking" that she has been taught. However, we also learn that the woman has "lost all taste for power" (22). Even though she went on for some time feeling like she had surrendered to the demand to "take in" a cat, that she had become the "owner" of a cat, this too was a misunderstanding. This time it was not a misunderstanding of Thea, but of herself and of the relation between them. In fact the woman was already in love and it was that love to which she had surrendered—something altogether different from taking and owning. As the narrator says: "She was already in love but she would only know this later on" (22). Once again, the structure maps the story of coming to love that Cixous told about Fips. Again, she comes late to the knowledge that she loves, though in this instance I think there is an important difference. This time she did also come late to the experience of love, but this time perhaps it was not too late. At stake in this observation is a clue to important differences between both Thea's and Fips's felicity with love as against the woman's fear. The temporal asymmetry between the woman "being" in love, and the woman "knowing" later that she is in love, reveals two different ways of living the self and the relation. One way, which I will shortly suggest is more open to the other as other, is the one that nearly perfectly characterizes Thea all along. The alternative way is more inclined to foreclose on difference. It denies difference and uses it as an armor through which the self can constitute itself as discrete and autonomous.

GLIMPSING BEYOND SACRIFICE

I want to suggest that all along in the story of the two arrivals, Thea's subjectivity is ordered by a feminine relation to difference. This is why for her there is only ever one arrival. As the quote with which I began this reading of Thea suggests, Thea is endlessly oriented toward living and the present. She is not counting the costs. She is not calculating her relation to the woman using herself as the measure. Nowhere is this more acutely illustrated than in the woman's incredulity that Thea, after her seeming abandonment by the woman and her subsequent fall into the violence of the garden, ends up thanking/gifting the woman for her hospitality, for saving her. How is this possible, you can hear the woman asking herself. It is possible because Thea has never subjected herself to a relation of slavery to the woman. She has never taken herself as the object of ownership. Indeed, she has never taken herself as object at all. It is the woman who has done this, the woman who took Thea to be animal/cat/thing. As subject of her own living in the present, Thea meets, and more importantly receives, the woman as an other to be loved beyond the categories the woman struggles with. We know this already from the woman's insistence that Thea does not love her, during the account of the first arrival, something that only makes sense if we understand that, at some level, the woman already recognizes Thea as loving. So from this we can conclude that as with every other situation, Thea seized her living in the garden, not unlike Eve, with the innocence of one who doesn't know there is a choice, indeed one for whom there really is no choice. Living in the present is without limits, and Thea's life is a life immersed in the present (23). At no point either do we get the sense that Thea ever saw the woman as the cause of what becomes her suffering at the hands of others. Thea welcomes the arrival of the woman on the other side of that suffering, and it is truly a welcome. There is no trace of accusation. Thea's primary orientation toward living and life, which is expressed as an immersion in the present, seems to permit her an extraordinary capacity to receive without calculation and subsequently to give in the same way. In the absence of an "I," or, to put this another way, of a subjectivity that grasps onto itself in calculating the risks of opening to the other, the risks of giving, Thea's giving is indistinguishable from Thea herself. In this sense, there is no "I" to give, no "I" to sacrifice itself for the other, and, by extension then, no "I" to whom a debt could be owed. Thus Thea simply is graceful giving.

Cixous is right, that it's all in the how and the why of giving that we find the possibility of gifts which arrive like grace, falling from the sky. Thea's gifts arrive like grace for the woman who is finally able to receive them, because, strictly speaking, Thea isn't giving any "thing." But so deeply immersed in her own, "masculine" subjectivity is the woman that she is guarded only against an other she can recognize. This in fact is how Thea slips by in the first place. Unlike Fips, Thea is neither finally reducible to animal/object/thing nor containable within those categories. It is no co-incidence, I think, that it is a kiss which signals the woman's lesson in her failures in hospitality, in gifts which ultimately do arrive, and in other love. The lips, as a mysteriously permeable boundary between inside and outside, are an appropriate site for the most affecting meeting between self and other, a meeting which itself challenges those very categories. For a moment, perhaps only in that moment, the woman receives the way Thea gives. Indeed there is no obvious "giver" or "receiver." All is giving, all is receiving, and the discrete boundary between self and other ceases to be a site of contest as the event calls for a different way of thinking of the subjectivities of the woman and the cat. In that moment which exceeds the opposition between self and other, Thea, as gift but not as giver, arrives and is received.

One of the most important differences in the stories of Fips and Thea, at least as I have read them here, concerns the place of sacrifice in the stories they tell of love, the gift, divinity, and subjectivity. While sacrifice remains an element in the story of Thea—and for me this is a disturbing element, for how else can we read the way the woman abandons her to the garden of dogs only to subsequently benefit from the suffering she endures—Thea nonetheless survives with her own capacity to love alterity intact. Recall that she has no resentment toward the woman who could quite reasonably be seen to be responsible for that suffering. Moreover, this very integrity, this capacity to love the other as other, is, finally, the occasion of the gift the woman receives through and with Thea. In that transgressive moment of the kiss, the moment through which all the categories of human, animal, and divinities get exceeded, the gift arrives. In this way the story of Thea is a very different story of love and gifting from the story of Fips; it is a story which I do think better, though still imperfectly, exemplifies Cixous's feminine economy of gifting. At the same time, it also reverberates with complex allusions to an alternative view of divinity and love; a view not based on the motif of the Messiah who arrives yet is sacrificed, but rather the Messiah who arrives and loves. If indeed Thea is Cixous's minuscule messiah, as well as her "prophet quotidian," then she is both a Jewish and a Christian divinity. She thus functions to condense the Messiah traditions of both Judaism and Christianity. In addition, I think she goes some way toward reconfiguring the relations between love, suffering, and sacrifice that are apparent, if differently so, in both traditions. Thea, being on the side of the gods, is immersed in life in the present. It is this relation to time and subjectivity that creates the conditions for the woman, if only momentarily to love divinely despite her "self." In this sense, and as the woman herself acknowledges, her lesson in a love without obligation, a love which unmistakably conforms to Cixous's feminine economy of desire, came from her cat. Thea's love is truly an other love.

> From morning until night the cat was busy living. Living! Living! Living! Living! To seek, sniff, stroke, to brush against the edge of the abyss, so near, to size up the celestial depths, eyes full of cloud-birds, crying with all its soul: Living! Living! Living! Living! On high! On high! On high, flying, divinity cloistered within feline finitude, behind its soul. A little ball of fur with a goddess inside. (Cixous 1996, 28)

The source of the first chapter epigraph, a remarkably prophetic comment made by Hélène Cixous, more or less in passing, is "The Laugh of the Medusa," [1975] 1980, 259. The source of the second chapter epigraph is *The Book of Promethea*, [1983] 1991, 105.

1. For well over thirty years Hélène Cixous has attempted to clarify her use of all the signifiers of sexual difference. Regardless of accusations to the contrary, and there have been many, particularly in North American feminist scholarship, her position is precisely the reverse of an essentialist one. She denies the essential/biological connection between masculine and male and feminine and female. Yet she also acknowledges that there is a social convention linking the two and that this convention produces real effects with which we can engage and which we can name. Hence, for example, she does make and has made claims about the way that a feminine libidinal economy is more easily found in women, but her explanation for why this is so is not an essentialist one. "We must take into account the fact that we are caught in daily reality in the stories of men and women, in the stories of a role. That is why I come back to the question of the terms masculine and feminine. Why those words? Why do they stay with us? Why do we not reject them? Because in spite of everything and for historical reasons, the economy said to be feminine which would be characterized by features, by traits, which are more adventurous, more on the side of spending, riskier, on the side of the body, is more livable in women than in men. Why? Because it is an economy which is socially dangerous in our times" (Cixous in Conley 1984b, 54).

2. Much of the inspiration for this section of the paper comes from Marta Segarra's wonderful and astute observations of Cixous's "first animal," Fips, in her article "Hélène Cixous's Other Animal: The Half-Sunken Dog" (2006).

3. Hélène Cixous's father died of tuberculosis when she was nine years old.

4. While sacrifice is associated with both Judaism and Christianity, I find the stronger associations with suffering lend themselves toward a more Christian interpretation here. Notwithstanding this association, it is important to also note that recent scholarship has witnessed a significant resistance to the sacrificial interpretation of Jesus in particular and Christianity in general. René Girard's work on sacrifice and the Gospels, for example, has been highly influential in building a case for rereading the Gospels as anything but an unambiguous affirmation of sacrifice as the measure/path to the divine within the Christian traditions.

5. The phrase "the little one" (as an English translation of the original French) is also used in reference to Fips when, soon after he is given to the children, he refuses to lie still in the box cradle they have made for him (187).

REFERENCES

Blyth, Ian, and Susan Sellers. 2004. *Hélène Cixous: Live Theory*. London: Continuum.

Cixous, Hélène. [1975] 1980. "The Laugh of the Medusa." Trans. K. and P. Cohen. In *New French Feminisms*, ed. Elaine Marks and Isabelle Courtivron. Brighton, UK: Harvester Press. 245–64.

———. [1975] 1986. "Sorties." In *The Newly Born Woman*, by Hélène Cixous and Catherine Clément. Trans. Betsy Wing. Minneapolis: University of Minnesota Press.

———. [1976] 1981. "Castration or Decapitation?" Trans. A. Kuhn. *Signs* 7 (1): 41–55.

———. [1983] 1991. *The Book of Promethea.* Trans. Betsy Wing. Lincoln: University of Nebraska Press.

———. 1998. "Stigmata, or Job the Dog." In *Stigmata: Escaping Texts.* New York: Routledge. 181–94.

———. 2006. "The Cat's Arrival." *Parallax* 12 (1): 21–42.

Cixous, Hélène, and Mirielle Calle-Gruber. 1997 [1994]. *Hélène Cixous Rootprints: Memory and Life Writing.* Trans. Eric Prenowitz. London: Routledge.

Conley, Verena Andermatt. 1984a. *Hélène Cixous: Writing the Feminine* Expanded edition. Lincoln: University of Nebraska Press.

———. 1984b. "voice i." *Boundary 2* 12 (2): 51–67.

Derrida, Jacques. [1991] 1992. *Given Time: I. Counterfeit Money.* Trans. Peggy Kamuf. Chicago: University of Chicago Press.

———. [1992] 1995. *The Gift of Death.* Trans. David Wills. Chicago: University of Chicago Press.

———. 1999. "On the Gift: A Discussion between Jacques Derrida and Jean-Luc Marion, Moderated by Richard Kearney." In *God, the Gift and Postmodernism,* ed. John D. Caputo and Michael J. Scanlon. Bloomington: Indiana University Press.

Fisher, Claudine. 1992. "Cixous' Concept of 'Brushing' as a Gift." In *Hélène Cixous: Critical Impressions,* ed. Lee A. Jacobus and Regina Barreca. Amsterdam: Gordon and Breach. 79–86.

Penrod, Lynn. 1996. *Hélène Cixous.* New York: Twayne.

Plate, Brent S., and Edna M. Rodríguez Mangual. 1999. "The Gift That Stops Giving: Hélène Cixous's 'Gift' and the Shunammite Woman." *Biblical Interpretation* 7 (2): 113–32.

Schrift, Alan. 1996. "Rethinking Exchange: Logics of the Gift in Cixous and Nietzsche." *Philosophy Today* 40 (1): 197–205.

Segarra, Marta. 2006. "Hélène Cixous's Other Animal: The Half-Sunken Dog." *New Literary History* 37: 119–34.

Shiach, Morag. 1991. *Hélène Cixous: A Politics of Writing.* London: Routledge.

Still, Judith. 1999. "The Gift: Hélène Cixous and Jacques Derrida." In *Hélène Cixous: Critical Impressions,* ed. Lee A. Jacobus and Regina Barreca. Amsterdam: Gordon and Breach. 123–39.

EIGHT

John Milbank and the Feminine Gift

Rachel Muers

John Milbank is well known in contemporary Christian thought for his critique and theological reworking of a wide range of recent literature on gift.[1] This reworking appears in the context of a larger project of recovering a Christian ontology and a Christian account of worldly reality, to expose and confront what he believes to be the nihilism and violence of secular modernity and its supposedly neutral public discourses. Milbank famously argues that Christian theology cannot expect to *argue* its case within a context that operates according to modern assumptions. Instead, it can and should attempt to "out-narrate" secular modernity, by putting forward an alternative ontology, ethics, and politics centered on Christian faith and practice.[2] The title "Radical Orthodoxy," given by Milbank and others to the theological movement centered around his work (Milbank, Ward, and Pickstock 1998), expresses both the claim that this work presents a real alternative to secular and liberal-Christian philosophies, and the concern to be faithful to Christian tradition. Milbank's work has always been interdisciplinary, engaging extensively with philosophical and social-scientific literature. Most often, this has been in order to uncover and criticize the alternative "theologies," the alternative accounts of truth, goodness, and beauty, which they put forward; but Milbank has also sought, in these non-theological discourses, signs of openness to the Christian "ontology of peace" he presents.

The focus of this paper is Milbank's account of "gift" and its gender implications. Gift is an extremely important theme in his recent work; indeed, he argues that gift is "a kind of transcendental category in relation to all the *topoi* of theology" (2003, ix). In other words, for Milbank, everything Christians have traditionally wanted to say about God and the world can be put in terms of gift. Alongside the theological reasons for focusing on gift, however, he sees the opportunity for a Christian "narration" of gift that might go beyond existing philosophical and ethnographic accounts. As Sarah Coakley has noted, Milbank's concerns in placing this idea at the center of his theological work are, at least in part, explicitly political and economic; he works against "the urgent economic backdrop of global capitalism . . . to demonstrate the remaining possibility of an alternative Christian socialism" (2004). In this chapter, I first explore the theological *rationale* for his focus on gift, and then turn to his use of ethnography. Although the question of gender is more obviously relevant to the latter, it is raised already by the former. In order to understand this, however, it is first necessary to see what "gift" does in Milbank's theology.

DIVINE GIFT

"Gift" appears in Milbank's work first and foremost as a name of God. He takes up Augustine of Hippo's naming of the Holy Spirit as gift, *donum.* "Gift" is a name for both God's relatedness to creation and God's relatedness in Godself—the relationships that constitute the Trinity. The key question Milbank wants to ask about gift is what the implications are of naming God as gift, of saying that God's life is about gift. His various engagements with non-theological literature on gift are all aimed at showing how creation participates in the giving and givenness of God.

There is plenty of material to enable him to do so. Milbank follows various ethnographic studies in assuming that gift-giving is a basic aspect of human sociality. Particularly important for him is the idea of gift-exchange and the gift economy. He wants to understand the gift not as exception to, or breach of, "normal life," but *as* normal life. For him, it is possible—and indeed necessary—to see gift-giving as the enduring context of human life and action. In terms of the literature on "gift," then, Milbank seeks a reappropriation of Mauss's seminal work on gift-exchange. This is over against, on the one hand, Derrida and others who speak of the impossibility of reciprocal gift-giving, and, on the other hand, anthropologists who read the ethnographic data in ways that marginalize or relativize gift-exchange.

Why is gift-exchange so central for Milbank? His most important reasons are theological. He wants to say that *time itself* is created by God and is hence a divine gift, and gift-exchange enables him to speak about how gift structures time—through the delay between the receipt of a gift and the return of a gift. He wants, as we have seen, to affirm that gift-giving is an appropriate way of describing the relationships *within* God, the relationships that in Christian theology constitute the Trinity. Gift-exchange enables him to speak about gift not just as event but also as ongoing relationship, and hence it provides a way of speaking about how the Persons of the Trinity are constituted by relationships, including the relationship of gift-giving. He also wants to explore creation's participation in the life of God. Gift-exchange opens up the possibility of speaking of this in terms of non-identical repetition—one "repeats" the gift by returning a gift—but one does not return *the same* gift. In the same way, as Milbank describes it, creation "gives back to God" what God gives, but gives in a way appropriate to its created existence.

The divine gift, in Milbank's account, is the only gift that is inexorable—that cannot *not* be gift once it is given. This is not—again contra Derrida—because it is non-returnable, but because it constitutes the being of the one who "receives" it; it is always received, always reaches its destination, and to that extent cannot fail. The creature can refuse to return gratitude, refuse to recognize its being as gift—but then this very refusal can be "accepted" by God in a way that draws the creature back into the relationship of gift-exchange. God can and does give the gift of "creation's return of the gift," in the face of the refusal of that return. Creation, sin, redemption, and reconciliation are narrated as divine gift given, refused, reaffirmed, and returned—and an economy of gift-exchange is opened up that was always already the basis of creaturely existence.

Theologically, then, gift-exchange proves a very fruitful nexus of reflection for Milbank. We should not, however, ignore the political and ethical dimensions of his emphasis on gift-exchange (as opposed to "the gift"). He believes that it is gift-exchange, the receipt and return of gifts, rather than the unilateral and non-returnable gift, that enables an escape from modern—individualistic, acquisitive, ultimately for Milbank nihilistic—ideas of subjectivity. The gift economy is the basis of his "alternative Christian socialism."

As I have already noted, Milbank takes up the naming of the Holy Spirit as *donum,* and centers his "theopneumatics"—his thinking of Christian belief beginning from the Holy Spirit (2003, ix)—on the idea of the gift. This link between Holy Spirit and gift is a useful starting point for thinking about his account of "the gender of the gift."[3] In his most recent work,[4] Milbank considers the question of gender in more detail, although it arises peripherally in several of his best-known writings.[5]

GENDERING THE GIFT: THE SPIRIT AND THE CHURCH

Why might Christian theologians in particular be interested in the gender of the gift? At least two reasons—both of them, as we shall see, potentially problematic from a feminist perspective—become apparent in Milbank's work. Firstly, the Holy Spirit, as well as being the Person of the Trinity to whom the name of "gift" is appropriated, and the Person who is most often within theological tradition characterized in feminine terms—or at any rate, whose gendering is most often a matter for comment and reflection. When Milbank names the Holy Spirit as "(relatively) feminine," he can draw on a long—and tangled and controversial—theological history;[6] there are numerous examples of historical[7] and contemporary[8] theology in which reflection on the economy of salvation and/or the inner-Trinitarian relations has led to the claim that the Spirit can rightfully be thought of as feminine.[9] Secondly, and linked to this, the traditional gendering of the Church as female/feminine invites reflection on the Church as divine gift, and as recipient and returner of the divine gift.

I begin by considering Milbank's characterization of the Holy Spirit, the divine *donum,* as "(relatively) feminine." Why does he make this association, and how should feminists—especially feminist theologians—respond to it? We should first note, as has Sarah Coakley, that Milbank does not always make clear why it is important to name the Holy Spirit specifically as gift, rather than (for example) to say that the Trinity is gift-exchange. In the introduction to *Being Reconciled* Milbank suggests that calling the Holy Spirit *donum* draws attention to how the closed "perfection" of the dyad of Father and Son is opened out—not to "amorous promiscuity" but to draw creation into the divine life. The Holy Spirit is not simply the unilateral divine gift, God as "given away" to creation, but is the "realisation of a perpetual exchange between Father and Son," and the desire through which the love between two (Father and Son) transcends the dyad towards "infinite and multiple reciprocities" (2003, x).

To understand what is going on here it is useful to note how Milbank defends and uses Mauss, against several of the latter's interpreters and critics, on the significance of the "spirit of the gift." For Mauss and Milbank, gifts themselves partake of subjectivity without ceasing to be objects of donation and exchange. It makes sense to talk about the effectiveness or the agency of gift-objects, and this is not just another way of talking about the effectiveness or agency of the people who give them. Milbank is looking for an account of gift that would overcome the rigid distinction between (acting) subject and (inert, passive) object. Thus to call the Holy Spirit "gift," *donum,* within the wider characterization of the divine life as "gift-exchange," is to give a theological basis to claims about the transformative effectiveness of gifts as such—an effectiveness that they have because of the gift relationships of which they are part, but which is not reducible to the agencies of the givers and recipients.[10] As we shall see, this move has implications for what he says elsewhere about the gender of the gift.

Before discussing that issue, however, it is important to be clear about what is and is not implied by the dual characterization of the Holy Spirit as gift and as "relatively" feminine. First, Milbank is clear that his adoption of feminine terms and pronouns for the Spirit "does not . . . mean that [he] think[s] that she is essentially feminine, any more than the Father and Son are essentially masculine" (1997, 190)—but she *is* "essentially" gift, because of the nature of the inner-divine relationships by which her personhood is constituted. The association between being gift and being female/feminine is not, then, a stable or necessary one for Milbank's theology; this is not straightforwardly a case of inscribing gendered categories onto God with the effect of reinforcing them in society.[11]

At the same time, however, Milbank does—as has become progressively clearer—want to develop a theology and anthropology within which sexual difference is recognized as "ontologically resistant," a "quality . . . of 'animality' as such, perhaps life as such" (2003, 206)—and to ground sexual difference, in some way, in Trinitarian difference (2003, 208; 1997, 190). Understandably, much feminist discussion of Milbank's recent published work has focused on the relatively short passage in *Being Reconciled* in which he outlines an understanding of sexual difference and complementarity, venturing with numerous caveats the claim that "[i]n general . . . men are more nomadic, direct, abstractive and forceful, women are more settled, subtle, particularising and beautiful" (2003, 207). Using Irigaray, he argues that sexual difference is a *basic* human (and more than human) difference, which cannot be eliminated or ignored without eliminating or ignoring all non-competitive human difference. More significant, for him if not for his critics, is the associated claim that this basic difference is reflected in—or, better, is a creaturely and therefore importantly non-identical reflection of—Trinitarian difference.

In the narrative of the economy of salvation—of the way in which God relates to creation and creation relates to God—the key link, for Milbank and others, between the Holy Spirit and femininity is found in the identification of the Church as "bride of Christ" and as locus of the work of the Holy Spirit. Milbank is prepared, with some others—and, notably, with explicit reference to Luce Irigaray—to speak of the "incarnation" of the Spirit in the Church, and of the Church, the embodiment of the Spirit, as eschatologically equal with Christ. The Spirit's embodiment in the Church is the embodiment of *reception-and-return of the divine gift,* the reception and return that ensures that the gift really and inevitably *is* gift. Often, and in connection with references to Irigaray, Milbank speaks of this move—co-equality of Christ and Church—as *necessary* for sexual equality-with-difference; but it would be unfair to read it in Feuerbachian terms, as a theology *in service of* a prior agenda of sexual difference. The co-equality of Christ and Church first appears in a piece in which the question of gender is scarcely discussed (1997, 171–93).

On the face of it, it might be possible to take up Milbank's account of the Church as the embodiment of the Spirit-as-gift and not to recognize any implications of this for gender relations. After all, it could be a set of uninteresting coincidences that the Church is (often) "feminine," that the Spirit is (sometimes) "feminine," and that there is considerable anthropological literature on "women as gifts."

The key move that stops Milbank himself from doing this is his highlighting of *sexual* difference in his account of how creation is, from the start, formed to participate in a divine economy of peaceable exchange-within-differentiation, of reciprocal giving. In Milbank's theology, if sexual difference is to be "built in," as it were, to the gift-exchange for which we are made, it must be both "built in to" created being and (in some sense) "built out of" God's being. It is here—with the "building in" of sexual difference to the account of divine life and hence of gift—that feminist challenges to Milbank's work become significant.

QUESTIONS ABOUT MILBANK'S GENDERED GIFT
The Subjectivity of the Gift/the Woman

Sarah Coakley has argued that Milbank's account of why the Holy Spirit is named as "gift"—summarized above—tends to domesticate both the difference of the Holy Spirit and the difference(s) of gender. She suggests that Milbank's "relatively feminine" Spirit gives divine sanction to a static and binary model of sexual difference. This has implications, according to Coakley, both for the theology of the Spirit and for understandings of sexual difference. Sexual difference is given a single authorized form, and the Spirit cannot be recognized as a genuinely transformative and disruptive "gift" to humanity— because gender relations themselves cannot be transformed or disrupted.

Looking at Milbank's brief account of the Trinitarian naming of the Spirit as "gift"—more precisely, as the gift-exchange between Father and Son—we can see how this problem might arise. There is a risk that the Spirit is reduced to whatever "exceeds" a masculine economy, to, perhaps, that which men exchange, or to that which preserves, by "complementing," a male-dominated order. This would make the Spirit fit neatly into a characterization of "women as gift" that has been the object of sustained feminist critique.

To be fair to Milbank here, we should recognize that he knows what he is doing; he has from an early stage taken up the issue of "woman as gift," partly because it helps him develop the idea of the subjectivity and agency of the gift-object. The way in which he takes up the issue, however, at least in his earlier work, tends if anything to strengthen the feminist critique.

Milbank makes extensive use of the work of Annette Weiner, whose *Inalienable Possessions* he suggests may be the most important anthropological book on gift since Mauss. He notes, at most length in "Can a Gift Be Given," Weiner's research into the work of the Trobriand women who are "given in marriage" in maintaining and developing relationships between their husbands' and their parents' families. To be a gift—thus Milbank paraphrases Weiner—is not to be objectified: "the fact that women are themselves often one of the most valuable 'gifts' does not necessarily render them passive objects, precisely because *the gift itself* was not an object, but imbued with subjectivity" (Milbank 1995, 160n75).

It is worth pausing to disentangle this claim, and, in particular, to ask about the relationship between its two halves. To say that women can be "given" and retain their agency—indeed, be (and be recognized as) agents of their own "givenness"—is a reasonable application of Weiner's ethnographic argument. Weiner's ethnography offers a way into thinking about a "gift that is a person"—and hence, about the Holy Spirit—without losing sight of either giftedness or personhood.

The problem is that "the gift itself was not an object, but imbued with subjectivity" can be taken in two ways. We could say that women are "imbued with subjectivity," so that when women, as opposed to yams or book tokens, are given, the gift is "not an object." This would make the "gift of women" something rather different from other gifts, because women are, obviously, also agents within gift-exchange; they produce giveable and non-giveable objects, they give gifts and receive them. This is not, as I read it, what Milbank wants to do, and this becomes clearer in a later article ("Socialism of the Gift, Socialism by Grace")[12] where he refers again to Weiner's work. He wants to say, for theological reasons, that "the giver is *in* the gift, he goes with the gift" (1996, 538) and that this is what makes the gift more than a passive, inert, and indefinitely manipulable object. The gift's being "imbued with subjectivity" is, then, a function of its *being gift*—and women, alongside (for example) a professional's gift of time or expertise, become *examples* of "gift imbued with subjectivity."

The risk here is that women are made to owe their "imbuing with subjectivity" to their status as gifts, and hence to their givers, or more precisely to the relationship between giver and recipient—that is, in the types of example Milbank discusses, to their fathers and their husbands. This is not, in any straightforward sense, what Weiner's work suggests. Nor, presumably, is it where Milbank wants his Trinitarian theology of the gift to end up—at least, not if it would mean the *subordination* of the "personal gift" (the Holy Spirit) to the "giver" (the Father). It is possible to read this entire reflection—which is, we should again recall, very much an "aside" in these earlier articles—as a proposal, specific to patriarchal contexts, for addressing simultaneously an imbalance in Trinitarian theology and a sexist model of gift-exchange.

However, if this is the case, the basic problem with the feminization of the "gift," and the reinscription of this into the Trinity, still remains. If "the gift" remains paradigmatically female/feminine—even "relatively" female/feminine—then the place of women within gift-exchange is still being determined in advance from a masculine perspective. The transformative dynamic that is supposed to enable distorted relational structures (such as patriarchy) to be overcome is instead reinforcing them.

This point can be explored further through a consideration of another theme in Milbank's account of gift, here in obvious relationship to Derrida—the strangeness of the gift.

The Strangeness of the Gift/the Woman

In Milbank's early discussions of "gift," women "given" in marriage are often used as paradigmatic gifts, or as revelatory of key characteristics of gift-exchange. Thus, in "Can a Gift Be Given?" Milbank uses Laban (Genesis 29–31) as an example of the "big man" described in Mauss's account of gift-exchange—the man whose status within and outside his family circle is secured by his capacity to give. This portrayal centers on Laban's "gift" of his daughters Leah and Rachel in marriage to Jacob. In "Socialism of the Gift, Socialism by Grace" women-as-gifts are taken as paradigmatic for the "strangeness" of the gift, the way in which the gift disrupts totalizing constructions of the self. Organicism, the representation of societies as single organisms (requiring and accepting, by implication, no additions from the "outside" in their self-perpetuating life), is presented as "a specifically *patriarchal* illusion, an attempt to expurgate the strangeness of wives." The wife who does not belong to the family or clan, who introduces something new in the succession of generations, disrupts the "totality" of the family. She represents and recalls the grounding of human existence in non-competitive difference—in relationships with others from whom gifts are received and to whom gifts can be given.

Ironically, Weiner's work on Trobriand kinship, mentioned earlier, demonstrates the limited applicability of Milbank's claims about organicism and the "strangeness of wives." According to Weiner, in Trobriand families, which are matrilineal, it is the father who is understood to provide the "external," additional or foreign, material for a growing fetus (and hence for the lineage that the child helps to perpetuate). The woman is the bearer of continuity, the reproducer of the "same" lineage; the man strengthens the lineage by bringing in difference. Precisely this aspect of Weiner's work—the identification of women as the maintainers and reproducers of the inalienable possessions by which a tribe or lineage is identified—has, in fact, been key to Milbank's most recent discussions of gift and gender. Here, Milbank has greatly extended his use of ethnographic material on "the gift"—in particular, of Weiner and of Maurice Godelier—in an attempt to secure sexual difference as a basic category of human being inescapably linked with gift-exchange. Goods that *cannot* be given away, that correspond to the continuity (or the reproduction, same for same) of the lineage or the tribe, are, for Weiner, particularly associated with the productive and reproductive work of women—and are, for Godelier, appropriated to the "sacred" in a way that conceals the work of women in producing and maintaining them.

Milbank is, as might be expected, interested in the place of the sacred in gift-exchange, and particularly in whether it is possible to rehabilitate, contra Godelier, a narrative in which sacredness is located within the gift-exchange rather than in what remains outside it. He is also, however, interested in narratives of the origins of patriarchy and/or of the erasure and denigration of sexual difference (which, agreeing with Irigaray, he takes to be closely connected). Weiner's work supplies the starting point by giving an account of how women produce and maintain *difference*—the inalienable that remains with the tribe or lineage and differentiates it from others. For various reasons, however, this narrative is inadequate for Milbank. It is not, he suggests, a particularly liberating narrative for women, in that it accords to women only the "power" to maintain existing hierarchies, reproducing existing difference as it stands. In any case, it relies on (what he suggests is) a very modern understanding of how difference and distinctiveness are established—through accumulation and possession, through hanging on to what is "one's own."

Milbank wants to take from Weiner a sense of the differentiated roles of men and women, but in a way that does not remove women, and their activities of production, from gift-exchange (as would happen if they were assigned to the category of the "inalienable"). He wants to claim that "inalienable possessions" are necessary neither for significant peaceable difference (including sexual difference) nor for "the sacred." His preferred narratives of the archaic, then, have nothing that is inalienable or "ungiveable." Gift-objects are "kept" by remaining within the community's circulation of gifts, not by becoming an individual's possession; and sacredness, as for Mauss with his much-criticized account of the "spirit of the gift," inheres in the gift-exchange and in the object *as gift,* rather than as inalienable possession. Within such a narrative, there is no need to postulate separate male and female spheres of economic activity (such that, for example, a male economy of exchange comes to dominate a female economy of production and reproduction); but there is the possibility of, and indeed the need for, sexual difference.

The relationship between the "strangeness of wives"—women as the *different* gift, the gift from outside that disrupts myths of the self-contained organic whole—and the "women as reproducers"—of the distinctive and self-same identity of a lineage—is nowhere made explicit in Milbank's discussion. It would not even be particularly important—because, as I shall discuss in more detail below, he is not committed to finding everything he wants to say about "gift" in the ethnographic material—were it not for the light it sheds on his theological grounding of gender.

Here I would take up Coakley's suggestion that what is going on here is a reincorporation of the "strange" gift into a larger self-contained and predetermined whole—through the allocation of a gender to the gift, and the inscription of this gendered gift into a narrative of sexual complementarity. The most obvious way to link the "strangeness of wives" to the idea of women as reproducers and bearers of continuity is by making marriage, and giving in marriage, a way to keep "strangeness" under control. Wives are, we might say, allowed to be "strange" in a patriarchal system because (in the end) they are wives; there is already a place allotted for their strangeness. They have subjectivity (even) as gift-objects, but they are not allowed or enabled to break the system of gift-exchange between men. This is an anthropological and political problem; but making the Holy Spirit both "gift" and "bride" turns it into a theological problem, because the gift of God then does not change the pattern of male-determined gift-exchange.

Milbank would argue—has argued—that the alternative to his grounding of gender difference in the divine life is a gender *in*difference that simply amounts to a repetition of patriarchy, that requires women to become subjects and agents on male terms. Irigaray can respond in similar terms to the similar criticisms made of her work. What is less clear in Milbank than in (at least some of) Irigaray, however, precisely because of his strong repudiation of the Feuerbachian aspects of her theology, is the sense that one speaks of two sexes to show that there are *at least* two sexes. Sexual difference, on a plausible reading of Irigaray's work, opens up the possibility of multiplicity—perhaps even of "amorous promiscuity." This is not, however, a plausible reading of Milbank's work. The Bridegroom and the Bride, Christ and the Church, are two, and only two, co-equal divine and incarnate "persons"; and what is learned from reflection on them is the centrality of heterosexual marriage to the "mystery" of the Church.[13]

Part of the difficulty here lies in Milbank's use of ethnography, and in particular of accounts of "primitive" or "archaic" societies. It is worth thinking more carefully about what is at stake in the theological use of ethnography.

WHAT ETHNOGRAPHY IN VIEW?

Non-theological reflections on gift, and especially those based on ethnography, have a particular and somewhat unstable location within Milbank's work. In one of his earliest articles on the subject, he compares the status of gift economies in non-Christian "primitive" societies, within Christian theology, to the status of non-Christian philosophies (1995). They are real prefigurations of, or prolegomena to, Christian theology, and Christian theology reconfigures them. They represent forms of human existence and thought that *do not exclude* the divine gift of transcendence, although they are also clearly *without* this divine gift.

Now, for this claim to be sustainable, Milbank does not need every preindustrial gift economy to fit all aspects of the theological claims he wants to make—just as he (or anyone else) does not need all non-Christian philosophy to "fit" with Christianity in order to be able to claim some such philosophies as real prolegomena to Christian theology. It is in fact unclear exactly what stake Milbank has in the accuracy, or non-accuracy, of presentations of "primitive" societies as exemplars of the gift economy. His account of creation by and for gift-exchange points to a "natural" (which does not, in his theology, mean either "automatic" or "godless") human capacity to exist and flourish in relationships of asymmetrical reciprocity. Gift-exchange, in its full development as participation in the relational life of God, is *what we are made for;* in becoming exchangers of gifts, and thus being freed from a solipsistic pattern of acquiring and keeping "for ourselves alone," human beings become truly human, truly themselves.

How is ethnography relevant to this kind of claim? On the one hand, at the simplest level, ethnographies that show the human importance of gift-exchange within a range of societies—its value, for example, as an organizing or explanatory principle, and particularly as a lens for understanding what makes "primitive" societies different from ours—might be taken as evidential support for the claim that humans are really "meant to be" exchangers of gifts. They would help to secure Milbank's claim to be talking about the *real world,* and to be (at least) putting forward a plausible narrative of what makes the real world work. The whole argument that "primitive" practices of gift-exchange have the status of *praeparatio evangelica,* indications of the preparedness of creation for its graced fulfillment, seems to assume the possibility of reliably identifying such practices through careful ethnographic description.

On the other hand, however, Milbank is as clear, critical, and unapologetic about the multiple interests of the ethnographers he discusses as are (for the most part) they themselves. Ethnography is not a setting out of "objective" evidence concerning the other as inert object of (ideally) disinterested reflection; to write ethnography is also to write oneself and one's "own" context. The ethnographic account of gift-exchange is already a critical intervention in, rather than merely a piece of "evidence" for, the debates in which Milbank is interested. Thus he can identify and criticize, for example, the persistence in the work of certain ethnographers of modern or capitalist notions of "ownership"; and, more pertinent to our discussion, he can comment on the ethical implications of patterns of gift-exchange described in ethnographies.

Milbank makes choices—as do others who use ethnographic work without doing it themselves—about whose accounts of "primitive" life to believe. The question is then on what grounds his choices are to be assessed, and which critiques of his preferred ethnographies are going to damage his argument.

Accounts of archaic societies have a well-known function as utopias—as ways of imagining alternative possibilities for human existence and interaction, and hence of prompting a critical examination of what we have now. Feminist retellings of prehistory, for example in the work of Gerda Lerner and (differently, and importantly for Milbank) Luce Irigaray, have been explicitly deployed as tools for deconstructing the "naturalness" of patriarchy. When such accounts are put forward in the service of particular political—or theological—projects, they are rightly subjected to historical and archaeological scrutiny—at least about whether they are *plausible* narrations of forms of historical human existence.

The issue of Milbank's investment in a particular account of archaic and/ or primitive societies—roughly, an account that owes more to Mauss than to any of his subsequent critics, though with important modifications from Annette Weiner—is important as we consider his account of gender and the gift. The question about which he appears to care most is whether we can develop a *usable* narrative of the archaic past—a narrative that will enable us to see beyond what he is prepared with Irigaray to call a "homosexual" (in the sense of "sexual sameness") capitalist economy and politics that excludes both sexual difference and gift-exchange, and a narrative that will cohere with a larger theological account of creation and its fulfillment.

Interestingly, at least in "Can a Gift Be Given?" the imperfections or short-comings of primitive gift-exchange vis-à-vis Christian theology appears to coincide at least in part with its "shortcomings" from a feminist perspective. The problem is that the circulation of gifts in fact only serves the mainte-nance of an existing society; the irruption of the genuinely new is problem-atic and carefully controlled. Gift-exchange serves patriarchy—and the reli-gion of patriarchy—and the women-as-gifts are not able to change it. This might, in other hands, serve as an indication of the great difference between humanly imaginable or practicable systems of gift-exchange and the gift-exchange made possible through divine gift. In Milbank's hands, however, as we have seen, it has led to the search for a *better* archaic past, something "naturally" human that might be a more adequate prefiguration of divine gift-exchange.

Theologically, there are of course major questions to be raised about any such attempt to narrate the archaic past—at least insofar as it claims to describe a society that actually existed. Is this supposed to be a society in which the gift of God could be received and returned without the reception-of-the-gift also having to be given—a society, in other words, without sin, or without sin as a fundamental distortion of human relationships? If so, what does this say about the universal significance of the "gift of the reception of the gift," described above? What relationship does this narrative of archaic origins bear to biblical narratives of divine blessings given and refused? This has deeper implications for questions of gender and the gift than might at first appear. There have been significant feminist theological appropriations of Irigaray that use her work to recover the importance of sexed embodiment in the *sanctified* life, life in communion with God, life that receives and returns the divine gift—but that are reluctant, on feminist as well as theological grounds, to accept any descrip-tion of actually existing "unfallen" gender relations.[14] Whatever is said about the nature or the naturalness of sexual difference, these feminist theologians suggest, can only at great risk predetermine the specific ways in which sexual difference can or should be lived. Something similar might be argued in rela-tion to Milbank's narrations of archaic societies.

Perhaps the best response to such theological uses of ethnographic narra-tions about sexual difference is, first, to say that one cannot decide in advance that they are *not* true, or at least plausible; to do so would be, from a feminist perspective, to naturalize patriarchy. Second, however, a feminist reading might well be suspicious of the attempt to provide a *single* account of "natu-ral" gift-exchange and right relation between the sexes. As an intervention in feminist debates, Milbank offers an attempt to imagine "original peace" between two sexes, which has much in common with Irigaray's later writings.

It has, I would suggest, at least some of the advantages of Irigaray's work, and not a few of the disadvantages. In focusing on sexual difference and the relationship between the sexes, Milbank, like Irigaray, raises important questions about the complicity of certain feminist discourses in modern erasures of real difference—and at the same time lays himself open to charges of heterosexism, and of reinscribing a logic of complementarity that has been damaging to women. In making claims about different male and female ways of inhabiting the world, he works to re-embody ethical and philosophical discourses—and raises worrying questions about biological essentialism. And in telling stories about the archaic past, he works to denaturalize modern stories of human "nature"—and raises questions about the truth and adequacy of his alternative stories, and their claims to reflect a more truthful understanding of what human beings *really are*.

Milbank, however, raises the stakes on his account of sexual difference, in a way that Irigaray has generally not been prepared to do, by explicitly rejecting "Feuerbachian" approaches. He eschews the project of constructing the God we "need" in order to make lived sexual difference possible. For Milbank, not only is transcendence-through-peaceable-differentiation (paradigmatically, through sexual difference) possible and desirable, it is—in its ecclesial form, at least, and to some extent in its supposed "archaic" form—a reflection of the reality of God. It is truly and most properly human insofar as it is that reflection. While we can think that Irigaray's alternative societies are constructed— like "the divine"—in order to create the space for new forms of self-realization, and do not need to be historically true (only believable or imaginable), it is not clear whether Milbank leaves himself that option. Of course his claims about sexual difference do not and should not have the same status as his theological claims—if only because the realities they peʀtain to do not have the same ontological status. God is *more truly* gift, reception and return of the gift, *more truly* non-competitive differentiation in gift relationship, than people are. At the same time, within Milbank's schema, if his stories of sexual difference and gift-exchange are to be of any use (in pointing to basic dimensions of created human being), they have at least not to be totally false—in terms that ethnographers or archaeologists would recognize.

Milbank's work, on this as on many other topics, raises basic questions about the relationship between theology and non-theological disciplines. Given the interest in religious symbolics within contemporary feminist thought, there might be scope for further dialogue with feminism in the context of his ongoing work on gift. Feminist thinkers may well be suspicious, however, of a theological rethinking of sexual difference—and indeed of the gift—that relies so much on the archaic and the archetype, and hence tends to circumscribe what can be said about real women—either in "primitive" societies or in the promised alternative politics.

NOTES

1. Sarah Coakley (2004) gave an overview of the background to Milbank's discussions of "gift." I am indebted to Sarah Coakley for a copy of this as-yet-unpublished paper.

2. For a (critical) discussion of Milbank's overall approach to theology and narrative, see Nicholas Adams 2006 (219–30).

3. To quote the title of the well-known work by Marilyn Strathern (1988)—a work to which Milbank, incidentally, makes only marginal and largely negative reference.

4. Much of this most recent work is unpublished at the time of this writing. I am very grateful to John Milbank for allowing me to read some relevant pieces in draft form. Occasional papers that give a good sense of Milbank's ongoing reflections on gender and the gift are, at the time of writing, to be found on the website of the University of Nottingham's Centre of Theology and Philosophy: http://theologyphilosophycentre .co.uk/online-papers/.

5. For example, in Milbank 1995 (119–61) the main explicit discussion of gender is in a footnote (160n75). See also, on the gender of the Holy Spirit, Milbank 1997 (190n3).

6. For summary discussions, see Congar 1983 (157–60); Johnson 1999 (82–86, 130–31). Note in particular the significance, in the history of pneumatology, of the multiple genders of "Spirit" in biblical and patristic languages: *ruah* (feminine) in Hebrew, *pneuma* (neuter) in Greek, *spiritus* (masculine) in Latin. See also the important treatment of this issue in D'Costa 2000 (39–47).

7. Two examples are pre-Nicene Syrian theology (see the discussion in D'Costa 2000 [41–47]) and the Pietist communities shaped by the theology of Zinzendorf (see Kinkel 1990).

8. Perhaps most famously in Latin American liberation theology, following in particular the (controversial) proposals of Leonardo Boff concerning pneumatology and mariology—see Boff 1988a and, for an example of its appropriation, Comblin 1989.

9. For an earlier connection between the gift and the "femininity" of the Spirit, see Lemonnyer (1936), quoted in Leonardo Boff 1988b (198), and also used by Congar: "[the Holy Spirit] is God's gift above all, and so bears that name . . . Now these qualities fit a mother rather than any other human figure . . . On earth we have no person *given* to us in the same way as our mother" (1983, 161).

10. Theologically, this move can lead Milbank into a discussion of sacraments—material objects that can both signify *and effect* new moments in the divine-human gift-exchange.

11. As does, it could be argued, Lemonnyer's discussion of the maternal character of the Spirit, cited above, and its reuse in later theology.

12. Milbank 1996 (532–48); an amended version appeared in Milbank 2003 (162–86).

13. In a particularly disturbing parenthesis, having linked maleness to "abstraction" and femaleness to "settledness" or "specificity," Milbank comments that "Christian abstraction is necessarily betrothed to Jewish specificity" (2003, 207). The long and largely disreputable history of the Christian feminization of Jews and Judaism need not be rehearsed here.

14. An example is Jones (2000). Jones works within the Reformed theological tradition, and hence within an account of divine gift very different to Milbank's; we would not expect their theologies to be compatible. The point is that there is no necessary correlation between his strong account of the traceable continuity between creation and sanctification, on the one hand, and a feminist concern for sexual difference, on the other.

REFERENCES

Adams, Nicholas. 2006. *Habermas and Theology*. Cambridge: Cambridge University Press.

Boff, Leonardo. 1988a. *The Maternal Face of God: The Feminine and Its Religious Expressions*. London: Collins.

———. 1988b. *Trinity and Society*. Tunbridge Wells, UK: Burns & Oates.

Coakley, Sarah. 2004. "Why Gift? Gift, Gender and Trinitarian Relations in Milbank and Tanner." Paper presented at the American Academy of Religion, November 20–23, San Antonio, Texas.

Comblin, Jose. 1989. *The Holy Spirit and Liberation*. Trans. Paul Burns. Tunbridge Wells, UK: Burns & Oates.

Congar, Yves. 1983. *I Believe in the Holy Spirit*. Trans. David Smith. London: Chapman.

D'Costa, Gavin. 2000. *Sexing the Trinity: Gender, Culture and the Divine*. London: SCM.

Godelier, Maurice. 1999. *The Enigma of the Gift*. Trans. Nora Scott. Chicago: University of Chicago Press.

Johnson, Elizabeth A. 1999. *She Who Is: The Mystery of God in Feminist Theological Discourse*. New York: Crossroad.

Jones, Serene. 2000. *Feminist Theory and Christian Theology: Cartographies of Grace*. Minneapolis: Fortress.

Kinkel, Gary. 1990. *Our Dear Mother the Spirit: An Investigation of the Theology of Count Zinzendorf*. Lanham, MD: University Press of America.

Lemonnyer, Antoine. 1936. *Notre Vie Divine*. Paris: Cerf.

Milbank, John. 1995. "Can a Gift Be Given? Prolegomena to a Future Trinitarian Metaphysic." *Modern Theology* 11 (1): 119–61.

———. 1996. "Socialism of the Gift, Socialism by Grace." *New Blackfriars* 77 (December): 532–48.

———. 1997. *The Word Made Strange: Theology, Language, Culture*. Oxford, UK: Blackwell.

———. 2003. *Being Reconciled: Ontology and Pardon*. London: Routledge.

———. Forthcoming. *The Ungiveable and the Spirit of the Gift*.

Milbank, John, Graham Ward, and Catherine Pickstock. 1998. *Radical Orthodoxy: A New Theology*. London: Routledge.

Strathern, Marilyn. 1988. *The Gender of the Gift: Problems with Women and Problems with Society in Melanesia*. Berkeley: University of California Press.

Weiner, Annette. 1992. *Inalienable Possessions: The Paradox of Keeping-While-Giving*. Berkeley: University of California Press.

NINE

De Beauvoir and the Myth of the Given

Victoria Barker

Nature is always value-less, but has been given value at some time, as a present—and it is we who gave and bestowed it. Only we have created the world that concerns man.

—NIETZSCHE, *THE GAY SCIENCE*

Man created woman—but what out of? Out of the rib of his God, of his ideal.
—NIETZSCHE, *THE TWILIGHT OF THE IDOLS*

EXISTENTIAL ANTHROPOLOGY?

In 1980, *Feminist Studies* published an article by Michèle Le Doeuff that invigorated debate about the originality of Simone de Beauvoir as a philosopher in her own right, beyond her reputation as a follower of Sartre. In "Simone de Beauvoir and Existentialism," Le Doeuff claimed that Beauvoir's approach effectively turns Sartrean existentialism on its head. Observing that it is not enough for Sartrean theory "to pass from a man's to a woman's hands to change from the phallocentic discourse it had hitherto been into the theoretical tool of a feminist investigation," Le Doeuff maintains that Beauvoir "operates a series of transformations on the existential problematic," the first and foremost being the transposition of existential worldview "from the status of a *system* . . . to that of a *point of view* orientated to a theoretical intent by being trained on *a* determinate and partial field of experience"—to wit, that of women (Le Doeuff 1980, 283). The effect of this transformation is revolutionary: whereas the existential ethic, according to Le Doeuff, "has the effect of expelling from the sphere of the person every possible determination, projecting them on to the exterior plane of the situation that is to be transcended," Beauvoirean perspectivism allows that "exteriority" may act as an obstacle to transcendence, a constraint on subjectivity, a grounds for alienation (Le Doeuff 1980, 284). Whereas existentialism demands "an annihilation of every anthropological determinedness," excluding in principle an existential anthropology, Beauvoir restores the anthropological problematic (Le Doeuff 1980, 284). Theorizing a relationship between "internal" states and "external" constraints, Beauvoir explores the questions that have dominated feminist philosophy ever since: questions about the meaning and significance of becoming a woman.

The anthropological perspective is evident throughout *The Second Sex,* particularly in the ethnographic studies of its first volume (Beauvoir 1972). This work draws heavily on the advances in that discipline that dominated French thought in the first half of the last century, heavily influenced by Émile Durkheim's *The Elementary Forms of Religious Life.* Beauvoir is clearly familiar with the work of Durkheim's followers, in particular that of her contemporary Claude Lévi-Strauss, whose *The Elementary Structures of Kinship* Beauvoir reports having read in manuscript during the writing of *The Second Sex* (Beauvoir 1965, 168). The anthropological perspective may also be traced to the influence of Alexandre Kojève, whose lectures in the 1930s had been attended by a number of Beauvoir's friends and colleagues, including Kojève's publisher, Raymond Queneau. Through this influence, the residue of earlier anthropologies may be discerned: both Sartre and Beauvoir are heavily indebted to the "anthropological reduction" of religion enacted by Ludwig Feuerbach a century before, which found renewed voice in the Kojèvean interpretation of Hegel. This anthropology is a significant influence on *The Second Sex,* informing Beauvoir's development of her key concept of the "other."

Just as Beauvoir may be said to have turned existential philosophy on its head, the same may be said of her existential anthropology. This is apparent from the outset: the anthropological "What is man?" becomes in her hands "What is woman?" The sexual specification signaling her claim that the anthropological quest has been implicitly gendered and falsely universalized all along. The real challenge to this burgeoning social science, however, lies in her answer to this question: woman, she maintains, is a mythical being, an artifice, a construct of a masculine imagination, a cipher for "masculine dreams and fears." She is "the mirror in which the male, Narcissus-like, contemplates himself; he bends over her in good or bad faith" (Beauvoir 1972, 217). Woman, in short, is an idol: "She is an idol, a servant, the source of life, a power of darkness; she is the elemental silence of truth, she is artifice, gossip, and falsehood; she is healing presence and sorceress; she is man's prey, his downfall, she is everything he is not and that he longs for, his negation and his *raison d'être*" (Beauvoir 1972, 175).[1] Man's idolatry consists in projecting onto woman the alienated properties of the masculine. She represents in positive form the "lack" that man confronts in himself, "and it is in seeking to be made whole through her that man hopes to attain self-realization" (Beauvoir 1972, 173).[2] Beauvoir posits woman as a "mytheme," to borrow (anachronistically) a term from Lévi-Strauss: an essential element of man's myths, a key figure or trope in the narratives that man constructs to found his subjective and social structures. With this hypothesis, Beauvoir invokes and challenges the key themes of received anthropologies: the concept of man's species-being, of his projection of this species-being onto the world, of his alienation in modern society. Each is subject to a form of suspicion that strikes to the heart of the anthropological quest: the suspicion of the myths of "man."

MAN'S IDOLATRY

The significance of *The Second Sex* for feminist philosophy lies, in part, in the scholarly distance that Beauvoir achieves in respect of the central object of its analysis: the figure of "woman." This is not widely regarded as one of its strengths, to be sure. Some of the most vociferous criticisms of this text concern Beauvoir's tendency to universalize her object, to treat "woman" as if it constituted a unitary category, spatial and temporal variation notwithstanding. Critics also note with consternation that Beauvoir appears to write at times as if she were not party to the group she is defining as feminine. While these tendencies may be disconcerting, it constitutes no objection to Beauvoir's approach to show that she is striving for unity and coherence in the concept of woman. The reason is that the principal object of her analysis in this text is not *women* but "*woman*"—the symbolic, rather than the empirical, entity. She is, of course, vitally interested in the *effect* on women of the abstract symbol "woman." But her prior aim, as I interpret it, is to understand how this symbolic entity is constructed: what it means, how it functions, whose interests it serves, and so on. Only once the meaning and significance of this symbolic construct "woman" is understood can its effects be identified and countered. Beauvoir's argument is that this "woman" does indeed admit of a certain unity, which may be discerned through the study of the cultural artifacts of our society: the discursive production of the myths of femininity and womanhood.[3] If it is possible to speak of "woman" in this symbolic sense, it is because we may make an ethnographical study of its construction. This, then, is a primary aim of *The Second Sex*—and also an explanation for its influence. By adopting a metadiscursive distance in relation to "woman,"

Beauvoir is able to theorize the role that this construct plays in society as a function of abstract gender categories.

The anthropological perspective provides valuable analytical tools in this task. *The Second Sex* is a pioneering exercise in what Marilyn Strathern has called "auto-anthropology," the exercise of directing the anthropological gaze toward one's own culture, rather than that of another (Strathern 1987, 17).[4] With the critical distance of the anthropologist describing alien practices, Beauvoir relates her shock at the revelation of woman's true status in society, her discovery that her world was "a masculine world" (Beauvoir 1965, 94).[5] The anthropological perspective reinforces and justifies the critical distance that she adopts in relation to the cultural formations she identifies. But this critical distance is demanded by a further consideration: Beauvoir's claim is that these cultural formations are constructed by men to their own ends. Resituating the anthropologists' "other" as a figure internal to her own society, Beauvoir finds it embodied in the figure of woman.[6] But, given that she is writing as a woman—as one who experiences the effects of the status of the other within her own society—her own relation to these cultural formations is already removed.[7]

This anthropological perspective is particularly evident in Beauvoir's discussion of myth, in particular the myth of woman. Durkheim's heirs viewed man as the creator of mythological frameworks that found and sustain the social structure.[8] Grounded in concrete social practices, myth condenses and represents a morphology of the social, expressing an emotional energy which is the key to its affectivity. The study of myth gives access to a logic which underlies and explains given social values. Myth is a collective representation, expressing "the way in which society represents man and the world . . . [It] is a moral system, and a cosmology as well as a history" (Durkheim 1915, 420). As an object of collective belief, created by a society that needs to believe it, a myth is in a sense "truer" than history. Indeed, a myth gives expression to a reality which transcends time and location, conjuring a sense of eternity in its ahistoricity. Interpreting the figure of woman as a mythical being, then, Beauvoir places woman at the heart of the cognitive and moral values that found society. Writing in the wake of the Nazi popularization of the *Volksgeist* myth, however, Beauvoir is perhaps more attuned than her predecessors to myth's pathological uses. By contrast with the Durkheimians, she shares with Lévi-Strauss a deep skepticism toward the ability of myth to reveal any deep metaphysical truth about mankind or to satisfy in any ultimate way man's existential yearnings. Beauvoir's account is in fact almost exclusively negative: the myths of woman are contradictory and confused, their aim is mystification and obfuscation.[9] They represent an illusion which is projected onto women—and introjected by them—so as to falsify the true circumstances of their existence. This is why we must seek the "reality the myths were intended to mask," "the exact truth beneath the surface of their interpretations" (Beauvoir 1965, 185).

Beauvoir's claim regarding woman's mythological status has been highly influential on later feminist philosophy. Le Doeuff develops it, for example, in describing the "philosophical imaginary" which constructs woman as "a mythological figure having nothing to do with real women" (Le Doeuff 1987, 52).[10] But there is a further dimension to this analysis, which has received rather less attention: by adding the charge of idolatry to her assessment of man's mythmaking, Beauvoir identifies the distinctively religious character of the myth of woman.[11] This, to my mind, is one of the most insightful, and yet neglected, aspects of Beauvoir's study of woman. This neglect is surprising, given that Beauvoir explicitly links the figure of woman to that of God, affirming a comment of Nietzsche: "Man created woman—but what out of? Out of the rib of his God, of his ideal" (Nietzsche 1968, 45; Beauvoir 1972, 218).[12] Beauvoir argues that the process by which the myth of woman is created is of a piece with that of the myth of God. First, the alienated properties of man are projected onto woman: "He [man] projects upon her what he desires and what he fears, what he loves and what he hates" (Beauvoir 1972, 229).[13] The incoherence that results is then also projected onto woman, so that the properties of ambiguity, contradiction and paradox come to be seen as "an intrinsic quality of the Eternal Feminine" (Beauvoir 1972, 284). The concept of woman that emerges transcends any possible instantiation by women themselves; it is essential, immutable, elemental, irrefutable; it is cast in the glow of divine ordination (Beauvoir 1972, 282–83). Woman thus comes to play a role akin to that of God, instantiating properties that are timeless and absolute, representing fundamental values which support man's self-image. Having diagnosed the quasi-religious character of man's belief in woman, Beauvoir responds to it as she does to man's belief in God. It is a form of idolatry and must be overcome.

The notion of idolatry at work here is of religious provenance; in rejecting idolatry, Beauvoir keeps faith with the entire corpus of Judeo-Christian thought. In Christian theology, truth and falsehood are distinguished by way of the contrast between icon and idol: whereas the icon shares the divine reality it represents, the idol fails to instantiate any reality at all.[14] The Greek *eidolon* refers to an insubstantial form or appearance, a reflection such as is found in a mirror. In biblical Greek, the term is used to refer to heathen gods and demonic powers and is consistently linked to the practice of sorcery and magic—and also, notably, to the *pharmakeia,* which Jacques Derrida associates with writing in the Platonic corpus (Galatians 5:19ff.; Ephesians 5:5; Colossians 3:5; Revelation 9:20ff. and 22:15; Derrida 1981, 71ff.).[15] Given these associations, idolatry is treated throughout the New Testament as one of the most serious of sins, against which the faithful must repeatedly be warned. The role of woman as the general author of sin underscores this concern in the writings of the Church Fathers since, as temptress and seducer, woman entices man from reality to appearance, compromising his status as *imago Dei*.[16]

While Beauvoir's appraisal of the nature of idolatry may be classical, her assessment of its prevalence is distinctly modern: she extends its ambit to include religious belief in its entirety. Her views on this are shared with Sartre, for whom "to be man means to reach toward being God. Or if you prefer, man fundamentally is the desire to be God" (Sartre 1958, 566). As the "value and supreme end of transcendence," God "represents the permanent limit in terms of which man makes known to himself what he is." God is "the one who identifies and defines him in his ultimate project" (Sartre 1958, 566). Beauvoir's contribution is to uncover the gender dynamic that motivates and propels this desire: man, she claims, "believes he is God, he wants to be God; and this because he is male" (Beauvoir 1972, 230). God affirms man by providing a transcendent ground for the values that he holds to be innermost to him. The idolatry of religious belief lies in the attempt to achieve transcendence by projecting these values onto an external source, rather than acknowledging them as his own. Religious belief is thus evidence of man's alienation, his failure to acknowledge the true source of his values. The transcendence man finds in his projections is thus illusory; so too, and by correlation, is the object onto which the projections are foisted.

As an object of a religious mode of thought—an object of man's quest to be God—woman shares with God the unenviable status of the "absolute other"—of the "Other." These two figures—God and woman—are "absolute" others in the thought of man, by contrast with the otherness of the other man, which is merely relative. Beauvoir explains: There are "two forms of alterity or otherness, which are mutually exclusive": first, the alterity of "the other who is also the same, with whom reciprocal relations are established"; second, the alterity of the "absolute Other" (Beauvoir 1972, 102). The first of these is "true alterity": "true alterity—otherness, is that of a consciousness separate from mine and substantially identical with mine" (Beauvoir 1972, 158). This form of otherness is properly governed by the dialogical model of subject/other relations inherited from Hegel. This model is held to be of potentially universal application, but Beauvoir's analysis suggests that it is of limited application in man/woman relations. In this context, a second model of the other arises, whose relation to Hegelian sources is debatable. Man/woman relations are governed by a structure of thought in which the subject projects a set of abstract features or qualities onto woman as other. The qualities projected are not created in the interaction of subject and other; they are a function of a social mythology modeled on abstract ideals of masculinity. Woman's otherness in this sense precedes her. Sonia Kruks suggests that the relation that Beauvoir describes in these terms is no longer a relation of subject to other, at least as Hegel identified it, since it is not intersubjective, as is the master/slave relation (Kruks 1995, 85–87). Certainly, Beauvoir's analysis of this relation is no longer a social ontology. It is the analysis of the cultural preconceptions to which both men and women are subject: an ideology or a mythology, as she terms it.[17] But Eva Lundgren-Gothlin follows the text of *The Second Sex* more closely in arguing that, in the concept of absolute otherness, Beauvoir introduces a second form of otherness, of a different order from that which obtains among men (Lundgren-Gothlin 1996, 72, 172).[18] Absolute otherness denotes a symbolic status in society's structures of thought, which is uninflected and intransigent.[19] It is this mode of otherness that gives woman her "mystical aura" (Beauvoir 1972, 102). It is this mode of otherness that links woman to sacral spheres—and ultimately to God.[20]

With the concept of absolute otherness, Beauvoir identifies a structure of thought in which God and woman play a joint role. The origins of this thought lie in classical bifurcations, wherein man is aligned with God in respect of his incorporeal, rational self, but opposed to God and aligned with woman in respect of his bodily, sensuous self. Beauvoir affirms the Nietzschean interpretation of Christianity as a metaphysical framework that suspends man between two sides of an abyss which cannot be crossed: between a "true" or ideal world and an "actual" or material world (Nietzsche 1968, 50ff.).[21] The two sides of this divide are paradigmatically represented by God and woman, God as man's ideal ego and woman as man's alter ego. Woman's role as man's other is a function of his attempt to reflect his otherworldly ideal, abandoning his worldly self to woman.[22] Or, more correctly, it is a function of the conflict caused by the failure of this attempt. For man finds himself caught between his two "others," barred from transcendence by virtue of his bond with immanence, yet unbefitting immanence by virtue of his idealization of transcendence. The upshot is that man comes to think of himself as a "fallen god," cursed to have been born of his mother's womb (Beauvoir 1972, 177).[23] Nietzsche famously locates the crisis of modernity in the schism between man and his God. For those who pursue Beauvoir's analysis, the crisis is a reflection of a further schism: the schism between man and woman. It is an effect of man's inability to unite with this further aspect of his projected self.

The account of the religious foundation of the myth of woman plays a critical role in Beauvoir's analysis. It explains why woman's status as other has proved insurmountable: it has a religious tenacity because it performs a functional role in man's quest for transcendence. Beauvoir shows how the myth of God as absolute other reflects and reinforces the myth of woman as absolute other, as twin effects of the same idolatrous structure of thought. It also explains Beauvoir's response to this situation: like the idol that is God, the idol that is woman must be overcome. The connection between these two figures explains her antagonism toward each. This is shown, for example, in a discussion of early man's belief in the Goddess. Beauvoir observes:

> The prestige she enjoys in men's eyes is bestowed by them; they kneel before the Other, they worship the Goddess Mother. But however puissant she may thus appear, it is only through the conceptions of the male mind that she is apprehended as such. All the idols made by man, however terrifying they may be, are in point of fact subordinate to him, and that is why he will always have it in his power to destroy them . . . once man acquires clearer self-consciousness, once he dares to assert himself.(Beauvoir 1972, 105)

Drawing a connection between these two figures of man's idolatry—the figure of the feminine other and that of the divine other—allows Beauvoir to conclude that modern man's idolatry of the first—the feminine—will go the way of ancient man's idolatry of the second—the feminine divine—once a "clearer self-consciousness" is attained. In this way, idolatry of woman will ultimately be overcome: "The more women assert themselves *as human beings,* the more the marvellous quality of the Other will die out in them" (Beauvoir 1972, 173; emphasis added).

THE LIMITS OF EXISTENTIAL ANTHROPOLOGY

But will it? This question fundamentally challenges Beauvoir's anthropology. Placing Beauvoir's analysis in the context of its sources will help to explain why this is so. The reference to the attainment of self-consciousness alerts us to the Hegelian roots of this discussion; so too, the use of the Hegelian notion of the other. As mentioned earlier, Beauvoir's left-leaning interpretation of Hegel is consonant with that popularized in France by Kojève in the late 1930s.[24] Kojève's influence is especially evident in Beauvoir's discussion of God. Kojève reads Hegelian philosophy "in the deepest sense" as radically atheistic:

Hegel understands and proclaims that what was called "God" is, in reality, humanity, taken in the completed totality of its historical evolution. Before the advent of Hegelian knowledge, "absolute consciousness *seems* to be *external*" to man. And that is precisely why pre-Hegelian man calls it "God." But that was only an illusion. In fact, theology always was an unconscious anthropology; man projected into the beyond, without realizing it, the idea that he had of himself, or the ideal of his own perfection that he pursued. (Kojève 1970, 26)

A number of the themes inherited from Feuerbach are evident in this passage: the projected nature of God's attributes; the idealized nature of these attributes as man's perfections; the illusory nature of the belief in the external source of value; and the evolution from an external to an internal source of values.[25] These are the principal themes of *The Essence of Christianity,* where Feuerbach argues that religious consciousness involves an act of projection on the part of the individual in which idealized species-attributes are reified and hypostatized on a transcendent plane as an immutable being (Feuerbach 1957). It is ultimately from Feuerbach that Beauvoir and her colleagues derive the thesis that the substance of religion is essentially anthropology, an expression of the human drive to realize itself in its ideality.

Van A. Harvey emphasizes that, while Feuerbach's anthropology is avowedly humanistic, it is not intended to discredit the values projected in religious belief; the task is rather to understand their true value (Harvey 1995, 90ff.).[26] While maintaining that the Christian God is a human projection, Feuerbach does not deny the "reality" of the divine attributes: "It does not follow that goodness, justice, wisdom, are chimeras because the existence of God is a chimera" (Feuerbach 1957, 22). On the contrary, the attributes "have an intrinsic, independent reality"—independent, that is, of the individual who reveres them (Feuerbach 1957, 21).[27] Their "independent reality" lies in the normative role they play in the moral framework of the society as a whole. This, says Feuerbach, is what distinguishes his position from atheism, as he understands it: "He alone is the true atheist to whom the predicates of the Divine Being,—for example, love, wisdom, justice,—are nothing; not he to whom merely the subject of these predicates is nothing" (Feuerbach 1957, 21). Defending himself against the accusation that he places man above God, Feuerbach protests: "[I]t is not I, but religion that worships man. It is not I, but religion that . . . makes God become man, and then constitutes this God, not distinguished from man, having a human form, human feelings, and human thoughts, the object of its worship and veneration" (Feuerbach 1957, xxxvi). Feuerbach presents himself as a messenger of the truth of religious consciousness: that it is a means for man to reflect upon himself. His point pertains not merely to a religious consciousness, however; it concerns man's metaphysical yearnings in general. Throughout the *Essence,* Feuerbach specifies the true object of his analysis as "the essential nature of man," which transcends the specificity and diversity of the religious traditions: "The eye that looks into the starry heavens, which gazes at that light . . . this eye sees in that light its own nature, its own origin" (Feuerbach 1957, 5).

The essential theme of the *Essence* is man's inability to exceed his own nature. It is expressed repeatedly, not merely as regards God but also, significantly, as regards other men:

> Man cannot get beyond his true nature. He may indeed by means of the imagination conceive individuals of another so-called higher kind, but he can never get loose from his species, his nature; the conditions of being, the positive final predicates which he gives to these other individuals, are always determinations of qualities drawn from his own nature—qualities in which he in truth only images and projects himself. (Feuerbach 1957, 11)

This is ultimately the weakness of Feuerbachian anthropology: its reduction of the other to an "image and projection" of the self. In what sense do the "images and projections" of religion have an "intrinsic, independent reality" distinguishable from the religious subject who credits their value? When, for example, Feuerbach claims that "the object to which a subject essentially, necessarily relates, is *nothing else than* this subject's own, but objective nature," can the subjective and the objective be distinguished with sufficient clarity for the two to operate as "independent" entities in dialogical relation (Feuerbach 1957, 4; emphasis added)?[28] Whereas Hegel conceived a dialogical relationship between subject and object, each constructed by way of its interaction with the other, the Feuerbachian model deprives the other of a substantive role in the construction of the subject. He allows that man's identity may derive from his interaction with the other, but the other, correctly identified, is "nothing else than" a projection of self.[29] Again: "The Divine being is *nothing else than* the human being, or rather, the human nature purified, freed from the limitations of the individual man" (Feuerbach 1957, 14; emphasis added). What has reality on the transcendent plane is explicable *entirely* in terms of the needs and desires that motivate man to construct it.

In the final account, the dependence of the other on the terms of the subject in Feuerbach's analysis is an upshot of the definition of the terms themselves. Stephen Thornton argues in this connection that "God" is "God" for Feuerbach only insofar as it instantiates certain attributes which are conceived anthropomorphically (Thornton 1996, 115).[30] God can be identified only by way of these attributes; no other definition is held to be possible. The idolatry of the other is overcome at the cost of the other's assimilation to the terms of the subject. This is why the religious antitheses collapse under Feuerbach's analysis: "[T]he antithesis of divine and human is altogether illusory, that is nothing else than the antithesis between the human nature in general and the human individual" (Feuerbach 1957, 13–14). As man achieves full self-consciousness, the illusory nature of the religious consciousness becomes apparent: "[C]onsciousness of God is self-consciousness, knowledge of God is self-knowledge. By God thou knowest the man, and by the man his God; the two are identical" (12). This is also why religion ultimately becomes obsolete: "[T]he historical progress of religion consists in this: that what by an earlier religion was regarded as objective is now recognised as subjective . . . What was at first religion becomes at a later period idolatry" (13).

Kojève, Sartre, and Beauvoir are major proponents of the Feuerbachian projection theory in twentieth-century thought. Through Beauvoir, the Feuerbachian projection theory has had a lasting impact on feminist thought on the other which is God. Significantly, however, this impact is also discernable at a deeper level of analysis: in feminist thought on the other which is woman. In Beauvoir's hands, the key Feuerbachian tenets are transposed from the analysis of God onto the analysis of woman: in her claim as to the projected nature of woman's attributes; in her claim that these attributes are products of man's quest for perfection; in her claim as to the illusory nature of belief in woman as the vehicle for these values; and in her belief in the evolution from an external to an internal source of values. It is a form of Feuerbachian suspicion that leads Beauvoir to identify in man's projections onto woman the religious fervor of idolatry. And it is a Feuerbachian optimism that fuels her belief that man's idolatry of woman, like man's idolatry of God, will one day be acknowledged and overcome.

The difficulties of Beauvoir's discussion of idolatry nevertheless lie in her adoption of this theory of projection.[31] They result from the fact that the Feuerbachian theory attributes to the other a tenuous existence at best. Feuerbach may have sought to substantiate the properties of the other, but his projection theory has the effect of reducing these properties to their functional role for a constituting ego. Accounting for the attributes of God purely by reference to the intentionality of the subject, it collapses into an egological model of subject/other relations, a model in which the other is defined and differentiated by reference to the terms of the subject.[32] The egological nature of this approach to the other has been much criticized by Hegelians; the criticism extends to Beauvoir's generation of French philosophers. Sartre's use of an egological framework in his social philoso-phy—in his theory of "The Look," for example—is a primary target of such criticism. Robert R. Williams goes so far as to doubt whether Sartre had even read Hegel, much less understood him (Williams 1992, 5).[33] The ego-logical approach is especially evident in Sartre's philosophy of religion, in which God is interpreted as a function of man's project to realize himself as a particular mode of being. Like Feuerbach, Sartre maintains that the "project of being God, which 'defines' man, comes close to being the same as a human 'nature' or an 'essence'" (Sartre 1958, 566). Sharing Sartre's views on this relation of man to "his" God, Beauvoir shares the difficulties of the egological model in the sphere of religion.

In her social philosophy, however, Beauvoir evidently seeks a dialogical model of subject/other relations so as to theorize the possibility of reciproc-ity between men and women—thereby remaining the more faithful reader of Hegel, as Lundgren-Gothlin suggests (Lundgren-Gothlin 1996, 70).[34] Yet Beauvoir's use of the Feuerbachian projection theory to describe woman's status as an idol of man is an obstacle to the success of this project. The pro-jection theory tends to reduce the object onto which man's projections are foisted. Adopting this model, Beauvoir interprets man's image of woman in self-reflective terms, having nothing to do with women themselves. Thus she arrives at a summation of man's misogyny: man "feels hostility for women because he is afraid of them, he is afraid of them because he is afraid of the personage, the image, with which he identifies himself" (Beauvoir 1972, 728). This theory of subject/other relations offers a poor basis for theorizing how man's idolatry of woman is to be identified and how the identification of idol-atry will bring about reciprocity between man and woman. Worse, it offers no grounds on which to figure woman in terms other than those identified as idolatrous. Beauvoir anticipates that woman's experience would support alternative terms of self-definition, but the projection theory tends to negate this possibility. Appealing to this theory, her thought tends to an egological model of subject/other relations and, correspondingly, to pessimism: "If the idols set up by her father, her brothers, her husband, are being torn down, she can offer no way of repopulating the heavens" (Beauvoir 1972, 612). The model reduces woman to an object of man's consciousness, a vehicle for his attainment of transcendence, a figure "given" to him by God. The egological nature of this theory undermines its value as an analysis of the other and its effectiveness in overcoming the idolatry it decries.

Beauvoir's difficulties in explaining how the idolatry of woman is to be overcome correspond to those of Feuerbach in overcoming the idolatry of God. For example: what incentive is there on this model for man to recognize and renounce religious idolatry? In the *Essence,* a consciousness of the projected nature of God is held to be sufficient to effect its overcoming, but this appears to rely on an overly optimistic view of man's rational motivations. Identifying the foundational role played by God in man's self-definition, Feuerbach presents grounds for the prolongation of religious belief, rather than its overcoming. What would cause the believer to abandon belief, where God serves a functional role in man's self-definition? What, indeed, is the connection between recognition of the role of God as other and the overcoming of religion? Does the recognition of God *as other* not work precisely to ensure the prolongation of belief *as an article of faith?*

Beauvoir is similarly incapable of explaining why man should come to recognize and renounce his idolatry of woman. If freedom is understood as the ability to construct the world in one's own image—to act as God, as Sartre would have it—what would cause man to abandon a mythology that has hitherto sustained his self-image? There is a powerful incentive for man to avoid self-consciousness on this theory, since it would require him to acknowledge the illusory basis of his transcendent values. And, where man refuses to abandon the myth of woman, this theory provides no means for women to rectify the situation. On Beauvoir's account, man's recognition of his idolatry is needed if woman's freedom from such idolatry is to be achieved—but without this freedom, women have no means to assert the demand for recognition needed to overcome man's idolatry. Amy Hollywood argues that this theory requires women to petition men for recognition, a petition that they are at liberty to ignore—which, *ex hypothesi,* it suits them to do. Whereas men may find transcendence in their objectification of women, women are placed by Beauvoir "in the impossible position of only being able to gain freedom through men's recognition of that very autonomy women have yet to attain" (Hollywood 1994, 167). Further difficulties surround the very possibility of woman's self-definition in terms other than those projected onto her. If "woman" is a product of man's idolatry, what is it that Beauvoir expects man to *recognize* in woman when she exhorts women to demand recognition from him? The disavowal of idolatry does not involve a recognition of *something else* in its place. On the contrary, it involves a recognition that what was formerly thought to be other is in fact not so.[35] Beauvoir attributes to man the capacity for the making of idols after his own fashion and so also the capacity for their preservation or destruction: "All the idols made by man, however terrifying they may be, are in point of fact subordinate to him and that is why he will always have it in his power to destroy them" (Beauvoir 1972, 105). But when man's disinclination to recognize his own projections is wedded to woman's inability to confront them with any alternatives, the basis for any optimism regarding man's abandonment of this idolatry is difficult to discern.

The difficulty may lie in the strength of the anthropological perspective that Beauvoir adopts. Beauvoir's concept of the myth of woman, we have seen, leads by degrees to the concept of idolatry and so displays the stubborn persistence of its religious provenance. Theorizing woman as a means to man's transcendence, Beauvoir appears to affirm Lévi-Strauss's assessment that the essential role of woman in society is sacrificial. Women are objects given among men in maintaining the systems of exchange that constitute the social structure. In *The Elementary Structures of Kinship*, Lévi-Strauss argues that, in the primitive societies he studied, woman serves as an object of exchange among men, traded in the same manner as money or other possessions: "[W]oman herself is nothing other than one of these gifts, the supreme gift among those that can only be obtained in the form of reciprocal gifts"—that is to say, gifts reciprocated among men (Lévi-Strauss 1969, 65).[36] Where woman acts as a "given" in this way, the meaning and values that she might potentially represent are sacrificed for the sake of man's self-representation, while she is deprived of the freedom to represent herself in alternative terms. Penelope Deutscher has noted that Beauvoir appears at times merely to concede the depressing truth that sexism and other forms of bad faith proliferate through, rather than despite, their exposure as such (Deutscher 2008, 92). When Beauvoir yields to pessimism in this way, the emancipatory message that is sought in *The Second Sex* is threatened. "The whole history of women has been made by men," she laments, and, despite women's apparent advances, "the social structure has not been profoundly modified by the evolution of woman's condition; this world . . . still retains the form that they [men] have given it" (Beauvoir 1972, 159, 689).

CONTRASTING PERSPECTIVES ON THE OTHER

At this point, it is important to stress that the anthropological perspective is not the sole perspective adopted by Beauvoir in approaching "the question of woman." *The Second Sex* is unusual in being composed of several contrasting perspectives, each informing and deepening the analyses of the others. The logical relation between these perspectives is at times difficult to clarify, but there can be little doubt about the efficacy of the strategy of keeping alternative perspectives in play, refusing to be "pinned down" on the subject of woman. There are several interpretative paths which offer a response to the apparent impasse of the anthropological approach. In the final sections of this chapter, I will briefly contrast three of these: the existential, the phenomenological, and the theological. I will suggest that the theological perspective offers feminist philosophy an avenue in which to consider a valuable critical role for the absolute otherness that Beauvoir predicates of woman.

The first interpretative path involves a return to Beauvoir's existentialist roots, which suggest that woman's freedom of self-representation is unassailable, prior to or despite her status as the other of man. The anthropological perspective indicates that this existentialist premise cannot be adopted a priori, in the manner of Sartre.[37] Approached in this way, the concept of woman's freedom would enfeeble Beauvoir's anthropology, undermining the claim that man's idolatry has the power to constrain women in the ways she describes. Beauvoir clearly needs a substantive concept of freedom so as to identify not only the adversity that women suffer as a result of the restrictions of their freedom but also the opportunities offered to women who assert a claim to freedom in the face of these adversities.[38] While this assertion may be inexplicable from the anthropological standpoint that has been considered, it is clear that Beauvoir intends the existential demand for freedom to perform a primary role in her philosophy. Having diagnosed the idolatry of man, and its impact upon the freedom of women, Beauvoir proceeds to make a firm ethical stance against it: "Every time transcendence falls back into immanence, stagnation, there is a degradation of existence into the 'en-soi'—the brutish life of subjection to given conditions—and liberty into constraint and contingence. This downfall represents a moral fault if the subject consents to it; if it is inflicted upon him, it spells frustration and oppression. In both cases, it is an absolute evil" (Beauvoir 1972, 28–29). Outlining the reasons for this "absolute evil," Beauvoir holds the denial of woman's freedom to be an act of bad faith on the part of man, revealing the limitations of subjectivity as traditionally defined, rather than any limitation on the part of the other itself. This approach renounces absolute otherness in favor of an existential affirmation of self-awareness and personal responsibility for one's own interpretations of the other.

A second interpretative path also involves an ethical redress, although on different grounds: it renounces absolute otherness not because it denies personal responsibility for the other but rather because it denies interpersonal mutuality with the other. This second approach involves a return to Beauvoir's phenomenological roots, which suggest that the "primordial conflict" of man and woman may in principle be overcome by way of mutual respect and understanding. The otherness of the other cannot be denied by man, in this approach, since it is present to and informs subjectivity. Sara Heinämaa argues that, for Beauvoir, men and women represent two variations of human embodiment, two different ways of relating to the world as embodied beings (Heinämaa 2003, 84, 91). Beauvoir's phenomenology is distinctive in laying stress on non-representational forms of interaction between subject and other, modeled on the erotic encounter of the lovers: "The erotic experience is one that most poignantly discloses to human beings the ambiguity of their condition; in it they are aware of themselves as flesh and as spirit, as the other and as the subject" (Beauvoir 1972, 449). Debra B. Bergoffen points out that the phenomenological perspective, like the existential, involves an ethical commitment. The reciprocity of the subject/other relation produces an "erotic ethic of generosity," in which love of the other is expressed in the active giving of self, rather than the passive state of being "given" as object: *The Second Sex,* she maintains, "links openness, joy, generosity, and the gift with the erotic's fleshed ethic of risk and vulnerability" (Bergoffen 1997, 190). It challenges a politics of sacrifice, where the status of the other involves appropriation by the subject. The ethic of generosity ultimately undermines the determinacy of the roles of subject and other. Thus: "It is possible to overcome this conflict if each individual freely recognizes the other, each regarding himself and the other simultaneously as object and as subject in a reciprocal manner" (Beauvoir 1972, 160).

These two interpretative paths respond to the egological construction of the other implied by the anthropological approach, suggesting two ways in which the absolute otherness of the other may be renounced. These two paths may be linked by way of their appeal to an ethic of the gift: the first demands that one recognize in the other the properties that one has given to her; the second demands that one recognize in the other the properties that she gives—and so reciprocate in turn.[39] The question here is whether these twin ethical demands constitute an adequate response to the anthropological impasse I have discussed: the egological construction of the other implicit in man's idolatry of woman. It seems to me that, where there exists a received power differential between subject and other, a dialogical relation modeled on an ethic of the gift is liable to corruption. The "economy" of the gift, as Jacques Derrida emphasized in his later work, is an extremely fragile one.[40] Consider: One cannot in good faith give a gift in the expectation of a return in kind; nor can one simply demand a gift from an other, whether it is "owed" or not; nor, lastly, can one demand acknowledgment of a debt arising from a gift that has been given. The gift, if given in good faith, is in principle debt-free. So, where a gift is given but not reciprocated, there appears to be little by way of grounds for redress. A dialogical relation established on the basis of the gift is, it seems, unilaterally severed in this situation. If this is so, then the gift appears to challenge, rather than to support, the very foundation of the dialogical relation.

The situation of woman described by Beauvoir is of this nature: woman's gift of self is a sacrifice in that it is given without return. But if this gift truly is a gift, there can in principle be no expectation of return. It is not clear, then, what the ethical grounds for redress may be when the return of this gift is not forthcoming. But this is not the end of it. For, even where a debt to the giver *is* acknowledged, this acknowledgment is by itself insufficient to establish reciprocity. Nothing less than a return of the gift suffices for the dialogical relation to be maintained between giver and receiver. But this is precisely what the subject denies the other in the given situation between man and woman that Beauvoir describes. It is, I think, telling that the paradigm of the reciprocal relation presented by Beauvoir is that of the lesbian lovers (Beauvoir 1972, 436).[41] Kruks has noted that Beauvoir's examples tend to rely on an assumption of social equality between the parties to the reciprocal relation. As soon as a power disparity is posited between them, the relations of oppression and subordination tend to reassert themselves and the possibility of reciprocal relation recedes (Kruks 1995, 84).[42] This suggests that the ethic of the gift provides a weak foundation for securing the dialogical relation between men and women.

This analysis also suggests that the problem of the lack of reciprocity between man and woman is not overcome merely by being brought to consciousness. Beauvoir embarks on a project of demystification of absolute otherness in the belief that, where the idolatry behind the myth of woman is understood, woman's absolute otherness will resolve into relative otherness, like that which relates men. The difficulty here is that this process of demystification does not, of itself, entail an overcoming of absolute otherness. Indeed, the representation of the other as other may in fact be sustained, rather than overcome, by way of its demystification. Beauvoir is responding to an exemplary statement of this strategy in Emmanuel Levinas's pronouncement that alterity reaches "its full flowering" in the feminine (Beauvoir 1972, 16; Levinas 1987, 85). Levinas's is by no means the first such statement of this position, though it may be one of the more explicit. The issue here is that the dialogical claim to recognize this other as essential to man's self-image remains perfectly compatible with the egological desire of man to define woman as the absolute other. The recognition of the role and function of sacrifice in no way mitigates the actuality of the sacrifice.[43] Indeed, it is precisely the recognition of the other as essential which may motivate the more emphatic statements of the other's otherness; Levinas provides a case in point. It is therefore unsurprising that, in those recent philosophies where the gift is extolled as an ethical paradigm, "it is the woman who has the dubious honour of being the victim *par excellence*," as Morny Joy has observed (Joy 1999, 323).[44] Men's acknowledgment of his projections onto woman, along with the sacrifice that this implies on the part of women, comfortably coexist with his ongoing assertion of woman's status as absolute other.

There is, however, a third interpretative path available to us, an alternative perspective on the status of the absolute other: the theological perspective. This perspective is suggested by several features of Beauvoir's analysis: her claim that the idolatry of man is an absolute evil and must be renounced; her claim that man's idolatry acts as a constraint on woman's freedom of self-expression; and her claim that the assertion of woman's freedom is to be understood as a quest for transcendence. The most explicit use of this perspective, however, lies in the appeal to the notion of absolute otherness, with the implied correlation between God and woman as two of its principal representatives. The identification of this correlation, I have suggested, leads Beauvoir to attempt a reduction of the absolute otherness of woman along the lines of her reduction of the absolute otherness of God. With the structure of her argument on woman as other reflecting the structure of her argument on God as other, de Beauvoir introduces into feminist philosophy a concept of the other with an implicit theological dimension—theological in the sense that it concerns the nature and status of our discourse on the absolute other, a paradigm of which is God.[45]

The theological perspective raises questions beyond those that Beauvoir explicitly addressed, with regard to the notion of absolute otherness. The foremost question is this: *Ought* absolute otherness to be reduced or overcome? Beauvoir takes it as axiomatic that the attainment of full subjectivity entails the overcoming of absolute otherness. But might there not be grounds for an affirmation of absolute otherness on the part of woman in Beauvoir's philosophy? Might absolute otherness not be attended by its own mode of subjectivity, of a different nature from that Beauvoir diagnoses as idolatrous? Specifically, might absolute otherness not provide the grounds for a mode of transcendence, of the very form that Beauvoir sought by way of the existential claim to freedom? For, in the face of man's projections onto woman—indeed, in the face of man's admission of indebtedness to the other qua other—the reassertion of woman's absolute otherness in respect of these projections—and in respect of this debt—may itself constitute a claim to autonomy and to transcendence.

This much, at least, is suggested by theological discussions of the absolute otherness of God. The autonomy of God in respect of man's idolatrous projections is a fundamental tenet of Judeo-Christian tradition. It is man, and man alone, who ultimately suffers the ramifications of his idolatry. Nothing compels the other to acknowledge these projections as pertaining to her. What I am suggesting is that the existential assertion of freedom may ultimately sit more comfortably with the claim of the absolute otherness of the other than with the demand for reciprocity between subject and other. After all, the dialogical relation between subject and other is severed not only at that point where the subject attempts to impose idolatrous projections onto the other. It is also severed at that point where the "gift" of the subject's idolatrous projections is simply not accepted. At that point, the freedom of the other from the subject's projections—and from the debt that the subject owes by virtue of its projections—may ultimately be secured.

CONCLUSION: THE RETURN OF A THEOLOGICAL MODE OF THOUGHT

Beauvoir's treatment of the concepts of absolute and relative otherness—and their differences—is highly schematic. So schematic is it that one wonders how she can arrive at the conclusion that absolute otherness is so assuredly to be overcome. Beauvoir maintains that, if absolute otherness is irreducible, then woman is destined to remain "mired in immanence," a "given" of the social structure, an eternal embodiment of "the myth of the given." However, if Beauvoir's correlation of God and woman holds, then a further possibility is implied: that the irreducibility of otherness may yield a model of woman's transcendence, such as Beauvoir sought. A theological perspective defends this possibility, offering an alternative model of the other and of subject/other relations. Eschewing both egological and dialogical models, a number of recent theologians, following Judeo-Christian tradition closely in this respect, develop a heterological approach to the other.[46] On this model, the absolute otherness of the other implies the other's autonomy from the idolatrous projections of the subject. The last generation of feminist philosophers, like their colleagues in theology, have explored the possibility that an assertion of absolute otherness might found a politics of freedom and autonomy—a mode of transcendence in relation to received structures of subjective and social identity. They have even ventured the possibility that absolute otherness may found alternative modes of subjectivity, beyond those that Beauvoir decries as idolatrous.

The work of Luce Irigaray is representative of this trend. Irigaray exploits the status of absolute otherness predicated of woman by Beauvoir to present an affirmative—quasi-transcendental—vision of woman as other. Irigaray borrows from the theological discourses of God's otherness to argue that there are forms of subjectivity that belong to women *in virtue of,* rather than *despite,* their received status as other (Irigaray 1993).[47] Across Irigaray's writings, the both/and of the cataphatic mode of speech is juxtaposed against the neither/nor of the apophatic mode, reflecting a self-critical stance which allows us to speak of the other without descent into idolatry—without reducing the other to the parameters of the anthropological quest to understand or appropriate.[48] The juxtaposition of these two modes of speech—the cataphatic "saying" and the apophatic "saying away"—fascinates Irigaray in the writings of the mystics. The influence of these religious texts is evident in Irigaray's quest to promote forms of speech that do justice to the other qua other.[49]

There remains a good deal of work to be done to exploit the theological resources available to feminist philosophy in theorizing the status of the absolute other. We might perhaps start by asking how a philosophy that sought so energetically to renounce the category of absolute otherness should have inspired a philosophy that seeks so innovatively to embrace it.[50] To my mind, the answer has to do with the fertility of the notion itself. In absolute otherness, Beauvoir finds a concept that has not only inspired a tradition of thought about the nature of transcendence, but admits of reinterpretation in the context of contemporary political concerns. It is ironic that, while Beauvoir sought to overcome a theological manner of thinking, her interpretation of woman as a pivotal figure of absolute otherness has made a feminist return to such thought a matter of some urgency.

NOTES

The first epigraph is from Nietzsche 1974 (203). The second is from Nietzsche 1968 (45), as quoted in Beauvoir 1972 (218).

1. Again: "Ambiguous idol! Man wishes her to be carnal, her beauty like that of fruits and flowers; but he would also have her smooth, hard, changeless as a pebble. The function of ornament is to make her share the more intimately in nature and at the same time to remove her from the natural, it is to lend palpitating life the rigour of artifice" (Beauvoir 1972, 190).

2. This theme of the myth of woman emerges over and again in Beauvoir's recollections of her writing of *The Second Sex.* In her autobiography, she describes how she devoted herself "to finding out about the condition of women in the broadest terms. I went to the Bibliothèque Nationale to do some reading and what I studied were the myths of woman" (Beauvoir 1965, 94–95). In a further interview, she reports: "I wanted to write about myself and he [Sartre] said, 'Don't forget to explain first of all what it is to be a woman.' And I told him, 'But that never bothered me, I was always equal to men,' and he said, 'yes, but even so, you were raised differently, with different myths and a different view of the world.' And I told him, 'that's true.' And that's how I began to work on the myths" (Beauvoir 1999, 55).

3. Beauvoir laments the ambiguities, contradictions, and paradoxes that afflict the received concept of woman, arguing that they are a function of woman's status as other: "[H]er ambiguity is that of the concept of the other" (Beauvoir 1972, 175). Woman lacks a determinate identity because the properties predicated of "woman" are not a function of women's self-definition but of her definition by man.

4. This is "anthropology carried out in the social context that produced it" (Strathern 1987, 17).

5. Responding to a suggestion of Sartre that she look into the question of woman's status, she reports: "I looked, and it was a revelation: this world was a masculine world, my childhood had been nourished by myths forged by men" (Beauvoir 1965, 94).

6. Beauvoir notes that natives of a given country are shocked to find themselves regarded as other in a foreign country. However, she continues, "wars, festivals, trading, treaties, and contests among tribes, nations, and classes tend to deprive the concept Other of its absolute sense and make manifest its relativity" (Beauvoir 1972, 16). Her question is why this process does not extend to men's relations with women.

7. Beauvoir's writing shows features of three auto-anthropological genres, outlined by Deborah E. Reed-Danahay: "native anthropology," written by those formerly subject to study but now turned author; "ethnic anthropology," written by members of ethnic minorities; and "autobiographical ethnography," written by anthropologists who interject personal experience into their writing (Reed-Danahay 1997, 2).

8. These included Marcel Mauss, Henri Hubert, and other contributors to the journal l'Année Sociologique, founded by Durkheim in 1898 as a way of publicizing his research and that of his colleagues and students.

9. Durkheim nevertheless also understands myths to be contradictory and confused, and that their role is to veil reality, rather than to reveal it (Durkheim 1915, 25f, 49f).

10. The mythological status of "woman" in no way mitigates the effect of this thought on "real" women: "[W]hatever a philosopher may say about islands, this will never do any harm to them, whereas what they say about women is generally an insult. As such, it has consequences" (Le Doeuff 1991, 86). The consequences stem from the fact that the myth is untenable and yet any deficiency in this regard is assumed to lie, not in the myth itself, but in the women who fail to "live up to" it.

11. Here, the influence of the thought of Durkheim is again apparent. Durkheim interpreted the bifurcations that are basic to Beauvoir's study—transcendence/immanence, icon/idol, spiritual/material, and so on—as rooted in the primary opposition of sacrality/profanity. The categories basic to thought, he argues, are "born in religion and of religion: they are a product of religious thought" (Durkheim 1915, 9). The values attached to this distinction carry across all thought, including that governing relations in the empirical world.

12. The neglect of Beauvoir's discussion of religion is also surprising, given its seminal influence on feminist theology by way of Mary Daly. From her first work, The Church and the Second Sex, Daly adopts key Beauvoirean themes: the radical nature of women's freedom, the necessity of choice, and transcendence as the surpassing of being (Daly 1985). In that work, Daly attributes to women the capacity to transcend "sexual differentiation" and so to nurture "the liberating, humanizing Church of the future" (Daly 1985, 221).

13. This theme of projection appears repeatedly, in various forms. For example: "In all civilizations and still in our day woman inspires man with horror; it is the horror of his own carnal contingence, which he projects onto her" (Beauvoir 1972, 180).

14. I analyze in greater depth the contrast between these two concepts and the implications for feminist philosophy in Barker (2000).

15. In "Plato's Pharmacy," Derrida argues that the pharmakeia is at once both poison and cure in the Platonic corpus—and undecidable between these two values (Derrida 1981, 71ff.).

16. Man alone is created *imago Dei*; only he can truly represent God's image on earth (Genesis 1:26; Wisdom 2:23; Romans 8:29; 1 Corinthians 11:7). Woman's metaphorical association with the negativity of imagery—with semblance, duplicity, appearance, deception, and so on—impedes her ability to act in God's image. One of the many implications of this is that the danger of idolatry is held to arise in the practice of representing God in the feminine—though not, apparently, in the masculine.

17. Beauvoir's discussion of woman as absolute other includes a social ontology: women, she claims, "have never composed a separate group set up *on its own account*" and "have never entered into a direct and autonomous relation with the men," and for this reason it is "impossible to consider her as another subject" (Beauvoir 1972, 102–103). But the analysis extends beyond this, to consider the abstract ways in which the meaning and significance of the symbol "woman" is produced.

18. Indeed, Beauvoir warns against the "confusion of two forms of alterity or otherness, which are mutually exclusive in point of fact," and proceeds to explain that woman is the absolute as opposed to the relative other because women have never established "direct and autonomous" relations with men (Beauvoir 1972, 102–103).

19. Beauvoir introduces the concept of absolute otherness in the context of a discussion on the work on mythology of Lévi-Strauss, whom she quotes: "Woman, in herself, is never more than the symbol of her line" (Beauvoir 1972, 103).

20. Outlining the history of the myth of woman, Beauvoir argues that the idolatry of woman emerged with the onset of patriarchy, with dramatic implications for women: "Supreme idol in the far realms of heaven and hell, woman is on earth surrounded with taboos like all sacred things; she herself is taboo" (Beauvoir 1972, 101).

21. From the first pages of *The Gay Science,* Nietzsche draws a number of metaphorical connections between God and woman to highlight man's weakness in depending on these twin props. This theme continues to his last writings: in *The Twilight of the Idols,* Nietzsche interprets man's projections as an expression of the real world/actual world binarism of Platonic metaphysics, the product of a "declining, debilitated, weary, condemned life" (Nietzsche 1968, 55).

22. God instantiates values held to be essential: "A god is no engendered being; his body, if he has one, is a will cast in firm and disciplined muscles, not a mass of flesh vulgarly subject to life and death" (Beauvoir 1972, 230–31). Beauvoir thereby explains both the attraction of God and the detraction of woman, who represents for man the inability to overcome his "perishable flesh, contingent, vulnerable, and disowned" (Beauvoir 1972, 23).

23. Man "sees himself as a fallen god: his curse is to be fallen from a bright and ordered heaven into the chaotic shadows of his mother's womb. This fire, this pure and active exhalation in which he likes to recognise himself, is imprisoned by woman in the mud of the earth" (Beauvoir 1972, 177).

24. Kojève's lectures were published by Beauvoir's friend Raymond Queneau in 1949, the same year as the publication of *The Second Sex.* These lectures were attended by a number of Beauvoir's associates, including Queneau himself and Maurice Merleau-Ponty. The influence of Kojève on Beauvoir is discussed in detail by Lundgren-Gothlin (1996, 67ff.).

25. Vincent Descombes is among those to note the similarities between Feuerbach's anthropology and Kojève's "humanist plea." He diagnoses difficulties with Kojève's concept of the absolute knowledge of man similar to those that confront

Feuerbach: "[H]ow can the totality [the identity of subject and object] imply man without leaving nature in the dialectical anticipation of its own negation by Mind?" (Descombes 1980, 46). Kojève's indebtedness to Feuerbach on the subject of God is also discussed by Shadia B. Drury (Drury 1994, 13).

26. Harvey defends Feuerbach against the objection of reductionism by noting that (unlike Freud, for example) Feuerbach pays close attention to the believer's consciousness, supporting his interpretation by means of Christian doctrine (Harvey 1996, 78–79). Insofar as Feuerbach defines the terms of the other as definable purely in terms of those of the subject, it may be argued that he performs an act of reduction of the other to the terms of the subject.

27. Feuerbach explains: "[I]n no wise is the negation of the subject [God] necessarily also a negation of the predicates [of God] considered in themselves. These have an intrinsic, independent reality; they force their recognition upon man by their very nature; they are self-evident truths to him; they prove, they attest themselves" (Feuerbach 1957, 21).

28. This theme that consciousness of the divine is "nothing else than" self-consciousness is repeated over and again in the *Essence*. For example: "[I]n the nature and consciousness of religion there is nothing else than what lies in the nature of man and in his consciousness of himself and the world" (Feuerbach 1957, 22).

29. This point is not substantially affected by Harvey's observation that Feuerbach does not standardly use the term "projection" as George Eliot's translation would have it, but a series of terms—with meanings closer to "objectification" or "externalization"—which point to the Hegelian underpinning of this theory (Harvey 1996, 75).

30. As an example of this strategy, Feuerbach redefines the contours of Christianity so as to exclude negative theology. The Christian, he asserts, *knows* that God has positive qualities; any theology that refuses the imagery of Christianity is merely a thinly veiled atheism (Feuerbach 1957, 15).

31. Harvey helpfully distinguishes two key theories of religious projection in modern thought: the "beam" theory and the "grid" theory (Harvey 1996). "Beam" theories image the act of projection as an externalization of some aspect of self that is "beamed" onto an object, whereas "grid" theories image the act of projection as the construction of a framework within which the understanding or experience of an object is made possible (Harvey 1996, 68–70). The former, Harvey notes, is more likely to treat the object of religious belief as an error or illusion; the latter is unable to arrive at such a conclusion, since questions of the truth of belief are necessarily internal to the grid itself (74). Beauvoir treats the idolatry of man as illusory because its object is itself "unreal."

32. This distinction between dialogical and egological readings of Hegel is developed by Theunissen (Theunissen 1984).

33. Williams points out that, in his "strange appropriation" of Hegel, Sartre approaches the problem of the other as a first-person analysis, approached in terms of the *cogito*, which he takes to be the "sole point of departure" in his study of intersubjective relations: "[E]ach one must be able by starting out from his own interiority, to rediscover the Other's being as a transcendence which conditions the very being of that interiority" (Williams 1992, 11; Sartre 1958, 244). From a Hegelian perspective, it is because Sartre sets up the ego as pure and unmediated identity that he undermines his ability to understand the problem of the other as a problem of intersubjectivity

(Williams 1992, 12). Tina Chanter makes a related assessment in noting that Beauvoir might have done better to observe the dialogical premises of Hegel's methodology which suggest, contra Sartre, that it is only at that point when the recognition of the other arises that man can assert himself as subject (Chanter 1995, 61).

34. Lundgren-Gothlin argues that Beauvoir was influenced by Kojève's reading of Hegel in her claim, against Sartre, that while the struggle for recognition is essential to human history, it may be transcended through reciprocal recognition (Lundgren-Gothlin 1996, 70–71).

35. Is there not also a question as to how Beauvoir's own thought could possibly have arisen? On this projection theory of "woman," the forms of self-definition that Beauvoir herself promotes would themselves be unfounded and inexplicable.

36. Lévi-Strauss's elaboration indicates that it is reciprocity between males that is understood here: "[T]he exchange of brides is merely the conclusion to an uninterrupted process of reciprocal gifts, which effects the transition from hostility to alliance, from anxiety to confidence, and from fear to friendship" (Lévi-Strauss 1969, 67–68). Beauvoir reports in her autobiography that *The Elementary Structures of Kinship* "confirmed my notion of woman as other; it showed how the male remains the essential being, even within the matrilineal societies generally termed matriarchal" (Beauvoir 1965, 168).

37. The internal conflict created in Beauvoir's philosophy by a categorical appeal to freedom is noted by a number of her commentators. Tina Chanter, for example, elucidates the conflict between the existentialist model of the absolute freedom of the individual to surmount his or her social situation and the Hegelian model of the irresolvable nature of the conflict between individuals (Chanter 1995, 49).

38. The existentialist claim to freedom of self-representation has heavily influenced subsequent thought, in the work of Judith Butler in particular. Butler pushes Beauvoir in the direction of voluntarism, maintaining that she substitutes individual choice for social constraint (Butler 1990, 8, 21). Butler emphasizes how women reposition their status within society by modifying the representations they have introjected.

39. Like Lévi-Strauss, Beauvoir is influenced by the account of the gift offered by Marcel Mauss, for whom the reciprocity of gifts in primitive societies has a far greater role than the economics of exchange (Mauss 1990).

40. Derrida argues, for example, that the gift cannot in principle be reciprocated, since it necessarily creates its own excess. The gift must in principle be at least equal to that which it seeks to repay, and so it gives rise to an escalating, or counterfeit, economy (Derrida 1992).

41. "Between women love is contemplative; caresses are intended less to gain possession of the other than gradually to re-create the self through her; separateness is abolished, there is no struggle, no victory, no defeat; in exact reciprocity each is at once subject and object, sovereign and slave, duality becomes mutuality" (Beauvoir 1972, 436).

42. Like Lundgren-Gothlin, Kruks identifies two different models of relationship to the other operating in *The Second Sex*. The first, which pertains to relations of equality such as the lovers, allows reciprocity because subject and other construct themselves in a state of mutuality. The second pertains to relations of inequality wherein "reciprocity is to a greater or lesser extent abolished and relations of oppression and submission take its place" (Kruks 1995, 84). In the latter case, otherness is

not created in the interaction of subject and other, as the Hegelian analysis would demand. Nor is woman responsible for her subjectification, as the existential analysis would demand. Woman's immanence precedes her; women are not the source of the problem and no fault accrues to them (Kruks 1995, 85–87). I interpret this as the state of "absolute otherness."

43. Butler makes this point in speaking of Hegel's response to the sacrifice of Antigone: while figuring woman as other, Hegel himself fully admits the necessity of woman's function within the state. This is what leads him to speak of woman as "the everlasting irony of the community" (Butler 2000, 149–50; Hegel 1977, 288).

44. Joy points out that this is especially so when the gift is modeled on sexual self-giving. Sacrifice—and especially women's self-sacrifice—is arguably "the prototype of the gift *par excellence*," she notes (Joy 1999, 321).

45. While his interpretation differs from my own, the theologian Karl Barth also interprets Feuerbach as making an essentially theological point about the anthropological element of religious speech: "We misinterpret Feuerbach if we see in [his philosophy] a deprecation of religion and theology: it is the essence of man that he emphatically and enthusiastically affirms," so that "[w]hen he identifies God with the essence of man, he thereby pays God the highest honour he can confer" (Barth 1957, xv).

46. The heterological is described by Mark C. Taylor as a mode of thought that resists incorporation, assimilation, and appropriation within the closed logical structures of classical thought (Taylor 1987, 133). Georges Bataille describes heterology as "the science of what is completely other (*tout autre*)," while admitting that the term is oxymoronic, in that the *heteros* is precisely what eludes the *logos* (Bataille 1985, 102). Heterology is figured as what "is opposed to any homogeneous representation of the world, in other words, to any philosophical system" (Bataille 1985, 97).

47. The work of Butler also deserves mention in this context, in her evocation of woman as the as yet unknown, beyond signification, beyond the epistemological and ontological discourses of the west: "The female sex is . . . *the subject* that is not one. The relation between masculine and feminine cannot be represented in a signifying economy in which the masculine constitutes the closed circle of signifier and signified" (Butler 1990, 11).

48. Irigaray thereby situates both divinity and femininity in a realm that, she insists, exceeds the determinations of the western symbolic (Irigaray 1993, 129).

49. Ann-Marie Priest claims that Irigaray leans heavily on the apophatic aspect of the negative theological way in her discussion of woman as other (Priest 2003).

50. The shadow of Feuerbach deserves attention here, as it arouses feminist concerns. Discussing Irigaray's claim in "Divine Woman" that "[i]t is essential that we be God *for ourselves* so that we can be divine for the other, not idols, fetishes, symbols that have already been outlined or determined," Serene Jones also accuses Irigaray of treating the transcendent as a function of the human needs for self-constitution, thus "swerving too close" to Feuerbach (Irigaray 1993, 71; Jones 1993, 127).

REFERENCES

Barker, Victoria. 2000. "The Duplicitous Idolatry of the Philosophical Imaginary." In *Michèle Le Doeuff: Operative Philosophy and Imaginary Practice*, ed. Max Deutscher. New York: Humanity Books. 127–46.
Barth, Karl. 1957. "An Introductory Essay." In Feuerbach 1957. x–xliv.

Bataille, Georges. 1985. *Visions of Excess: Selected Writings, 1927–39.* Trans. A. Stoekl. Minneapolis: University of Minnesota Press.

Beauvoir, Simone de. 1965. *Force of Circumstance.* Trans. Richard Howard. London: André Deutsch.

———. 1972. *The Second Sex.* Trans. H. M. Parshley. Harmondsworth, UK: Penguin.

———. 1999. "Beauvoir Interview 1982." In *Beauvoir and* The Second Sex: *Feminism, Race, and the Origins of Existentialism,* ed. Margaret A. Simons. Lanham, MD: Rowman & Littlefield. 55–59.

Bergoffen, Debra B. 1997. *The Philosophy of Simone de Beauvoir: Gendered Phenomenologies, Erotic Generosities.* Albany: State University of New York Press.

Butler, Judith. 1987. *Subject of Desire: Hegelian Reflections in Twentieth Century France.* New York: Columbia University Press.

———. 1990. *Gender Trouble: Feminism and the Subversion of Identity.* New York: Routledge.

———. 2000. *Antigone's Claim: Kinship between Life and Death.* New York: Columbia University Press.

Chanter, Tina. 1995. *Ethics of Eros: Irigaray's Rewriting of the Philosophers.* New York: Routledge.

Daly, Mary. 1985. *The Church and the Second Sex* 2nd ed. Boston: Beacon Press.

Derrida, Jacques. 1981. *Dissemination.* Trans. B. Johnson. Chicago: University of Chicago Press.

———. 1992. *Given Time: I. Counterfeit Money.* Trans. Peggy Kamuf. Chicago: University of Chicago Press.

Descombes, Vincent. 1980. *Modern French Philosophy* Trans. L. Scott-Fox and J. M. Harding. Cambridge: Cambridge University Press.

Deutscher, Penelope. 2008. *The Philosophy of Simone de Beauvoir: Ambiguity, Conversion, Resistance.* London: Cambridge University Press.

Drury, Shadia B. 1994. *Alexandre Kojève: The Roots of Postmodern Politics.* New York: St. Martin's Press.

Durkheim, Émile. 1915. *The Elementary Forms of Religious Life.* Trans. J. W. Swain. New York: George Allen & Unwin.

Feuerbach, Ludwig. 1957. *The Essence of Christianity.* Trans. G. Eliot. New York: Harper & Row.

Harvey, Van A. 1995. *Feuerbach and the Interpretation of Religion.* Cambridge: Cambridge University Press.

———. 1996. "Projection: A Metaphor in Search of a Theory?" In *Can Religion Be Explained Away?* ed. D. Z. Philips. New York: St. Martin's Press. 66–82.

Hegel, G. W. F. 1977. *Phenomenology of Spirit.* Trans. A. V. Miller. Oxford, UK: Clarendon Press.

Heinämaa, Sara. 2003. *Toward a Phenomenology of Sexual Difference: Husserl, Merleau-Ponty, Beauvoir.* Lanham, MD: Rowman & Littlefield.

Hollywood, Amy. 1994. "Beauvoir, Irigaray, and the Mystical," *Hypatia* 9 (4): 158–85.

Irigaray, Luce. 1993. *Sexes and Genealogies.* Trans. Gillian C. Gill. New York: Columbia University Press.

Jones, Serene. 1993. "This God Which Is Not One: Irigaray and Barth on the Divine." In *Transfigurations: Theology and the French Feminists,* ed. C. W. Maggie Kim, Susan M. St. Ville, and Susan M. Simonaitis. Minneapolis: Fortress. 109–42.

Joy, Morny. 1999. "Beyond the Given and the All-Giving: Reflections on Women and the Gift." *Australian Feminist Studies* 14 (30): 315–32.

Kojève, Alexandre. 1969. *Introduction to the Reading of Hegel.* Trans. James H. Nichols Jr. Ithaca, NY: Cornell University Press.

———. 1970. "Hegel, Marx, and Christianity." *Interpretation: A Journal of Political Philosophy* 1 (1): 21–42.

Kruks, Sonia. 1995. "Simone de Beauvoir: Teaching Sartre about Freedom." In *Feminist Interpretations of Simone de Beauvoir,* ed. Margaret A. Simons. University Park: Penn State University Press. 79–95.

Le Doeuff, Michèle. 1980. "Simone de Beauvoir and Existentialism." *Feminist Studies* 6 (2): 276–89.

———. 1991. *Hipparchia's Choice: An Essay Concerning Women, Philosophy, etc.* Trans. T. Selous. Oxford, UK: Blackwell.

Lévi-Strauss, Claude. 1969. *The Elementary Structures of Kinship.* Trans. James Harle Bell et al. Boston: Beacon Press.

Levinas, Emmanuel. 1987. *Time and the Other.* Trans. Richard A. Cohen. Pittsburgh: Duquesne University Press.

Lundgren-Gothlin, Eva. 1996. *Sex and Existence: Simone de Beauvoir's* The Second Sex. Trans. Linda Schenck. London: Athlone Press.

Mauss, Marcel. 1990. *The Gift: The Form and Reason for Exchange in Archaic Societies.* Trans. W. D. Halls. London: Routledge.

Nietzsche, Friedrich. 1968. *The Twilight of the Idols and The Anti-Christ.* Trans. R. J. Hollingdale. Harmondsworth, UK: Penguin.

———. 1974. *The Gay Science.* Trans. W. Kaufmann. New York: Vintage.

Priest, Ann-Marie. 2003. "Woman as God, God as Woman: Mysticism, Negative Theology, and Luce Irigaray." *Journal of Religion* 83 (1): 1–23.

Reed-Danahay, Deborah E. 1997. "Introduction." In *Auto/Ethnography: Rewriting the Self and the Social,* ed. Deborah E. Reed-Danahay. Oxford, UK: Berg.

Sartre, Jean-Paul. 1958. *Being and Nothingness.* Trans. Hazel Barnes. London: Methuen.

Strathern, Marilyn. 1987. "The Limits of Auto-Anthropology" In *Anthropology at Home,* ed. Anthony Jackson. London: Tavistock.

Taylor, Mark C. 1987. *Altarity.* Chicago: University of Chicago Press.

Theunissen, Michael. 1984. *The Other: Studies in the Social Ontology of Husserl, Heidegger, Sartre, and Buber.* Trans. Christopher Macann. Cambridge, MA: MIT Press.

Thornton, Stephen P. 1996. "Facing Up to Feuerbach." *International Journal for Philosophy of Religion* 39 (2): 103–20.

Williams, Robert R. 1992. "Sartre's Strange Appropriation of Hegel." *The Owl of Minerva* 23 (2): 5–14.

TEN

Women and the Gift: Speculations on the "Given" and the "All-Giving"

Morny Joy

Sexual relations between man and woman are an aspect of the total presta-
tions[1] of which marriage provides both an example and the occasion. . . . In the
total prestations of which woman is only a part, there is one category whose
fulfilment depends primarily on her good will, viz., personal services, whether
they be sexual or domestic. The lack of reciprocity which seems to characterize
these services in the Trobriand Islands, as in most human societies, is the mere
counterpart of a universal fact, that the relationship of reciprocity which is the
basis of marriage is not established between men and women, but between
men by means of women, who are merely the occasion of this relationship.
　　　—CLAUDE LÉVI-STRAUSS, *THE ELEMENTARY STRUCTURES OF KINSHIP*

In the couple sexuality finds its actualization, its realization, an in-itself and a
for-itself corresponding to the poles needed for the perfect incarnation of every
man and woman's humanity. The task is realized separately and together.
　　　　　　　—LUCE IRIGARAY, *I LOVE TO YOU*

Contemporary discussions of the gift, be they in secular or religious set-
tings, are entangled in an elaborate web of discourses, ranging from that of a
posited pre-market system of exchange (Mauss [1924] 1990, 26–42); to hal-
lowed invocations of gratuitous giving (Bataille 1985; Cixous 1986); to rhetor-
ical conundrums regarding its assumed definition (Derrida [1991] 1992) or to
mutually enhancing relations (Irigaray [1992] 1996). These discussions, from
a postcolonial perspective, entail a dubious agenda, inherited from earlier
anthropological exercises, where other peoples' cultures provided the occasion for confirming certain preconceptions or musings about alternative utopian scenarios.

Women, perfunctorily observed or idealized, have since figured in many male analyses of the phenomenon of the gift. Their status in most of these anthropological/sociological studies is one indicator of their own culture's received attitudes toward women. These theories thus reveal not just an insensitivity to other cultures, but an assumed superiority that has permitted western men predominantly to assume dominance over women in their own culture. In this context, the attributes of the "given" (as an involuntary offering) and the "all-giving" (as a voluntary, gratuitous action) were customary in religion and society as indicators of women's status. At the same time, these men have also pronounced on the status of women in other cultures in a universal fashion using the conventions of their own. Since the seventies, women anthropologists, such as Annette Weiner (1976, 1992), Eleanor Leacock (1981), and Marilyn Strathern (1988), have disputed these misinterpretations. Certain other contemporary women theorists, such as Hélène Cixous and Clément (1986) and Luce Irigaray ([1974] 1985a, [1978] 1985c), have also attempted to rebut the prevailing tendencies and provide alternative theories regarding women. There is, however, a danger that these women theorists could fall into similar colonializing or essentialist pitfalls as did the male scholars. In a feminist, postmodern, and postcolonial setting, perhaps the only way to approach the topic of the gift is to examine some of the exegetical burdens it has borne, and continues to bear, concerning the situation of women, while also exploring alternative possibilities.

It could be said that any discussion of the gift in contemporary western scholarship reveals the predicament that continues to ensnare anyone who approaches it—entangled as it is with the baggage of colonialist attitudes that can further implicate even those who attempt to provide a different model.[2] I intend to orient the discussion in this chapter with reference to the relation of women to definitions of the gift, especially the two predominant ideas regarding their status as either "given" or "all-giving."[3]

PREOCCUPATIONS WITH THE GIFT

Perhaps the most influential study of the twentieth century about the gift, and the impetus for much recent theorizing, is the sociologist Marcel Mauss's small volume, *The Gift* (Mauss [1924] 1990), which was informed by his readings of anthropologist Franz Boas's *On the North-Western Tribes of Canada* ([1894] 1981) and *Kwakiutl Ethnography* (1966), as well as of Malinowski's *Argonauts of the Western Pacific* (1922). In both the Kwakiutl potlatch (Boas)[4] and the Melanesian *kula* ring (Malinowski),[5] Mauss detected an elaborate and delicate balance of giving, receiving, and repayment which sustained a religious dimension that was interconnected to the social, political, and economic domains. Mauss was fascinated by these pre-monetary systems of exchange, but his work did not remain simply on the level of a theoretical analysis. He extolled the communal aspect involved, as opposed to the utilitarian and individualistic interests he felt dominated contemporary western commercial transactions. In his "Moral Conclusions," Mauss ends with an endorsement of this "archaic" economy as inculcating a generous disposition that is "less sad, less serious, less miserly and less personal than we are" (Mauss [1924] 1990, 104), as well as less predisposed to war. "It is by opposing reason to feeling, by pitting the will to peace against sudden outbursts of insanity of this kind that peoples succeed in substituting alliance, gifts, and trade for wars, isolation and stagnation" (Mauss [1924] 1990, 105).

While this is a generous endorsement, such a retrospective projection reflected more Mauss's own preoccupations at the time of writing in post–World War I Europe than a critical evaluation of the actual data. Contemporary reservations about such interpretations, especially regarding the definition of potlatch, have been expressed by the scholar of religion Jonathan Z. Smith:

> The problem for me, and I've taught three courses where we read potlatch material, has to do with the ethnography and the category. . . . What's happened is that the opportunity to go back to Boas' notes at Columbia and see what he wrote, as opposed to what he thought he wrote twenty years later, has had the result that the Kwakiutl turn out no longer to have a potlatch. (Smith 1987, 214–15)

Apart from registering this sobering observation, it is beyond the scope of this essay to undertake a thorough investigation of the reliability of the original data concerned with potlatch itself.[6] But Smith's words indicate that a major revision of all such imposed categories is imperative. A beginning has been made in the important study by Christopher Bracken, *The Potlatch Papers: A Colonial Case History* (1997).[7]

In the last thirty years, feminist anthropologists have also been attempting to rectify the misguided and erroneous evaluation of women's position in the work of Boas and Malinowski, particularly regarding the latter's statements regarding women's lack of significant power. Annette Weiner, in her own study of Trobriand society, has challenged such conjectures:

> Beyond the ethnographic data, however, the "discovery" that Trobriand women have power and that women enact roles which are symbolically,

structurally, and functionally significant to the ordering of Trobriand society, and to the roles that men play, should give us, as anthropologists, cause
for concern . . . [W]e have accepted almost without question the nineteenth
century Western legacy that had effectively segregated women from positions of power . . . [W]e have led ourselves to believe that, if women are not
dominant in the political sphere of interaction, their power remains at best
peripheral. (Weiner 1976, 228)

Weiner's findings regarding the work of women in the Trobriand society,
where they do exercise power within a mutually reinforcing network (that is,
a wider cultural configuration that includes not just men, but crucial issues of
regeneration and immortality), puts into question in a radical way the work
of Mauss, as well as the more contemporary discussions by non-anthropol-
ogists, such as Jacques Derrida and Georges Bataille, on the status of the gift
and its connection to women.[8]

Although Mauss does not add any of his own theoretical elaboration to
earlier observations from the field by Boas and Malinowski regarding wom-
en's role, he is content to replicate their findings: "All these institutions express
one fact alone, one social system, one precise state of mind: everything—food,
women, children, property, talismans, land, labour services, priestly functions,
and ranks—is there for passing on, and for balancing accounts" (Mauss [1924]
1990, 18). There does not appear to be any independent status for women.
Lévi-Strauss's position is similar to that of Mauss, in that he generalizes from
Malinowski's Trobriand work on the *kula* ring. However, he does make an
addition by positing that the commercial exchange of women is fundamental
to the functioning of incest prohibition. "The prohibition of incest is less a rule
prohibiting marriage with the mother, sister or daughter, than a rule obliging
the mother, sister or daughter to be given to others. It is the supreme rule of
the gift, and it is clearly in this aspect, too often unrecognized, which allows
its nature to be understood" (Lévi-Strauss [1949] 1969, 481).

The unfortunate fact is that Malinowski, Mauss, and Lévi-Strauss were
all influenced by Durkheim's model of a sacred and profane dichotomy. As
women were regarded as profane, they were deemed as not meriting serious
study.[9] Thus, in the work of these social scientists and that of recent theorists
of the gift, there is an obvious additional layer of personal embellishment that
has been identified by Weiner in the anthropological records:

If we return for a moment to the anthropologists who have devised theories
about exchange, we find an interesting series of dependencies. The Trobriand
informants who say they exchange for "love" or "generosity" are following a

myth that serves their society to hide a reality of self-interest. The anthropologist who then insists on labeling this act as a "gift" seems to be perpetuating the Trobriand natives' myth. But this is probably only incidental to what she or he is doing. In weaving the "gift" myth, is not the anthropologist hiding a reality that concerns *his* or *her* role in *his* or *her* society? Is he or she not perpetuating and creating an image of "the primitive" as a person, or "primitive society" as a way of life, that has survived on some fundamental principle *other than self-interest*? (Weiner 1976, 221)

It is in this connection that the warning of the anthropologist Marilyn Strathern is particularly relevant as she is addressing certain feminist extrapolations which, similarly to those of the male theorists, do not take into consideration the original cultural context of the gift:

> The difference between Western and Melanesian (we/they) sociality means that one cannot simply extend Western feminist insights to the Melanesian case; the difference between anthropological/feminist viewpoints means that the knowledge anthropologists construct of Melanesia is not to be taken for granted; the difference between gift/commodity is expanded as a metaphorical base on which difference itself may be apprehended and put to use for both anthropologist and feminist purposes, yet remains rooted in Western metaphysics. (Strathern 1988, 7)

It is from this perspective that the work of both Luce Irigaray and Hélène Cixous needs to be considered carefully. While they are both critical of the male-centered adaptations of the gift and of Western metaphysics, their own work can also seem circumscribed at times by the same western shortcomings to which they are reacting. In their own different deliberations, regarding women and the gift, although they contest the ideas of Mauss, Lévi-Strauss, and Bataille, they do not interrogate the colonial attitudes involved. Yet a discriminating cultural critique as well as self-reflexive stance would seem to be a necessary element in any contemporary discussion of the gift. Thus far, however, these elements have been lacking in current western preoccupations with revisions of the nature of the gift.

THE GIVEN

It is against this backdrop that I would like to take up Irigaray's indictment of certain western male formulations of the gift. When Irigaray refers to Lévi-Strauss, in particular in "Women on the Market" (Irigaray [1978] 1985c), she details the exploitation of women whom she describes as providing the unacknowledged infrastructure of the entire sociocultural-economic apparatus of patriarchy. Though she specifically faults Lévi-Strauss, Irigaray views the problem simply as indicative of an ingrained masculine disposition of control.

> Why exchange women? Because they are "scarce [commodities] . . . essential to the life of the group," the anthropologist [Lévi-Strauss] tells us. Why this characteristic of scarcity, given the biological equilibrium between male and female births? Because the "deep polygamous tendency," which exists among all men, always makes the number of available women seem insufficient. (Irigaray [1978] 1985c, 170)

Irigaray understands this situation as symptomatic of "History" and of other social structures with their male-centered system that inscribes the exploitation of women.

> All the social regimes of "History" are based upon the exploitation of one "class" of producers, namely women. Their reproductive use value (reproductive of children and of the labor force) and their constitution as exchange value underwrite the symbolic order as such, without any compensation in kind going to them for that "work." (Irigaray [1978] 1985c, 173; translation modified)

Though Irigaray's criticism of Lévi-Strauss's descriptions of women may be on target, her universal assumption that this is the same case in all varieties of cultures—that women have been alienated from their own "labor" and valued only as (re-)productive cogs in a workforce controlled by men—is suspect. It is particularly problematic in the light of Weiner's research. In contrast to Irigaray's generalized description, Weiner describes a society where women exert control over a sphere, both material and spiritual, upon which no man may encroach. Such women's work also provides a necessary complementarity as central to the maintenance of society. Weiner's evaluation that "the female domain, the regenesis of human life, is accorded primary value" (Weiner 1976, 234) makes the automatic assignation of women to secondary status, as a passive token of exchange, appear simplistic and condescending. It also indicates a troublesome element in Irigaray's position in that as she takes male scholars at their word and does not investigate further the accuracy of their findings, especially in the light of women anthropologists' findings. Irigaray's position is dependent on her appreciation of all women/mothers as the repressed element that sustains the patriarchal order. Accordingly, she deems that all women's service is in the thrall of the Phallus/Father/God and does not consider that there may be exceptions (Irigaray [1974] 1985a, 42, 359–60).[10]

Irigaray's position is also at odds with the work of anthropologist Eleanor Leacock, who specifically takes Lévi-Strauss to task for the omission in his work of matrilineal societies, such as the Iroquois. Leacock states that Lévi-Strauss would have been aware of these societies but chose to ignore them.

> The stubborn fact remains that even in its own terms Lévi-Strauss's entire scheme founders on those societies that are matrilineal . . . and matrilocal.
> . . . It is therefore not surprising that in the space of a page and a half in *The Elementary Structures of Kinship,* there are four (incorrect) statements about such forms as extremely rare and transitory (116–17). (Leacock 1981, 235)

Perhaps a more thorough questioning by Irigaray of the implicit western orientation involved in the work of male anthropologists such as Lévi-Strauss would have revealed a far more complex set of assumptions at work. These would have significance not just for the interpretation of Melanesian society, but of other peoples where women have negotiated and do negotiate their social standing from positions of influence (Etienne and Leacock 1980). In this way Eurocentric blind spots and their imperialistic bias could be revealed.

THE ALL-GIVING AND THE ULTIMATE GIFT-SACRIFICE

Another problematic aspect of women's situation was also prompted by Mauss's reflections on the gift. This arose from the fact that there is an ambivalent agenda in Mauss's account between the description of economic and social system of checks and balances that regulates the gift, and his elaboration of an impulse to make an unreserved offering. This impulse was assigned by Mauss to the place of sacrifice within a masculine economy.

The connection of exchange contracts among men with those between men and gods explains a certain aspect of the theory of sacrifice. It is best seen in those societies where contractual and economic ritual is practiced by men. According to Mauss, this occurs mainly when men, as masked incarnations in shamanistic rituals, are possessed by the spirit whose name they bear. They here act as representatives of the spirits. In this case the exchanges and contracts concern not only men and things, but also the sacred beings that are associated with them (Mauss 1990, 13). It would seem that the only way

Mauss could accommodate the profligate waste and destruction of a potlatch was by associating it with a religious realm of sacrifice.

> Sacrificial destruction implies giving something that is to be repaid. . . . It is not simply to show power and wealth and unselfishness that a man puts his slaves to death, burns his precious oil, throws coppers into the sea, and sets his house on fire. In doing this he is also sacrificing to the gods and spirits, who appear incarnate in the men who are at once their namesakes and ritual allies. (Mauss 1990, 14)

Mauss did not expand in any detail on the spiritual underpinnings of this sacrificial impulse—but he located them within a dynamic of an anticipated divine recompense, with an added incentive of divine protection from covetous evil spirits. The work of René Girard (1979) was strongly influenced by this interpretation of Mauss of an extreme notion of the gift as sacrifice. Irigaray, in "Women, the Sacred and Money" ([1984] 1993b), is extremely critical of Girard's interpretation. Girard's work acknowledges an original human propensity to ward off the potential malevolence of deistic figures and spirits by sacrifice. He is more interested, however, in embellishing this rudimentary gesture of placation by locating the beginnings of a religious sacrificial impulse in more complex motivations.

In Girard's reading of a primal act of violence, it is not guilt or appeasement for the murder of the father (which would imply some sort of compensatory ritual and gift), as in *Totem and Taboo* (Freud 1918), that instigates an immemorial compensatory gesture. Girard locates the origin of this impulse in what he posits as a desire for the fullness of being. Yet this desire does not seem to be satisfied by basic moves of auto-affection. Instead, the subject's desire becomes fixated on another, who seemingly manifests the plenitude that the subject is lacking. Such fixation on another and the cupidity of another's goods instigates a form of mimetic behavior. Unfortunately, this desire can escalate out of proportion, unless it is contained by the sacrifice of a substitute figure—the scapegoat—which defuses the situation.[11] As with Freud, this archaic projection would seem an implausible explanation on many counts (Frear 1992).

In Girard's script, however, in contrast to Freud's conclusions, which concern the repetition compulsion of religion, there is the intervention of the Christ figure, the ultimate innocent victim. Christ inverts and revolutionizes the established order by revealing the mercenary machinations involved in all former sacrifices. Christ thus alters the violent inauguration of religion forever. Girard's theories, however, as those of the previously mentioned male anthropologists, exhibit a distinct bias in favor of male behavior, which is the basis for Irigaray's criticism. Not once does he refer to women's participation (or lack of it) in this ritual of immolation—except for a casual, even dismissive reference to Dionysian maenads. In addition, Girard is not concerned with non-western practices, and his work as it progresses becomes a vindication of Christianity.[12]

In her reaction to Girard, Luce Irigaray ([1984] 1993b, 73–88) does not remark on this theory as being in any way an exceptional case, for she regards it as simply one more illustration of the disregard or suppression by men of the female of the species—both theoretically and/or practically. In the context of sacrifice, however, Irigaray is especially concerned to stress that beneath Girard's speculations regarding the scapegoat figure—the sacrifice of whom restores equilibrium—there is another unacknowledged victim: woman. This female figure does not feature as an overt offering on an altar, but as a victim of covert deprivation and denial. Her flesh, her integrity, her special place in the social order are all effaced by man's emphasis on his gender's role not just as primordial in the religious, but also in the social scheme of things.

In this connection, Irigaray also makes another observation of profound significance with regard to the institution of sacrifice—and, in this particular instance, her insight is incisive with reference to western religions. Irigaray reports that women have rarely, if ever, been involved in either the preliminary protocols of sacrifice, or in its public rituals, even in their contemporary "tamed" versions.

> One other thing is obvious: in the religions of sacrifice, religious and social *ceremonies are almost universally performed by men.* Men alone perform the rite, not women or children (though male children can sometimes act as acolytes). Women have no right to officiate in public worship in most traditions, even though that worship serves as the basis and structure for the society. (Irigaray [1984] 1993a, 78)

A similar judgment has also been made by Nancy Jay in the conclusion of her detailed study of numerous sacrificially oriented societies: *Throughout Your Generations Forever: Sacrifice, Religion and Paternity* (Jay 1992). Jay's conclusions are even more specific than Irigaray's:

> Sacrifice may be performed for many reasons. But it is beautifully adapted for integrating patrilineal descent groups, a goal that can only be accomplished by differentiation from all other lines of descent. Sacrifice can both expiate descent from women (along with other dangers) and integrate the

"pure and eternal patrilineage. . . . There is necessarily an either- or about lineage membership (members must be distinguished from non-members), and for patrilineages this either/or requires transcending descent from women. This is one way to understand why child bearing women must not sacrifice and also why the pollution of childbirth so commonly needs to be expiated sacrificially." (Jay 1985, 296–97)

Both Jay and Irigaray see these rubrics governing sacrifice as still alive and well today, with Jay in particular analyzing the controversies concerning contemporary women's ordination:

> In the sacrificing churches, resistance to ordination of women is not just psychological. . . . Both sides of the controversy over women's ordination appear to share an understanding with sacrificing patrilineage members around the world: recognition of the power of sacrifice as a ritual instrument for establishing and maintaining an enduring male-dominated social order. (Jay 1985, 304)

While initially such statements by Irigaray and Jay might seem somewhat simplistic in their explanatory power, they nonetheless strike a chord with many women who have struggled against what seem to be inflexible and insuperable obstacles in their quest to become ordained priests, ministers, or rabbis in contemporary religious institutions. In many ways the above pronouncements might seem a digression from the normal ritual observances of the gift—but it can be argued that, from a religious perspective, sacrifice is perhaps regarded as the most highly esteemed prototype of the gift. Basically, it would seem that many of the mechanisms involved in sacrifice, particularly their symbolic remnants in most western religions, are geared to guard the boundaries within which the requisite public, male-dominated rituals can be observed. As a result, the fact that women are placed externally to the exercise of such power, rather than acting as ritual specialists, could then appear to depend on a deep-rooted and unconscious prejudice. Aspects of this systematic exclusion, which has been thoroughly investigated in Mary Douglas's work *Purity and Danger* (1966), posits the bifurcation of purity and danger, sacred and profane, culture and nature. In both the theoretical and the practical applications of this binary division to male and female, as evident in the work of western female scholars, women have tended to be identified with the less valued side of the pair. Irigaray argues that societies that operate according to this system, with its denigration and effacement of women, need to become aware of the psychological roots of this foundational sacrifice rather than continue to repeat their self-protective rituals.

Another example of such extravagant gestures of substitution can be found in the work of Georges Bataille, who also read Mauss's analysis of the gift. Bataille proposes a model of giving that, as unconstrained largesse, he pronounces as characteristic of women: "To give is the fundamental feminine attitude" (Bataille [1957] 1987, 127). This unconditional abundance as *dépense* (expenditure) is Bataille's revision of what he viewed as Mauss's theoretical domestication of the profligate waste evident in Boas's description of potlatch celebrations. Bataille was concerned that any emphasis on the value of objects of exchange weakened the energy he felt was at the core of a needed or even natural process of reckless abandon. This process, according to Bataille, did not reckon on reciprocity, but operated according to a communal "logic" of immediate and immoderate consumption. In such a transgressive economy, it was not simply the civilized (that is, bourgeois) or utilitarian value of objects that Bataille wished primarily to counter. Instead, he wanted to (re)introduce a worldview, untarnished by rational calculations, where an economy of superabundance—be it in its rituals of sacrifice, in its squandering of riches, or in its dissolution of assets—witnesses to a sacred universe.

This sacred reality has nothing to do with the orthodoxies of organized religion, which Bataille designates as profane. For Bataille, religion, specifically Christianity, has eradicated the innate human propensity for sacrality by the imposition of categories which deny the superabundant energy that Bataille considers the essence of life. Doctrines such as salvation and original sin are the antithesis of transgression—which, according to Bataille, is the movement of this exorbitant expenditure, a cathartic expression of a natural surplus of energy that challenges the confining calculations of religion and society.

Eroticism will play a central role in Bataille's approach. He has read Lévi-Strauss, and he laments the fact that Lévi-Strauss did not make any connection between the exchange of women and eroticism (Guerlac 1990, 101). Eroticism and the role of women are central motifs in Bataille's exposition of transgression. Michael Richardson depicts this relation: "Eroticism serves the purposes of love; it is an explosion, a bursting of life, and it needs to be returned to its rightful place, which lies at the heart of the sacred. It represents both a mediation point between ourselves and the forces of nature and at the same time both differentiates as well as emphasizing our essential unity" (Richardson 1994, 109).

The essential link, however, that conjoins eroticism and woman is one that inevitably involves sacrifice—a phenomenon which Bataille invested with the most intense release of both violence and dread, yet which, at the same time, affirmed the essential sacred nature of life. As Bataille asserts in his essay "Hegel, Death and Sacrifice": "It must be said too that sacrifice, like tragedy, was an element of a celebration; it bespoke a blind, pernicious joy and all the danger of that joy, and yet this is precisely the principle of *human joy*; it wears out and threatens with death all who get caught up in its movement" (Bataille 1990, 23). This seeming paradox, of death as the ultimate exaltation of life, is the vindication of *dépense,* the ecstatic testimony of transgression, the defiant act contra all profane and homogenized religion. It is a gesture that, for Bataille, is made in the name of that unfathomable and dangerous abyss that undermines all systems that ensure security. "It is the common business of sacrifice to bring life and death into harmony, to give death the upsurge of life, life the momentousness and the vertigo of death opening onto the unknown" (Bataille [1957] 1987, 91).

It is important to stress, however, that though there has been reference to Bataille wishing to undertake an actual human sacrifice under the auspices of the group Acéphale (Richardson 1994, 116–17), and though he has stated, "Violence alone can burst the barriers of the rational world" (Bataille [1957] 1987, 54), Bataille's relation to sacrifice is primarily one of allegiance to abstract heterogeneous forces that sabotage what he considers the staid and sanctimonious, the acquisitive orientation of regulated societies. "Sacrifice is the antithesis of production, which is accomplished with a view to the future; it is consumption that is concerned only with the moment" (Bataille [1973] 1992, 49).

Yet though sacrifice is extolled, Bataille's version would seem to have one major drawback. This is because, in the sacrificial act of sexuality, it is the woman who has the dubious honor of being the victim par excellence: "The lover strips bare the beloved of her identity no less than the blood-stained priest his human or animal victim. The woman in the hands of her assailant is despoiled of her being" (Bataille [1957] 1987, 90). Though Irigaray does not address Bataille specifically, she would certainly view his formulation as not transgressive, but as simply one more manifestation of the sacrificial exploitation of women. Bataille's excess can thus be understood as just another instance of conduct responsible for maintaining a male-centered system, particularly that of a quasi-religious nature—be it sacred or profane. Irigaray deems this a very suspect foundation. "Clearly, religion is a figure for a social universe organized by men. But this organization is founded upon a sacrifice of nature, of the sexed body, especially of women. It imposes a spirituality that has been cut off from its roots in the natural environment. Thus it cannot fulfill humanity" (Irigaray [1984] 1993b, 191). It is for this reason that Irigaray believes that religion itself needs a drastic overhaul, because as she observes:

"[R]eligious structures, categories, initiations, rules, and utopias, all . . . have been masculine for centuries" (Irigaray [1984] 1993a, 75).

While Irigaray would not appreciate his motives, it is perhaps important to stress that the abasement of women is, ironically, a position of honor for Bataille in his conception of the sacred. It is a positive dereliction for women insofar as she exemplifies the ultimate *offering*—annihilation of her being as the perfect token of communion, of giving. It needs also to be acknowledged that, in this sublime sacrifice, the sacrificer also abandons himself. Both participants are ecstatic violators of the limit. For Bataille this inaugurates a Nietzschean moment—a joyous affirmation of life in death, achieved by risking everything in defying all conventions/limits. Yet there are certain problems of both appropriation and projection in this process. The woman remains at the mercy of the desires of man. The male sacrificer is the agent of her "salvation":

> *Intimately,* I belong to the sovereign world of gods and myths, to the world of violent and uncalculated generosity, just as my wife belongs to my desires. I withdraw you, victim, from the world in which you were and could only be reduced to the condition of a thing having a meaning that was foreign to your intimate nature. I call you back to the intimacy of the divine world, of the profound *immanence* of all that is. (Bataille [1973] 1992, 44)

Michele Richman succinctly indicates the role of woman as both given and all-giving in the context of Bataille's elaborations on Mauss's *The Gift*:

> Generosity flows not just from the father who makes the gift of his daughter to the community; the real don [sic] is the gift a woman makes of herself. By turning to eroticism as the form of *dépense* most accessible in contemporary society, Bataille focuses on what appears as the greater potential for erotic exuberance among women. (Richman 1982, 81)

She then continues, raising perhaps the most contentious item in Bataille's approach: "The possible relation of their [women's] transgressive sexuality to the position ascribed them in the exchange system of patriarchal society is never explicitly considered" (81). Bataille's idealized portrayal of women as beneficent, to the point of immolation, ultimately projects a fantasy that takes women's exploitation for granted. Yet he will venture even further. In another essay, "The Notion of Expenditure" (1985), Bataille draws attention to the figure of the prostitute as the ultimate representative of a mode of gratuitous expenditure. The irony of this exaltation, from a contemporary position, is that, if there was ever a woman held in the subjection of societal forces beyond her control (both symbolic and material), no matter the extent of her exuberance or dedication to the moment, it is the figure of the prostitute. Transgressive though she may be, such procurement of women sustains, if not contributes directly to, the maintenance of the system of capitalistic extortion that Bataille wishes to subvert.

And so it is that for Bataille, as for Mauss and Lévi-Strauss, the blind spot in the old dream of symmetry distorts not just men's attempts to define the operations of a society, but their experiments that seek to express an idealized divergent order. This occurs despite Bataille's resistance to Lévi-Strauss's structuralist commodification of women, although he acknowledges his accomplishment in discerning the relationship between the incest taboo and the requisite structures of exchange of women. Bataille himself appears to be caught within that same binary mode that pervaded Lévi-Strauss's work—particularly that of the sacred and profane. This is evident especially when he glorifies (fetishizes) women in what amounts to a caricature of erotic excess that is inevitably both masochistic and self-destructive.

Bataille thus mobilizes the figure of woman to conform with his own romantic projections. In addition, his observations on the gift, in the same manner as Mauss and Lévi-Strauss, demonstrate a tenuous relation to the primary anthropological data—already distorted by the lens of western colonial perspectives. Nor does Bataille's work seem to be related to the lives of actual women in any of the societies studied. Yet it is this trajectory of the gift and its questionable connection to women themselves, so indicative of Eurocentric self-preoccupations, that still continues to exercise a perverse fascination for many western thinkers.

It could also be argued that Derrida's various recent extrapolations proclaiming the paradox of the gift were initiated by his encounter with the enigma of woman—by way of Nietzsche and Bataille (Derrida [1991] 1992).[13] Derrida's first foray into this troubled area finds its most striking expression in his indeterminate explorations of the idea of women in *Spurs*: "Either, at times, woman is woman because she gives, *because she gives herself,* while the man for his part takes, possesses, indeed takes possession. Or else, at the other times, she is woman because, in giving, she is in fact *giving herself for,* is simulating, and consequently assuring the possessive mastery for herself" (Derrida [1978] 1979, 109). Here woman is cast as a conundrum, but either way she is a male construct rather than a being who is responsible for her own actions. While it could be argued that Derrida, in this earlier excursion regarding the feminine and *différance,* does attempt to locate woman as an indefinable deconstructive element—thus disturbing the binary logic of a male-determined economy, metaphysical or otherwise—there is also an implicit appeal, à la Bataille, to a wild, transgressive element. This suggests that for Derrida not only do women simply escape definition, but they surpass the constricted circumstances dictated by customary meanings and structures. In a later evocation of women, in *Given Time* ([1991] 1992), there is further equivocation as Derrida attempts to situate the figure of woman (herself an anomaly) with reference to the somewhat checkered history of more recent interpretations of the gift. Yet all of this equivocation has led to charges by contemporary feminist theorists that men continue to assign them to theoretical position(s), without consultation. Or, as Rosi Braidotti has so astutely observed:

> Why do men, when their system appears on the brink of collapse, appeal to the "feminine," as emblematic of a force, external to their system, which may provide a viable alternative? The ultimate irony is that this "feminine" has no relation whatsoever to flesh and blood women. (Braidotti 1994, 124)

It would seem that the time has come for women to reclaim the right to make their own statements of their relation to the gift.

CREATIVE RESPONSES

In recent years, women thinkers have indeed taken it upon themselves to present their own understandings of the role of women and the gift. The early work of Luce Irigaray, with her use of the term "*jouissance,*"[14] and of Hélène Cixous, with her deployment of the term "*l'écriture féminine,*"[15] demonstrate that these French women thinkers were both disposed to the notion of "woman" as a term that eluded, in its expansiveness, "phallogocentric" confinement/repression. Both waxed lyrical, in a quasi-deconstructive style, about the possibilities of female recalcitrance to control and the exorbitance of female sexuality. Cixous rejected the debased form of giving that has been exploited by men in the past, citing as counter-examples women, such as the figure of Ariadne, who live "without calculating, without hesitating, but believing, taking everything as far as it goes, giving everything, renouncing all security" (Cixous 1986, 75). Cixous thus believes that there is a form of female economy that can be distinguished from that of the male. In this capacity, Cixous appreciates that it is possible for a woman to still give of herself endlessly and without reserve, but, in this refashioned model, she is never taken advantage of, nor desecrated.

If there is a self proper to women, paradoxically, it is her capacity to depropriate herself without self-interest: endless body, without "end," without principal "parts"; if she is a whole, it is a whole made up of parts that are whole, not simple, partial objects but varied entirety, moving and boundless change, a cosmos where eros never stops travelling, vast astral space. (Cixous 1986, 87)

This idealized heterogeneous female economy does not count the gains to be made, does not calculate the dividend. Yet while Cixous's vocabulary of extravagance is reminiscent of the prodigality recommended by Bataille, in this case there is no need for compensation. But is there nonetheless a cost involved? It would seem that such utopian alternatives are in need of extremely careful scrutiny by women before they are adopted today. Otherwise women could easily find themselves squandering their precious resources, and being expropriated to serve the ends of the capitalistic system. This system continues to operate so that, while paying lip service to a new nomenclature of free market, it simply conducts its coemptive business as usual.

Irigaray, at once influenced by, yet critical of, both Lacan and Derrida, sought initially to affirm *jouissance* as a mode of access to the Real (that dimension of reality beyond conscious control or coherent expression) which escapes representation, but which also provides a disruptive energy to undermine the patriarchal symbolic system:

Turn everything upside down, inside out, back to front. *Rack it with radical convulsions,* carry back, reimport, those crises that her "body" suffers in her impotence to say what disturbs her . . . Not by means of a growing complexity of the same, of course, but by the irruption of other circuits, by the intervention at times of short-circuits that will disperse, diffract, deflect endlessly, making energy explode sometimes, with no possibility of returning to one single origin. (Irigaray [1974] 1985a, 142)

These various images of refractory activity were galvanized in Irigaray's own work in the service of dismantling the foundations of a monolithic philosophical/religious and social order, but there seemed something awry in these appeals to complete destruction in the name of infinite possibility. In the same way that Cixous's "giving without reserve" could easily be co-opted into the service of the exploitative structures, Irigaray's dispersions initially seemed to run a similar risk of playing into the hands of established structures that could reclaim women's alleged natural gratuitousness for their own benefit.[16] The questions need to be asked: To whom, and for what purpose, does woman give? Does excess necessarily work in the service of women themselves? The figure of woman, exulting in her hypothetical status as totally removed from the existing system, may not necessarily be in control of the exploitative maneuvres that could inevitably consume her.

There is, however, a change in the direction of Irigaray's work from approximately the time of her essay "The Universal as Meditation" ([1984] 1993a), when she began to reflect on the work of Hegel and propose a new understanding of the negative phase of the dialectic. Irigaray, in her assessment of both western philosophy and religion, concluded that she could not find in their constructs the resources that would assist her in formulating a version of the negative that did not demean women. She began to seek a position that would not simply be a reactive move within a restrictive dialectic: "If neither absolute spirit nor the traditional western monotheistic God seem to be the paths of a becoming, how can we ensure that the negative does not entail martyrdom?" (Irigaray [1992] 1996, 13). Irigaray does not wish to remain with fixated categories of a Hegelian dialectic and the realm of Absolute Being as she pursues an appreciation of the divine that is manifested in a process of becoming. This process both acknowledges women in their own right and facilitates relationships with men. In contrast to Hegel, she wants to reconceive the negative so that any encounter with difference will be based on a recognition of the other that confirms a person in his or her utter alterity (Irigaray [1992] 1996, 103). This is a rejection of the previous Hegelian rules of exchange, from "the sacrifice of sexed identity to a universal defined by man with death as its master" (Irigaray [1992] 1996, 26). To achieve this, Irigaray states that:

> She [woman] should not comply with a model of identity imposed upon her by anyone, neither [by] her parents, her lover, her children, the State, religion or culture in general. That does not mean she can lapse into capriciousness, dispersion, the multiplicity of her desires, or a loss of identity. She should, quite the contrary, gather herself within herself in order to accomplish her gender's perfection for herself, for the man she loves, for her children, but equally for civil society, for the world of culture, for a definition of the universal correspondence, to reality. (Irigaray [1992] 1996, 27)

Irigaray's reworking of Hegel is a complex project, especially her reconfiguration of the dialectic with reference not just to woman herself but to the relation between women and men.[17] In their respective ways, Irigaray and Bataille are both preoccupied with the consequences of Hegel's dialectic, principally as it was expressed in Alexandre Kojève's more anthropological and Marxist interpretation of the master/slave relationship (Kojève [1947] 1969).[18] Bataille's work is in so many ways a gesture of defiance against what Jean-Michel Besnier terms "the tortures of negativity without a cause" (Besnier 1995, 21). In his florid execrations, Bataille rails against the regimes of reason and profane (that is, orthodox) religion. For Bataille, Hegel's mode of negativity, as the mode of mediation which brings about reflexive consciousness, leads to a triumph of rationality, and thus enacts a provisional death, a deformed sacrifice that is in the service of morality. Bataille spurns this moribund mechanism and proposes his own exaltation of sacrifice, mysticism, eroticism. In this context, otherness/negativity is not only subsumed without remainder, but an unfettered energy is also generated. Despite Bataille's efforts, this vindication, as described earlier, remains circumscribed by the terms of the system it seeks to surpass. Separation still dominates. So, despite the pleasures of sexual abandon, there remains a sacrificer and a victim. There is never a mutual recognition or return that rejects a oppositional relationship. Thus Bataille, in seeking an alternative to Hegel, seems to conclude by consolidating the very dialectic he seeks to dismantle.

Irigaray, on the other hand, seeking to renegotiate Hegel, intends to turn "the negative, that is, the limit of one gender in relation to the other, into a possibility of love and creation" (Irigaray [1992] 1996, 11). She wants to rethink the dialectic structure and its engagement with negativity. To do this, she takes the relationship of the human couple as her ideal model. There are many who, in these days of sophisticated and complex theories of gender-bending, find this exemplar of heterosexuality something of a sentimental, if not retrogressive, step, particularly with its refusal to acknowledge lesbian couples as being of comparable worth (Irigaray [1992] 1996, 3). Irigaray's rejoinder to this objection is to state that she is striving to reverse the predominant western dynamic that has theoretically and practically (as evidenced in the work of Mauss, Lévi-Strauss, Girard, and Bataille) tended to relegate women to the expendable element (no matter how glorious her end) in a sacrificial economy. Irigaray's vision, in contrast, is one that proposes a mode of recognition where the absolute otherness of each partner is affirmed. She also believes that this requires another level of consciousness and of communication. This alone can effect a transformation of the current soulless standard model. Irigaray describes the terms of this vital encounter:

> It would entail, beyond the enslavement to property, beyond the subject's submission to the object (which does not mean to objectivity), becoming capable of giving and receiving, of being active and passive, of having an intention

that stays attuned to interactions, that is, of seeking a new economy of existence or being which is neither that of mastery nor that of slavery but rather of exchange with no preconstituted object—vital exchange . . . an exchange thus able to *communicate* at times, commune . . . beyond any exchange of objects. (Irigaray [1992] 1996, 45)

In response to Bataille's profligacy, Irigaray also wants to move beyond "instinctive expenditure" (Irigaray [1992] 1996, 138). But for such a vital exchange, a woman has first to come into her own, and realize her own version of Hegel's universal. "I have to realize myself as what and who I am: a woman. This woman I am has to realize the female as universal" (Irigaray [1992] 1996, 144–45). This realization of the universal will encourage women's autonomy so that they need not be determined by external forces, but will act as their own agents in relationships. Essential to her process of reform is a return, a *récueillement,* which has novel implications for the Hegelian phase of recognition.[19] This *récueillement,* on the part of a woman, involves a self-reflexive discipline—of both mind and body, and that has definite spiritual overtones—whereby one evaluates one's socialization as a dependent being. In this way, a woman can achieve a realization of her own integrity. Only by attaining this insight can one recognize the other as a person who is entitled to remain an "other" and who must not be assimilated. Negativity from this perspective does not automatically entail appropriation. As a result, an exchange without absolutes or teleological designs can occur. There is a constant process of becoming where the other is encountered in a space of respect and recognition that fosters mutual integrity and fecundity.

The interdependency of the two subjects in such a relationship is one where neither is an object—according to the existing formulas entailed in commercial transactions. It involves instead a manner of living so as to enhance difference, of which, for Irigaray, the most important form is that of sexual difference.

Interdependency between subjects is no longer reduced to questions of possessing, of exchanging or sharing objects, cash, or an already existing meaning. It is, rather, regulated by the constitution of subjectivity. The subject does not vest its own value in any form of property whatsoever. No longer is it objecthood, having or the cost of having that governs the becoming of a subject or subjects or the relation among them. They are engaged in a relationship from which they emerge altered, the objective being the accomplishment of their subjectivity while remaining faithful to their nature. (Irigaray [1992] 1996, 127)

There are certain problems with Irigaray's postulate of sexual difference, and with her assertion that there exists a separate natural or ontological identity of both women and men, which I have reviewed elsewhere.[20] My intention in this chapter, however, is more to explain Irigaray's fruitful criticism of the way that notions of the gift have been designated so as to subordinate women. I believe that her recasting of the process of recognition can be understood as accepting the absolute integrity of any "other" without necessarily invoking naturalistic appeals to "feminine" or "masculine" identity. In this way, the work of Irigaray can be appreciated as reframing the dynamics of human relationships. In so doing, she has changed the basic forms of encounter in a manner that refuses appropriation by an oppositional dialectical form of negativity. At the same time, it rejects any model of transaction initiated by fear, power, or mercantile motives. Her work thus poses a major challenge to previous theories of the gift and sacrifice with their refusal to acknowledge women in their own right.

CONCLUSION

Irigaray's critical analysis is a strong indictment of many western male theorists' propensity either to neglect women or to appropriate their identity and position, and pronounce the terms of their existence. This has been nowhere more evident than in the ascription of women within the category of gift. If they have not been ignored entirely, women appear to have been expropriated in two ways. In the first, women have been accorded the dubious achievement of providing the resources which fuel the economy, but denied any authority in the allocation of those resources. Alternatively, they have remained largely a pawn in the services of various schemes devised by men—of either divine or human provenance—that not only determine their value, but also organize the rules which admit or exclude their participation in their rituals. While women anthropologists such as Leacock, Strathern, and Weiner have written persuasively to dispute the problematic conclusions of in-the-field anthropologists such as Boas, Malinowski, and Lévi-Strauss, this has not prevented the armchair synthesizers Bataille and Derrida, as commentators on the work of Mauss, from undertaking further uncritical adaptations. In these studies women have been regarded as simply tokens of exchange—albeit occasionally valuable ones—or projected as figures of excess. Both of these characterizations reflect the writers' own indulgences more than reality. Contemporary French women thinkers such as Irigaray and Cixous have criticized this male tendency either to manipulate the terms of engagement or to envisage scenarios of a sacrificial or deregulated nature. They have also supplied their own creative alternatives.

Yet there remain problematic issues. In the case of the gift, when it involves a female, treated as an object with no access to fair jurisdiction, Irigaray's analysis would seem to be especially apt, though principally applicable in modern western Christian cultures. I think it is false, however, in the light of the data provided by the women anthropologists, among them Leacock, Strathern, and Weiner, to assume that such restrictions have been ubiquitously imposed throughout all histories and cultures. Also, from a secular perspective, many do not feel that Irigaray's challenge to women, to finally attain an alterity appropriate to their gender, is an adequate response to reorder societal abuses.[21] Thus, while I understand that Irigaray's work has been helpful in indicating the stereotypical sexual constructions that have been evident in Eurocentric deliberations on the gift, Irigaray's own solutions, with their emphasis on heterosexual difference, do not satisfy those with concern for other modalities of gender identity or other modes of difference, specifically those designated by race, ethnicity, and class. Perhaps this is a common predicament when the Eurocentric mindset is confronted by both its formerly colonized peoples and its own internalized forms of negativity/difference. It is not simply the fact that the "gift" as it has existed in other cultures escapes the categories that have been imposed on it. The gift, emblematic of an ideal of utter gratuitousness, still has currency in the western mindset. Whether secular or religious, it remains an intangible index of heterogeneity in a culture that, because of its own repressions or defense mechanisms, is reluctant to confront its controlling and colonial impulses—whether the object is women or peoples of other cultures/ethnicities. Thus the gift will remain an enigma to an acquisitive society, exemplified by contemporary capitalism in its neoconservative and/or globalizing guises. Twentieth-first-century capitalism with its rapacious need for more of the same is hesitant to acknowledge its blind spots. By opposing an idealized version of the gift to such profiteering, its critics tend to eulogize its sheer gratuity. Subtle differences become elided, and dichotomies prevail. This hinders careful analysis of the facile generalizations that continue to prevail. This is especially evident in the case of women in relation to the gift. My hope is that the essays by the women contributors in this volume have provided testimony that this need not be the case and that human beings can aspire to live differently.

These do provide evidence that women today can finally make claim to their inheritance as full participants in human existence. They have moved beyond the banalizations and indiscriminate distortions of the past. They aspire to have reciprocal relationships that can flourish. They have provided models for being otherwise than simply decorous or servile. They have enriched our ways of celebrating life in this world. These are gifts that women can now offer to enrich the world. In the past, male speculations on women and the gift did not honor them, but depicted them according to men's own desires and needs. Perhaps it is time to call for a respite from any further deliberations concerning Mauss's notion of the gift, especially if it features men's views about women. This is because all available evidence points to the fact that such discussions inevitably evoke the past. This past became a virtual palimpsest where men have recorded their fantasies of women. Occasionally these were not demeaning, but spoke to alternative futures for women where they were free to make their own life decisions. This time has indeed come, for certain fortunate women in the contemporary world. Admittedly there are still blocks, backlash, opposition, glass ceilings, and blighted intolerance. There are regions in this world where women suffer from gross abuse and degradation. Their plight must ever be present to our consciousness and conscience.

Yet for the fortunate inhabitants of the "One-Third" world, things do continue to change, even if at times the improvements seem minimal at best. The critical turn in theory nonetheless has provided a forum to communicate and debate different viewpoints. The digital revolution also assures that this communication can be fast and furious. Part of this shifting reality is the bonus that women can also reflect anew on dimensions of the gift as a means of recognizing the integrity of others—both in intimate relationships of care and in more communal struggles for justice. Such deliberation could provide the basis for other more egalitarian modes of conceiving and analyzing notions of the gift that need no longer be gender-specific. This book is but an initial step. As such, it introduces both an exciting and challenging prospect.

NOTES

Earlier versions of this paper appeared as "Beyond the Given and the All-Giving: Speculations on Women and the Gift," in *Approaching Religion,* part 1, ed. Tore Ahlbäck (Turku, Finland: Donner Institute, 1999):109–25, and *Australian Feminist Studies* 14 (30) (1999): 315–32. Reprinted with permission.

The first epigraph is from Lévi-Strauss [1947] 1969 (115–16). The second is from Irigaray [1992] 1996 (29).

1. There is no exact English translation for the French term *prestation.* It is usually translated by the term "total services" as the intention is to focus on the role of gifts as a requisite element in the entire social network of a specific society.

2. I intend a double reading of the term "colonial," referring both to the traditional subservient evaluation of colonized peoples and to that of women.

3. See my introduction to this volume for further discussion of these terms.

4. The term "potlatch" has been used both to describe a system of limitless gift-giving and a counter-movement of wanton destruction of property. There have been quite a number of debates in recent years regarding the accuracy of this definition. As an example, see Bracken 1997 (33–162).

5. *Kula* activity, as described by Malinowski in the Trobriand Islands, involved an elaborate system of inter-island trade of precious objects, such as shells. Weiner

(1992, 131–55) is highly critical of Malinowski's limited conclusions about this process.

6. Smith refers to the work of Irving Goldman, *The Mouth of Heaven.* In regard to the work of Boas, Goldman claims: "Strictly speaking, the term 'potlatch' has no valid place in the vocabulary of professional writing on Kwakiutl simply because it is local jargon and not a Kwakiutl word. Used in the place of the real Kwakiutl terms for property distributions it obscures their indigenous meanings. Boas's use of 'potlatch' is particularly incomprehensible . . . because it did not arise from the texts. . . . There never were, at least in precontact days, such events as 'potlatches'" (1975, 131).

7. Bracken locates Boas's work within a colonialist discourse of the nineteenth and early twentieth centuries. He views it as part of an assimiliationist policy where the difference of the indigenous people as "other" was exaggerated so as to reinforce the Eurocentric identity of the white colonizer—be it an anthropologist, a government agent, or a settler (Bracken 1997, 231).

8. Weiner states strongly her own conclusions concerning women's power: "Throughout the Pacific and other societies of similar political scale, women as sisters and spouses gain their own domains of power through controlling economic resources and protecting inalienable possessions and the various cosmological phenomena that provided authentication of historical, ancestral linkages" (Weiner 1992, 152).

9. Anthropologist Diane Bell in her work *Daughters of the Dreaming* illustrates how Australian aboriginal women have suffered from the limitations of many western men's circumscribed view of the women of their own society (particularly with reference to Durkheim's categories of sacred and profane). For example, Bell's work relates how Australian aboriginal women were judged profane according to Durkheim's binary structure, thus as lacking the necessary attributes for partaking in sacred rituals and myths, and therefore not particularly worthy of being studied (Bell 1994, 36, 242–48).

10. It must be admitted that in her most recent work, such as *I Love to You* ([1992] 1996), Irigaray does appeal to non-western cultures for examples of certain societies in Asia, where she believes that women have been honored and not exploited, but even here her work displays colonialist or Orientalistic tendencies. See Joy 2006 (124–41).

11. Martha Reineke discusses the work of Girard in her book *Sacrificed Lives* (1997). See particularly 74–81.

12. There are a number of recent volumes which, while not following explicitly in Girard's footsteps, take up the question of the Christian God in relation to the gift and /or sacrifice. See Caputo and Scanlon (1999), Keenan (2005), Horner (2001), and Webb (1996).

13. The whole saga of the gift in French thought could be described as somewhat incestuous—beginning with Mauss, followed by Lévi-Strauss's and Bataille's commentaries, and Derrida's further writings on all of them. See especially Derrida (1998).

14. This is a term used by Jacques Lacan to refer to the superabundant expression of female sexual pleasure. Irigaray refines its meaning so that it does not simply refer to genital pleasure. She understands it as indicating that a woman's body can be sensually responsive in myriad ways.

15. Cixous uses this term in connection with a mode of writing that reflected a mode of consciousness that was not restricted to rational processes or linear expression.

16. Irigaray also runs the risk, especially in her mimetic/hysteric posture (which is a form of parody), of simply reinforcing women's eccentricity and incapability of

challenging in any practical way the present nature of women's situation. See Chisholm (1994) for a careful treatment of this danger.

17. For a more detailed analysis of Irigaray's engagement with Hegel, see Joy 1996 (3–101).

18. Irigaray's work can be viewed as part of a large rethinking of Hegel in France. This began as a result of the lectures on Hegel in Paris in the thirties by Alexandre Kojève (1969). See Bruce Baugh (2003).

19. Irigaray's understanding of *Récueillement* involves a form of return to the self by means of a form of critical contemplation that would foster self-awareness. In her own practice she also follows a form of Hindu yoga and meditation that has spiritual implications. See Irigaray 1996 (24).

20. I have expanded on what I consider the major difficulties in Irigaray's work in Joy 2006 (146–51).

21. There is also the problem of whether Irigaray's elaboration of living the (sexual) difference, which sustains her creative project (with all its post-Hegelian implications), can be reconciled with her exaltation of the heterosexual couple, and the ontological difference that, in *I Love to You* (Irigaray 1996), she posits as the foundation of a new order between male and female. This is a topic that needs further discerning examination and deliberation as the delicate task of renegotiation between the traditional categories of sexes and gender construction continues to unfold.

REFERENCES

Bataille, Georges. [1957] 1987. *Eroticism*. Trans. M. Dalwood. London: Marion Boyars.
———. [1967] 1988. *The Accursed Share: An Essay on General Economy*. Vol. 1, *Consumption*. Trans. Robert Hurley. New York: Zone Books.
———. [1973] 1992. *Theory of Religion*. Trans. R. Hurley. New York: Zone Books.
———. [1976] 1991. *The Accursed Share*. Vol. 2, *The History of Eroticism.*, Vol. 3, *Sovereignty*. Trans. R. Hurley. New York: Zone Books.
———. 1985 *Visions of Excess: Selected Writings, 1927–1939*. Trans. A. Stoekl. Manchester, UK: Manchester University Press.
———. 1990. "Hegel, Death and Sacrifice." In *On Bataille*, ed. A. Stoekl. Yale French Studies 78. New Haven, CT: Yale University Press. 9–30.
Baugh, Bruce. 2003. *French Hegel: From Surrealism to Postmodernism*. New York: Routledge.
Bell, Diane. 1994. *Daughters of the Dreaming*. Minneapolis: University of Minnesota Press.
Besnier, J.-M. 1995. "Bataille, the Emotive Intellectual." In *Bataille: Writing the Sacred*, ed. C. B. Gill. New York: Routledge.
Boas, Franz. [1916] 1923. "Tsimshian Mythology." Washington, DC: 31st Annual Report of the American Bureau of Ethnology.
Boas, Franz, and Gordon Hunt. 1921. *Ethnology of the Kwakiutl*. Washington, DC: 35th Annual Report of the American Bureau of Ethnology.
Bracken, Christopher. 1997. *The Potlatch Papers: A Colonial Case History*. Chicago: University of Chicago Press.
Braidotti, Rosi. 1994. *Nomadic Subjects: Embodiment and Sexual Difference in Contemporary Feminist Theory*. New York: Columbia University Press.

Caputo, John D., and Michael J. Scanlon, eds. 1999. *God, the Gift and Postmodernism.* Bloomington: Indiana University Press.

Chisholm, Dianne. 1994. "Irigaray's Hysteria." In *Engaging with Irigaray: Feminist Philosophy and Modern European Thought, Gender and Culture,* ed. C. Burke, N. Schor, and M. Whitford. New York: Columbia University Press. 263–83.

Cixous, Hélène. 1986. "Sorties." In *The Newly Born Woman,* by Hélène Cixous and Catherine Clément. Trans. B. Wing. Minneapolis: University of Minnesota Press. 63–134.

Derrida, Jacques. [1972] 1981. *Positions.* Trans. A. Bass. Chicago: University of Chicago Press.

———. [1978] 1979. *Spurs: Nietzsche's Styles.* Trans. B. Harlow. Chicago: University of Chicago Press.

———. [1991] 1992. *Given Time: 1. Counterfeit Money.* Trans. P. Kamuf. Chicago: University of Chicago Press.

———. [1992] 1995. *The Gift of Death.* Trans. David Wills. Chicago: University of Chicago Press.

———. 1998. "From a Restricted to General Economy: A Hegelianism without Reserve." In *Bataille: A Critical Reader,* ed. Fred Botting and Scott Wilson. Oxford, UK: Blackwell. 102–38.

Douglas, Mary. 1966. *Purity and Danger: An Analysis of Concepts of Pollution and Taboo.* London: Routledge & Kegan Paul.

Etienne, M., and E. Leacock, eds. 1980. *Women and Colonization: Anthropological Perspectives.* Brooklyn: Praeger.

Frear, G. L., Jr. 1992. "René Girard on Mimesis, Scapegoats, and Ethics," *The Annual of the Society of Christian Ethics.* Washington, DC: Georgetown University Press. 115–33.

Freud, Sigmund. 1918. *Totem and Taboo.* Trans. A. A. Brill. New York: Random House.

Girard, René. 1979. *Violence and the Sacred.* Baltimore: Johns Hopkins University Press.

———. [1982] 1986. *The Scapegoat.* Baltimore: Johns Hopkins University Press.

Goldman, Irving. 1975. *The Mouth of Heaven: An Introduction to Kwakiutl Religious Thought.* New York: John Wiley & Sons.

Guerlac, Suzanne. 1990. "'Recognition' by a Woman!: A Reading of Bataille's *l'Erotisme.*" In *On Bataille,* ed. A. Stoekl. Yale French Studies 78. New Haven, CT: Yale University Press. 90–105.

Hénaff, Marcel. [2002] 2010. *The Price of Truth: Gift, Money, and Philosophy.* Stanford, CA: Stanford University Press.

Horner, Robyn. 2001. *Rethinking God as Gift. Marion, Derrida and the Limits of Phenomenology.* New York: Fordham University Press.

Irigaray, Luce. [1974] 1985a. *Speculum of the Other Woman.* Trans. G. C. Gill. Ithaca, NY: Cornell University Press.

———. [1975] 1985b. "Commodities among Themselves." In *This Sex Which Is Not One.* Trans. C. Porter with C. Burke. Ithaca, NY: Cornell University Press.

———. [1978] 1985c. "Women on the Market." In *This Sex Which Is Not One.* Trans. C. Porter with C. Burke. Ithaca, NY: Cornell University Press.

———. [1984] 1993a. "Universal as Meditation." In *Sexes and Genealogies.* Trans. G. C. Gill. New York: Columbia University Press.

——. [1984] 1993b. "Women, the Sacred and Money." In *Sexes and Genealogies*. Trans. G. C. Gill. New York: Columbia University Press.

——. [1992] 1996. *I Love to You*. Trans. A. Martin. New York: Routledge.

Jay, Nancy. 1985. "Sacrifice as a Remedy for Having Been Born of Woman." In *Immaculate and Powerful*, ed. Clarissa Atkinson et al. Boston: Beacon Press.

——. 1992. *Throughout Your Generations Forever: Sacrifice, Religion, and Paternity*. Chicago: University of Chicago Press.

Joy, Morny. 1998. "What's God Got to Do with It?" In *Bodies, Lives, Voices: Gender in Theology, Theology*, ed. Kathleen O'Grady, Ann Gilroy and Janette Gray. Sheffield, UK: Sheffield Academic Press. 213–65.

——. 2006. *Divine Love: Luce Irigaray, Women, Gender and Religion*. Manchester, UK: Manchester University Press.

Keenan, Dennis King. 2005. *The Question of Sacrifice*. Bloomington: Indiana University Press.

Kojève, Alexandre. [1947] 1969. *Introduction to the Reading of Hegel*. Trans. J. H. Nichols Jr. New York: Basic Books.

Leacock, Eleanor Burke. 1981. *Myths of Male Dominance: Collected Articles on Women Cross-Culturally*. New York: Monthly Review Press.

Lévi-Strauss, C. [1949] 1969. *The Elementary Structures of Kinship*. Trans. J. H. Bell et al. Boston: Beacon Press.

Malinowski, Bronislaw K. 1922. *Argonauts of the Western Pacific: An Account of Native Enterprise and Adventure in the Archipelagoes of Melanesian New Guinea*. Studies in Economics and Political Science, No. 65. London: G. Routledge.

Mauss, Marcel. [1924] 1990. *The Gift: Forms and Functions of Exchange in Archaic Societies*. Trans. W. D. Halls. London: Routledge. Published in France as "Essai sur le don," in *Sociologie et Anthropologie*, Paris: Presses Universitaires de France, 1950.

Reineke, Martha Jane. 1997. *Sacrificed Lives: Kristeva on Women and Violence*. Bloomington: Indiana University Press.

Richardson, Michael. 1994. *Georges Bataille*. New York: Routledge.

Richman, Michele H. 1982. *Reading Georges Bataille: Beyond the Gift*. Baltimore: Johns Hopkins University Press.

——. 1990. "Anthropology and Modernism in France: From Durkheim to the 'Collège de Sociologie.'" In *Modernist Anthropology: From Fieldwork to Text*, ed. Marc Manganaro. Princeton, NJ: Princeton University Press. 183–214.

Roudinesco, Elisabeth. 1990. *Jacques Lacan & Co.: A History of Psychoanalysis in France*. Trans. J. Mehlman. Chicago: University of Chicago Press.

Smith, Jonathan Z., with W. Burkhert and R. Girard. 1987. *Violent Origins: Ritual Killing and Cultural Formation*. Stanford, CA: Stanford University Press.

Strathern, Marilyn. 1988. *The Gender of the Gift: Problems with Women and Problems with Society in Melanesia*. Berkeley: University of California Press.

Walter Natasha. 2010. *Living Dolls: The Return of Sexism*. London: Virago.

Webb, Stephen H. 1996. *The Gifting God: A Trinitarian Ethics of Excess*. Oxford: Oxford University Press.

Weiner, Annette. B. 1976. *Women of Value, Men of Renown: New Perspectives in Trobriand Exchange*. Austin: University of Texas Press.

——. 1992. *Inalienable Possessions: The Paradox of Keeping-While-Giving*. Berkeley: University of California Press.

CONTRIBUTORS

Victoria Barker is Honorary Research Associate and former Lecturer of the Department of Studies in Religion at the University of Sydney. She has published widely in the fields of philosophy of religion and feminist philosophy of religion, most recently in the *Journal of Religious History* and the *Journal of Feminist Theology*. Her present focus is on the influence of theological models of God's otherness on feminist philosophy of woman's otherness.

Maria Cimitile is Associate Professor and Academic Program and Development Officer in the Office of the Provost at Grand Valley State University in Michigan. Her scholarship explores the relationship between Irigaray and Heidegger, Kristeva's psychoanalytic and political theories, contemporary political theory, and psychoanalysis. Her co-edited volume (with Elaine Miller), *Returning to Irigaray,* is a critical assessment of Irigaray's early poetic writings and her later political works. Currently, she is working on a manuscript that demonstrates the relevance of Kristeva's psychoanalysis and Enlightenment political philosophy to contemporary nationalism. She also works in academic administration and publishes and presents in the areas of leadership for women, and strategic planning for diversity goals.

Nancy J. Holland is Chair of the Department of Philosophy at Hamline University in St. Paul, Minnesota. Her main research areas are contemporary European philosophy and postmodern feminism. Recent articles include "Thoughts on Thirty Years in the Society for Phenomenology and Existential Philosophy," in *Journal of Speculative Philosophy,* and "Looking Backwards: A Feminist Revisits Herbert Marcuse's *Eros and Civilization,*" in *Hypatia.* Her latest book is *Ontological Humility: Lord Voldemort and the Philosophers.*

Morny Joy is University Professor in the Department of Religious Studies, University of Calgary. Her principal areas of research are philosophy and religion, especially continental philosophy, as well as postcolonialism and intercultural studies in South and Southeast Asia. She has also written and edited numerous books and articles in the area of women and religion, more recently in connection with rights and religion. Her most recent publications are *Continental Philosophy and Philosophy of Religion* and *After Appropriation: Explorations in Intercultural Philosophy and Religion*. In 2011, she was awarded an honorary doctorate by the University of Helsinki.

Deborah Lyons is Associate Professor of Classics at Miami University. She is the author of *Gender and Immortality: Heroines in Ancient Greek Myth and Culture*. Her *Dangerous Gifts: Gender and Exchange in Ancient Greece* takes an anthropological approach to ideological constructions of gender, production, marriage, and exchange in Greek myth and thought. Her "The Scandal of Women's Ritual" won the Women's Classical Caucus article prize for 2009. She is currently working on a project entitled "Immortality and Its Discontents."

Lorraine Markotic is Associate Professor in the Department of Philosophy at the University of Calgary. She has published articles on Nietzsche in *New Nietzsche Studies, Nietzsche Studien,* and the *Deutsche Zeitschrift für Philosophie*. She has also published in *American Imago, German Life and Letters, Modern Drama, Modern Austrian Literature, Paragraph, Seminar, symplokē,* and elsewhere. In addition, she has written on Irigaray, Kristeva, Lacan, Derrida, Badiou, and Freud's Dora.

Rachel Muers is Senior Lecturer in Christian Studies at the University of Leeds. She previously held posts at the University of Exeter and at Girton College, Cambridge. Her publications include *Keeping God's Silence: Towards a Theological Ethics of Communication, Living for the Future: Theological Ethics for Future Generations* (with Mike Higton), *The Text In Play: Experiments in Reading Scripture,* and (again with Mike Higton) *The Routledge Critical Introduction to Modern Theology.*

Kathleen O'Grady is a Research Associate at the Simone de Beauvoir Institute, Concordia University, Montreal, Quebec. She is also a policy research and communications strategy consultant for a member of the Canadian Senate and several national and international nonprofit organizations. O'Grady has written extensively in the mainstream and academic press on women's and cultural issues. She lives in Ottawa with her family. Details of her publications can be viewed at www.kathleenogrady.com.

Mariana Ortega is Professor of Philosophy at John Carroll University, University Heights, Ohio. She received her Ph.D. from the University of California, San Diego. Her main areas of research are twentieth-century continental philosophy, specifically Heideggerian phenomenology, Latina feminism, and race theory. Her research focuses on questions of self and sociality, visual representations of race, and the question of identity. She has published articles in journals such as *Hypatia, International Journal of Philosophical Studies, International Philosophical Quarterly,* and *Radical Philosophy Review.* She is co-editor, with Linda Martín-Alcoff, of the anthology *Constructing the Nation: A Race and Nationalism Reader.* She is currently working on a monograph that elaborates a notion of self as multiplicitous subjectivity in light of existential phenomenological views and Latina feminisms.

Sal Renshaw is an Associate Professor at Nipissing University, Canada, and is Chair of the Department of Gender Equality and Social Justice, cross-appointed in the Department of Religions and Cultures. She is author of *The Subject of Love: Hélène Cixous and the Feminine Divine,* and her research interests range from philosophies of love to representations of sexuality and ethics in contemporary media. She has most recently published on representations of queer sexuality in the HBO series *The L Word* and is currently working on a collection of feminist essays, *Screening the Canon,* a critical reading through film of key theological concepts such as grace and sacrifice.

41, 119, 127–28; language and, 125–27.
See also Ereignis
Being and Time (Heidegger), 117–19, 121,
126
being or Being: desire for, 200; gift of,
40–41, 96, 125–26, 156; and humanity,
127; language and, 41, 117–18, 125–27;
meaning of, 118–20, 126; multicultural ways of, 40, 45; of presence, 118,
126; and time, 113–14, 119. See also
Dasein; Ereignis; Heidegger, Martin
Being Reconciled: Ontology and Pardon
(Milbank), 42, 153–54
Being-in-relation, 124
Bell, Diane, 215n9
Besnier, Jean-Michel, 210
betrayal, 37, 138
biological essentialism, 17, 25, 148n1, 163
birth, giving, 31–32
Black Sun (Kristeva), 102. *See also*
melancholia
Boas, Franz, 2, 194–96, 203, 215nn6–7
body image, 6–7
Boundas, Constantin, 4, 46nn4–5
Bracken, Christopher, 19, 44, 215n7; *The
Potlatch Papers: A Colonial Case His-
tory,* 2, 195
Braidotti, Rosi, 207
brain-sex determinants, 25–26
Brizendine, Louann, 25–26
Butler, Judith, 25, 189n38, 190n43, 190n47

capitalism, 1, 27, 151, 213; gift-giving and,
18–20. *See also* commodities
caring, 21–23, 83; and empathy, 26–27;
women's identity and, 24
Chambri people (Papua New Guinea):
Golden Girl myth, 55, 59–64, 67;
marriage transactions, 59, 61–62,
68n13
Chanter, Tina, 189n33, 189n37
choice, reproductive, 22–23, 31
Christ, 154–55, 200
Christianity, 164n13, 201, 203; elements
in Cixous's stories, 136, 139, 147,
148n4; Feuerbach on, 188n30; the gift
and, 97; Nietzsche's views of, 86–87,

172; sacrifice in, 148n4; theology, 150–
51, 160, 162, 170; Trinity, 151–53, 157
Church, the, 153–55, 159–60
Church Fathers, 5, 171
Cimitile, Maria, 41
circle/cycle of exchange, 95–97, 132–33,
162
circulation of women, 36–37, 62
Cixous, Hélène, 15, 44, 85–86, 212; "The
Cat's Arrival," 141–47; childhood
in Algeria, 135; on the gift of love,
41–42, 134; law of return, 106; on
male feelings of obligation, 79, 84; on
masculine and feminine economies,
17, 78, 131–32, 140–41, 147, 148n1; religious allusions in writings, 136, 139,
147, 148n4; on sexual difference, 131,
148n1; shortcomings of work, 197;
"Sorties," 2, 131, 140, 142; "Stigmata, or
Job the Dog," 136–41; on women's giving without reserve, 207–208
Coakley, Sarah, 151, 153, 155, 159
colonialism, 46n3; and indigenous peoples, 20, 48n26
colonialist views, 2, 22, 44, 194, 197
commodities: family continuity and, 37,
54; gifts as, 106, 197; women as, 12, 15,
54, 64, 206
consciousness, 177, 182, 214, 215n15; absolute, 174; religious, 174–76; self-, 173,
176, 178, 188n28
contradictory nature of woman, 37, 54,
73, 169
cosmic connection, 12
creation: for gift-exchange, 160; God
and, 151–55; of humankind, 68n20;
and sacrifice, 114; of women in myth,
53, 55–56, 59–60, 64
Crittenden, Ann, 22–23
cultural formations, 169

Daly, Mary, 186n12
Dankbarkeit, 84
Dasein, 40, 113, 126; Being of, 97, 118–19;
and being-there, 123, 125; relationality
of, 121; subjectivity of, 117, 127; temporality of, 118–20, 124

de Waal, Frans, 27

Derrida, Jacques, 1–3, 13, 189n40; Adorno prize address (2001), 39, 98; on blindness in men, 98; "Choreographies," 92, 94–95, 98; on *différance,* 92, 96, 98, 206; economy of gift/exchange, 80, 82–83, 97, 181; on the forgotten gift, 81–82, 90n6; *Geschlecht* arguments, 94–96; and the gift as selfless, 33–34; on giving and receiving gifts, 81, 83, 90n5, 151–52; ideal of justice, 30; on the impossibility of the gift, 39, 80, 95–96, 111, 132–33; "Plato's Pharmacy," 93, 170–71, 186n15; on recognition of the gift, 81, 95, 132; on the sacrifice of Isaac, 98–99; on women and the gift, 14, 39, 206–207; on women and truth, 14, 73

Descombes, Vincent, 187n25

desire: for being, 200; mother's, 106–109; women as objects of, 15, 39, 102, 122, 205; women's, 39–40, 67n10, 102

Destruktion, 117

Deutscher, Penelope, 179

dialectic, 209–10, 212

différance, 92, 96, 98, 206

difference(s): gender, 17, 26, 55, 155, 159; "ineradicable," 28, 35; modern erasures of, 42, 163; ontological, 94, 216n21; of the other, 128; recognition of, 3, 121, 123, 127, 137; temporality of, 120, 123; women's maintenance of, 158. *See also* sexual difference

Diprose, Rosalyn, 27–35, 48n30

divine, the: animal and, 135; antithesis of, 176; attributes, 174; being, 174–75; consciousness of, 188n28; feminine, 173, 190n48; gift, 151–53, 160, 162, 165n14

division of labor, 23, 36, 53, 64, 66

Douglas, Mary, 47n18, 202

Durkheim, Émile, 167, 169, 186nn8–9; model of sacred and profane, 186n11, 196, 215n9

earth: creation of humankind from, 68n20; gifts from, 57; and origin of

mythical beings, 56, 59, 62–64, 67n6, 68n27; women's association with, 17

economies of exchange, 17, 106, 108, 133, 159; Derrida on, 80, 82–83

ego, 48n35, 172, 176, 188n33; melancholia and, 103, 107

Elementary Structures of Kinship, The (Lévi-Strauss), 46n13, 167, 193, 199; women as gifts given in marriage, 2, 6, 46n13; women as objects of exchange, 179, 189n36. *See also* Lévi-Strauss, Claude

Emerson, Ralph Waldo, 41, 88, 116, 129

Empathic Civilization, The (Rifkin), 27

Empathizing Quotient (EQ), 26

empathy studies, 26–27

Ensler, Eve, 6, 47n15

equality, 82, 154–55, 189n42; biological features and, 17

Ereignis, 40; definition/translation of, 113, 118, 128; gift of, 126–27; Irigaray's critique of, 122–24, 127; language is, 125; and subjectivity, 126

Errington, Frederick, 59–61, 63, 68nn13–14

Essence of Christianity (Feuerbach), 174–75, 178, 188n28

ethics, 27–33

ethnography, 151, 156, 160–61

Eurocentrism, 2, 22, 199, 206, 213

excess, 204, 206; of the gift, 111, 113, 133, 189n40; women and, 1, 209, 212

exchange contracts, 199

exchange of women, 48n27, 65, 196, 203, 206

exclusion, 4, 43, 97–98, 202

existentialism: anthropology and, 167, 180; and freedom, 183; transformation and, 166

exploitation, 15, 198, 204–205

external/internal values, 174

fantasy, 61, 63, 68n18, 205, 214

Father and Son dyad, 153–55

Fausto-Sterling, Anne, 25–26

feminine, the: and *différance,* 206; as divine, 173, 187n16; God as, 187n16;

Holy Spirit as, 153–55; killing, 128; Nietzsche's notion of, 38, 73, 84, 89n2; ontology and ethics and, 33; and the other, 173; and paternity, 31; term usage, 45n1, 48n24, 48n33; woman and, 1, 31, 89n2, 207. *See also* masculine and feminine relation

feminine economy, 38, 74; Cixous's, 17, 131–32, 140–41, 147, 148n1

feminism, 43, 84, 98, 163

Feminism and Emotion: Readings in Moral and Political Philosophy (Mendus), 21–22

feminist critique, 3; of anthropological methods, 195–97; of mothering and gift-giving, 21–22; of sexual difference, 163, 165n14; of women as gift, 155–56

feminist philosophy: on the meaning of woman, 167–68, 170; and theological concepts of otherness, 180, 183–85

Feuerbach, Ludwig, 167, 188n27, 188n30, 190n50; anthropological perspectives, 174–75, 187n25, 190n45; on the idolatry of God, 177–78; projection theory, 176–77, 188n29; reductionism, 188n26; on religious belief, 174–75, 178; on subject and object relations, 175

fichu, 98

fidelity, 37, 54

Fine, Cordelia, 25–26, 44

forgetting, 90nn6–7; and the gift, 81–82; of the mother, 121–22, 127

forgiveness: impossibility/possibility of, 39, 99; melancholia and, 40, 102, 107–109

Foucault, Michel, 24, 48n28

free gift, 8, 14, 106, 131

freedom, 189nn37–38; and absolute otherness, 183–84; of animals, 138; and rights, 34; women's, 14, 178–80, 183

Freud, Sigmund, 23, 106, 200; on mourning and melancholia, 102–103

gender difference, 17, 45n1; and indifference, 159; predetermined before birth, 25–26

gender of the gift, 42, 152–53, 158–59, 161–62

gender-bending, 25, 210

gendering, 153

generosity: corporeal, 29–30; economy of, 17, 78; ethics of, 35, 181; extravagant, 3, 77–78, 80, 89; and the gift, 17, 28, 30, 32, 38, 205; Nietzsche's concept of, 38, 73–78, 80, 89; and obligation, 79, 132; and subjectivity, 28, 48n30. *See also* giving and receiving; gratitude

Gewertz, Deborah, 59–61, 63, 68nn13–14

gift, the: asymmetry of, 29; of being, 40–41, 96, 125–26, 156; contemporary discussion of, 193–94, 197; different understandings of, 1, 111–12; economy of, 39, 41, 97, 101–102, 116, 181; endless theorizing of, 45; as an event, 41; as feminine, 73–74, 153–55, 157; forgetting, 81–82; forgiveness as, 108–109; as graceful, 135, 141; gratuitousness of, 213; illusion of, 40; impossibility of, 39, 80, 95–96, 111, 132–33; of life and death, 10, 45, 97, 113, 128; of the mother's desire, 106–109; multiplicitous understanding of, 40–41; recognition of, 34–36, 81; of self, 115, 128–29; as selfless, 33, 35; of sexual services, 39, 101–102; strangeness of, 157, 159; as a symbol, 116; taken for granted, 23, 74, 83–85, 89. *See also* generosity; giving and receiving; gratitude; poisonous gifts; women and the gift

Gift, The (Mauss), 1–2, 47n19, 194–95; contemporary critique of, 8; economy of the gift, 102, 116; salary for sexual services *(mapula)*, 39, 101–102. *See also* Mauss, Marcel

gift economy, 8, 18, 41, 106; exchange and, 48n25, 151–52, 160

gift exchange: anthropology of, 95; and capitalism, 18–20; ceremonial or ritualistic, 9–10, 12, 14; Christian theology and, 151–53, 157, 164n10; circulation and, 79–80; dichotomy of, 14, 16, 33; ethnographic account of, 160–61;

theories, 8–9, 18–20, 33, 35; on human-deity relationship, 9–10, 47n20

Hesiod. *See Theogony; Works and Days*

heterology, 184, 190n46

"History," 198

Holland, Nancy J., 39

Hollywood, Amy, 178

Holy Spirit: and femininity, 154; and gender difference, 155; as gift *(donum)*, 151–53, 156–57, 159. *See also* God

Homer. *See Iliad* (Homer); *Odyssey* (Homer)

hospitality, 141–46; gift of, 30, 99; Jewish codes of, 139; maternal, 32–33; women's, 31

human nature, 163, 175–76

human survival, 11

human/animal boundary, 135, 137, 142–43

human-deity relationship, 9–10, 47n20

Hyde, Lewis, 20

Hypatia, 21–22

identity, 47n22, 61; bodily, 29; man's, 175; masculine and feminine, 212; women's, 16, 22, 24, 185n3, 209, 212

idolatry: in Christian theology, 170–71, 183; of the "other," 176; and patriarchy, 187n20; projections of, 184; of religious belief, 171; woman as a product of man's, 168, 173, 176–78, 180–81

Iliad (Homer), 36, 64–65

independence, 38, 85–87, 89

indigenous peoples: appropriation, 2; Australian aboriginal women, 215n9; colonialism and, 48n26; and gift-giving in matriarchal cultures, 20, 22; of Northwest Coast Canada, 15; as "other," 215n7

integrity: recognition of, 25, 34, 211–12, 214; in relationships, 16, 24

intercorporeality, 29

intersubjectivity, 27, 29, 188n33; notion of the self and, 78; recognition and the gift and, 34, 48n35

Irigaray, Luce, 44, 190n48; analysis of Heidegger, 41, 116–28, 129nn6–7,

130n8; cataphatic and apophatic modes of speech, 184–85; criticism of Lévi-Strauss, 197–99; criticism of René Girard, 200–201; on the female as universal, 211; on the institution of sacrifice, 201–202; on market value of women, 15–16; on the negative phase of the dialectic, 209–10, 211; on obtaining perfection of gender, 16–17; philosophy of relationality, 117–18, 120–21, 123, 128–29; on *récueillement*, 211, 216n19; on relationships, 211–12; self-analysis, 16; on sexual difference, 41, 123, 129n3, 159, 211–13, 216n21; shortcomings of work, 197, 213; on silence and language, 125–28; similarities to Milbank, 42, 159, 161, 163; on status of woman as "other," 184, 190n49; threshold metaphor, 123–24; use of "ek-sisting" and "letting-be," 127; use of *jouissance*, 207–208, 215n14; view of religion, 204–205, 209

Irigaray, Luce, works: "Divine Woman," 190n50; *The Forgetting of Air in Martin Heidegger*, 117; *I Love To You*, 193, 215n10, 216n21; *Sharing the World*, 117–18, 129n3, 129n7; "The Universal as Meditation," 209; *The Way of Love*, 117; "Women on the Market," 15, 129n1, 197; "Women, the Sacred and Money," 200

jar *(pithos)* symbolism, 54–58, 62–63, 67n3, 68n19

Jay, Nancy, 201–202

Jones, Serene, 165n14, 190n50

Jordan-Young, Rebecca, 25–26, 44

jouissance, 207–208, 215n14

Joy, Morny, 182, 190n44

Judaism, 147, 148n4, 164n13

justice, 28–33, 35, 214

Kaufmann, Walter, 84

Klein, Melanie, 103

knowledge, gifting and, 133–34

Kofman, Sarah, 39, 92

Kojève, Alexandre, 187n25, 210; on

Hegelian philosophy, 173–74; lectures (1930s), 16, 167, 187n24

Komter, Aafke E., 24

Kristeva, Julia, 44, 109nn2–3; on the gift of love and forgiveness, 39–40, 108–109; melancholia theory, 102–105; on mother's desire and the gift, 106–109; works by, 102

Kruks, Sonia, 172, 182, 189n42

Kwakiutl, 194–95, 215n6

Lacan, Jacques, 102–103, 105, 215n14

language: and Being, 117–18, 125–27; and logic of the gift, 47n19, 96, 102; melancholia as a, 104–105, 108; and the mother's desire, 106–107; silence and, 125–28

law of return, 106, 108

Law of the Father, 15–16

Le Doeuff, Michèle, 166–67, 170

Leacock, Eleanor Burke, 15, 194, 199, 212–13

Levinas, Emmanuel: ethics, 27–28; on the feminine, 33, 48n33, 182; notion of justice, 29–30; on paternity and maternity, 31–32; philosophy of the gift, 28, 48n30; position of passivity, 29

Lévi-Strauss, Claude, 54, 167, 193, 196, 212; Bataille's readings of, 203, 206; Irigaray's criticism of, 197–99; on women as gifts given away, 2, 6, 46n13, 179, 189n36

Logic of the Gift, The (Schrift), 4, 8

Longfellow, Erica, 6, 46n11

loss, 88, 103

love: and aggression, 103; for animals (the other), 134, 140–42, 145–47; asymmetry of, 145; between autonomous individuals, 41; and forgiveness, 39–40; gift of, 39–42, 106

Lugones, María, 22

Lundgren-Gothlin, Eva, 172, 177, 189n34

Lyons, Deborah, 5, 36–37

magnanimity, 75–77, 89

male dominance, 194, 202

Malinowski, Bronislaw K., 63, 101, 194–96, 214n5

man/woman relations: conflict, 180; economic activity, 158–59; new order of categories, 216n21; and otherness, 171–72; and realization of humanity, 119; reciprocity and, 177, 182, 189n36; sexual relations, 193; and variations of human embodiment, 180–81. *See also* masculine and feminine relation

mapula, 39, 101

market value, 15–16

Markotic, Lorraine, 37–38

marriage: in Chambri myth and society, 55, 59, 61–64; cycle of exchange in, 96–97; in Greek myth, 37, 56–57, 61–64; heterosexual, 160; incest rules and, 46n13, 196; and reciprocity, 193; women as gifts given/exchanged in, 2, 6, 9, 54, 156–57, 159; women's participation in, 10–12, 47n14

Mary (mother of Jesus), 5

masculine and feminine relation: attribution, 39; brain-sex determinants in, 25–26; divisions, 17–18; identity, 212; Judith Butler on, 190n47; social convention of, 148n1

masculine economy, 155, 199; Cixous's, 17, 78, 131–32, 140

masculine world, 120, 123, 169, 186n5

masculinity, 4–5, 94, 172

maternity. *See* mothering/motherhood

matriarchal cultures, 20–21, 189n36

matrilineal societies, 11, 158, 189n36, 199. *See also* Trobriand society

Maushart, Susan, 22–23

Mauss, Marcel, 93, 196, 215n13; on the archaic economy, 195; commentaries on his writings, 1–3, 8–9, 18–20, 203, 206, 214; economy of gift/exchange, 39, 41, 101–102, 106, 108, 116, 189n39; focus on potlatch ceremonies, 2, 15, 80, 200; on *mapula* (sexual services), 39, 101–102; "Moral Conclusions," 195; and recognition of the gift, 20, 33, 35; on sacrifice, 9, 199–200; spirit of the gift, 153, 158–59; on time, 96

McDonald, Christie V., 94

melancholia: compared to mourning, 102–103; and forgiveness, 39, 107–109; as a kind of mystic, 104; as a linguistic disorder, 104; pre-Oedipal and Oedipal stages of, 103–106

Mendus, Susan, 21–22

Merleau-Ponty, Maurice, 28–29, 187n24

mermera erga, 58, 62

metaphysics, 116; of closure, 124; of presence, 117, 123; and subjectivity, 128; Western, 197

Milbank, John, 164n13; accounts of "primitive" or "archaic" societies, 160–62; Christian theology and the gift, 150–51; on the divine gift, 151–53, 160, 162; on the Holy Spirit as feminine, 153–55; on organicism and the strangeness of wives, 157, 159; on sexual/gender difference, 42, 154–55, 158–59, 163; theopneumatics, 42, 152; use of ethnography, 158, 160–61

misogyny, 25, 177; in Greek culture, 64; in Greek literature, 54–55, 60, 62–63; in Nietzsche's writings, 37, 72

modernity, 172; secular, 150

mother, the: desire of, 106–109; forgetting/rejection of, 121–22, 127; and other/otherness, 120–21, 123, 127

mother-child dyad, 105–107

mothering/motherhood: caring and, 21–22; femininity and, 84; as the gift of the Other, 31; gift-giving and, 18, 20–21; maternal hospitality, 32–33; public support systems and, 22–23; redemption through, 5

mourning, 102–103

Muers, Rachel, 42

myth: charter, 63; as contradictory, 186n9; of femininity, 168; of gift, 13, 197; of the given, 184; of God, 43, 170, 173; of the Golden Girl, 55, 59–63, 67; study of, 169; of woman, 43, 167–70, 173, 178–79, 182, 185, 185n2, 186n10. *See also* Pandora

nature of man, 175, 188n28

Nauckhoff, Josefine, 84

negativity, 209–12

neocolonialism, 2, 46n3

Nietzsche, Friedrich: admiration for Emerson, 88; aphoristic writing style, 37–38, 72; on charity, 74; concept of woman, 73, 93; on connection between God and woman, 187n21; emphasis on pessimism, 88; on extravagant generosity, 77–78, 80, 89; generosity concept, 38, 73–76; on giving and receiving, 38, 74, 80, 83, 85; "God is dead" phrase, 87; gratitude concept, 38, 73, 83–84, 86–89; hostility toward Socrates, 87; on magnanimity, 75–77, 89; misogyny and sexism in writings, 37, 72; notion of the feminine, 38, 73, 84, 89n2; on the relationship between men and women, 82; on self-interest and altruism, 76–77; value of independence and self-reliance, 86, 89; views of Christianity, 86–87, 172; Zarathustra's gift-giving, 74, 78–80, 85

Nietzsche, Friedrich, works, 89–90; *Beyond Good and Evil,* 74, 76–77, 87; *The Birth of Tragedy,* 87–88; *Daybreak,* 76, 80, 87; *The Gay Science,* 75–77, 84–88, 166, 170, 187n21; *On the Genealogy of Morals,* 77–78; *Thus Spoke Zarathustra,* 74, 78–80, 85; *Twilight of the Idols,* 88, 166, 187n21; *The Will to Power,* 82, 88

objects, women as: of exchange, 36–37, 53, 58, 65, 179; of man's consciousness, 177; of sexual desire, 39, 102; and subjects, 54

Odyssey (Homer), 36–37, 57, 64–66

Oedipal process, 103–106

O'Grady, Kathleen, 39–40

Oliver, Kelly, 34

ontology: Christian, 150; and ethics, 33; of the gift, 28; and politics and justice, 29; social, 172, 187n17; subordination of, 94

organicism, 157

Ortega, Mariana, 40–41, 45

other/otherness: Beauvoir's concept of,

gift-objects, 156, 159; masculine, 146; metaphysics and, 128; and the mother's desire, 106; in the Oedipal realm, 105; and other/otherness, 133, 180, 183–84; in projections of the world, 122; of women, 16

suffering, 75, 148n4; animal, 135–40, 146–47; melancholia and, 108

suspicion, 5, 37, 168

symbolic worth, 10–11

Systemizing Quotient (SQ), 26

temporality: of *Dasein*, 118–21, 124; of other, 128; and relationality, 120, 123

Theogony (Hesiod), 53, 55–58

theology, 174, 190n45; and absolute otherness, 183–85; Christian, 150–51, 153, 160, 162, 170, 188n30; feminist thinkers and, 163–64, 184, 186n12; of idolatry, 170–71, 183; and sexual difference, 154–55, 163; of the Spirit, 155; Trinitarian, 157

theopneumatics, 42, 152

Thornton, Stephen, 175

Totality and Infinity (Levinas), 27, 31

transcendence, 122, 180; man's quest for, 171–73, 177–79; of Other, 129n4, 188n33; woman's, 183–84, 186n12

transformation, 28–29, 45, 210; and existentialism, 166–67; justice and, 30, 35

transgression, 15, 139, 203–205

Trobriand society, 101, 156; anthropologists' presumptions of, 13, 196–97; *kula* ring, 194, 196, 214n5; lineage, 157–58; women's power and participation in, 6, 10–11, 24, 195–96, 198

true or pure gift, 133; Emerson's view of, 41, 116; Kristeva's concept of, 106–107

truth: of Being, 125–26, 130n8; women and, 14, 73

universalism, 209, 211; of mothering and caring, 21–22, 32

Vagina Monologues, The, 6, 47n15

Vaughan, Genevieve, 2, 27; on gift-giving, 18–22

Vernant, Jean-Pierre, 37, 54, 67n1

Walter, Natasha, 6–7

wealth: in Greek myth, 36, 57–58, 66; in Trobriand society, 11

Weiner, Annette, 2, 15, 47n14, 198; on bias and embellishment in anthropology, 12–13, 44, 196–97, 212–13; concerning women's power, 12, 195 -96, 215n8; inalienable goods, 10. *See also* Trobriand society

western thought, 2, 46n2, 116–18, 206

wife-takers/wife-givers, 59, 61–62, 68n13

Williams, Robert R., 177, 188n33

woman, concept of, 170, 180, 185n3; Nietzsche's, 73, 93; symbolic constructs, 168–69, 187n17

"womanness," 10–12

women and the gift: contemporary reflections on, 2–3, 15, 213–14; as "the given," 6; male scholarly work on, 7, 13–15; presumptions on, 4; and the Spirit, 155; tied to the impossibility of the gift, 94; and women thinkers, 15, 207. *See also* gift, the

women's voices, 7, 44–45

Works and Days (Hesiod), 53–56, 58, 67n10

Work of the Gift, The (Shershow), 18–19

worldhood, 117, 119–21, 125, 128

Zarathustra (from Nietzsche's novel), 74, 78–80, 85

Zeus, 53, 55–56, 66

CPSIA information can be obtained at www.ICGtesting.com
Printed in the USA
LVOW08s0539210813

348779LV00005B/14/P